BORIS PASTERNAK

BY BORIS PASTERNAK
AND PUBLISHED IN HARVILL EDITIONS

Doctor Zhivago
Poems 1955-1959 and *An Essay in Autobiography*

BORIS PASTERNAK
THE TRAGIC YEARS 1930-60

Evgeny Pasternak

Translated from the Russian by
Michael Duncan
The Poetry of Boris Pasternak translated by
Ann Pasternak Slater and Craig Raine

COLLINS HARVILL
8 Grafton Street, London W1
1990

COLLINS HARVILL
William Collins Sons and Co. Ltd
London · Glasgow · Sydney · Auckland
Toronto · Johannesburg

BRITISH LIBRARY CATALOGUING IN PUBLICATION DATA

Pasternak, E. B. (Evgeny Borisovich) 1923–
Boris Pasternak:
1. Fiction in Russian. Pasternak, Boris, 1890–1960
Biographies
I. Title
891.73′42

ISBN 0-00-272045-0

First published in Great Britain by Collins Harvill 1990
© VAAP 1990
Translation © William Collins Sons and Co. Ltd 1990

Photoset in Linotron Bembo by
Rowland Phototypesetting Limited
Bury St Edmunds, Suffolk
Printed and bound in Great Britain by
Hartnolls Limited, Bodmin, Cornwall

CONTENTS

Translator's Preface

The present book is part of the author's tribute to his father. Wherever possible Evgeny Pasternak has let his father be his own witness and has kept his own authorial presence in the background.

As previous translators know better than I, Boris Pasternak's prose style can stray into the convoluted, the apparently obscure, even the prolix. I have sought to retain his ambiguities, his images and his devices – without, as it were, tidying up. The result may be to leave him a little less clear-cut than in some previous versions.

I have consulted and, wherever appropriate, benefitted from Elliott Mossman's *Pasternak's Correspondence with Olga Freidenberg*, as well as other books by my friend, the late Max Hayward. I have tried to keep footnotes to a minimum.

The harder part – the translation of the numerous extracts from Pasternak's poetry – has been bravely and elegantly undertaken by Craig Raine and Ann Pasternak Slater. (In cases where the author has omitted a line or one or more stanzas from a poem he has quoted in the text, the absence has been marked thus: [. . .].)

I am deeply indebted to Evgeny Pasternak and his co-author and wife, Elena Pasternak, for their patient, unstinting help; to the scholarship of Dr Christopher. Barnes; and to John Coldstream for eliminating infelicities from my English. For those that remain I am penitently responsible.

MICHAEL DUNCAN
Otford
September 1989

Author's Foreword

An artist's biography is bound to serve as an overall commentary on his works. This is all the more true of the life of a writer. An exception might be made for the years of childhood, boyhood and youth. But Boris Pasternak, like the greatest of his predecessors, paid enormous tribute in his work to that particular period.

In *Safe Conduct* (1931) and *An Essay in Autobiography* (1957)* he created an integrated, convincing image of his formation and growth; of how he arrived at artistic independence – in other words, how he prevailed in his vocation and won for himself an unchallenged place in the history of his generation.

This account of his early development also acts as a footnote to what he himself has written of how in his "own individual case, life became converted into art and art was born of life and experience."*

Pasternak's autobiographical prose breaks off at the beginning of the 1930s. It was, as he said, impossible to carry on with it. During that period of collectivization and mass terror, the question of the fate of the individual ceased to have meaning. Life lost its absolute value. It is not by chance that the hero of *Doctor Zhivago* dies in 1929. Reality started to require some other means of communication – either by some prose-related structure capable of rendering abstract horror, or by tragically stark, chronological narrative.

Little is generally known of Pasternak's own life during these years. And judgments are made about it on the basis of fragmentary, melodramatic, oversimplified memoirs. This has evidently prompted Collins Harvill – who had it in mind to publish a short volume about Pasternak for his hundredth anniversary – to bring out an English translation of the second part of my book *Materials for a Biography of Boris Pasternak*, which is ready and waiting to be

---

* *An Essay in Autobiography* is published in one volume as *Poems 1955–1959 and An Essay in Autobiography*, Collins Harvill, London, 1990, p. 61.

printed in Russia. This second part begins in 1930 when Pasternak wrote the book of poems he entitled *Second Birth*.

Like the best of his contemporaries who also had occasion to appreciate the price to be paid for preserving personal dignity and independence in their creative vocation, Pasternak remained true to himself in those harsh times.

My own – secondary – biographical research task, of verifying the places and times of events in his life and comparing literary texts, memoirs and documents, has opened up unexpected perspectives. In their chronological order and set within the framework of the historic events he observed and experienced, the scenes and thoughts recorded by the artist acquire added dimension and comprehensiveness. The apparently complex becomes intelligible; what is unclear and, at first sight, fortuitous acquires a moral and historical rationale.

During the historically eventful years of Pasternak's life, the actual conditions under which people had to exist changed as never before. He was twenty-four years old when the period of military and revolutionary turmoil started. He had some literary experience to his credit, and a great deal more artistic and philosophic experience acquired in peacetime conditions in prewar Russia.

The artistic, i.e. primarily lyric and philosophic, tasks of that period affected him more closely than they did many others of his own age. He was born and bred into a family of professional artists, not well off materially and obliged to earn their living by combining their own work with endless private teaching.

The highly diverse, intense life of Moscow households, gardens, parks and streets provided the background against which the Pasternaks' close-knit, hardworking artistic circle moved and was the concomitant, the milieu and the co-partner of Pasternak's activity, his artistic activity in particular.

As a child Pasternak met Lev Tolstoy, Scriabin, Rilke, Rachmaninov, Serov, Levitan, Vrubel, Polenov, Korovin, Klyuchevsky and many other well-known people of his time. For him their existence was, on the one hand, an everyday feature of family life, and on the other, a marker and a measuring rod for his own future activity.

For a long time Pasternak sought to avoid supplying any autobiographical detail in public. The very first such disclosure in print was one he made in 1922. One third of the text is taken up with personal matters:

I was born in Moscow on 29 January [old style] 1890. I owe a great deal – if not all – to my father, Member of the Academy of Painting, Leonid Osipovich Pasternak, and my mother, a superb pianist.

There follows a list of educational establishments, at which he had studied and the books he had written up to that time. After reading this entry among those on other authors listed in the handbook *Writers. Autobiographies and Portraits of Contemporary Prose Writers. Moscow 1926*, Marina Tsvetayeva commented:

. . . that was how Marcus Aurelius began his book Meditations. In our time (which I hate), when every fledgling that falls out of the nest considers itself a visitant from heaven, such a confession – in the full sense of the word – is unheard of, and emphasizes the supreme nobility of its author. Greatness never attributes its origins to itself, and this is undoubtedly right and proper. The crux of the matter lies in acknowledging one's filial origins – whether from our father in heaven or from one's father here on earth.

The details assembled in this book from a variety of sources help recreate the atmosphere and surroundings of the living drama of which Pasternak became both participant and recorder. The first half of his biography is equally studded – if not more so – with an ever-changing sequence of family ties and friendships, of names and places – in times which allowed far greater ease of movement.

In 1922, with the appearance of his book *My Sister, Life* Pasternak received wide literary acclaim. His reputation kept growing. By the end of the Twenties his literary authority was widely recognized. Journals and publishing houses readily printed his poems and his prose work. The Press carried favourable reviews, acknowledging his enormous poetical talent, despite his "stylistic difficulty" and his "subjectivism". Before him lay the comforting prospect of official recognition and a pre-eminent position in Soviet poetry. Not only was he unattracted by the prospect: he regarded it as suicidal. Pasternak considered it dishonest to be in a privileged position against a background of universal deprivation. He said so openly. This was taking risks, and brought counter attacks and noises of displeasure down upon him.

The tragic succession of events in our country's history necessitated his adopting a new attitude to his work – one full of risk-taking and determined by moral imperatives. The artist had to become the witness to truth and the conscience-bearer for his age. In the mid-Thirties, after speaking out boldly on a number of occasions, Pasternak withdrew from public activity – it was already leading nowhere. He earned a living doing translations. Between times he kept up his prose work in which he wanted to give an integral and morally vital account of the fate of his generation. In 1940 he discovered for himself in his poem "Peredelkino" a simple, clear style in keeping with the evolution of his poetics.

In the years of unbearable tension Pasternak's intense, candid, selfless life found its outlet in his novel *Doctor Zhivago*.

The following brief survey of the events of this creatively-inspired period in Pasternak's life has been put together largely on the basis of material from the family papers kept in Moscow and in London. It is accompanied by a concurrent analysis of his literary works which, with the exception of *Doctor Zhivago*, are little known to Western readers. The Russian language edition of *Materials for a Biography of Boris Pasternak* has been held up for a variety of reasons. In the meantime a number of studies have appeared and new, hitherto unknown documents have been discovered. This allows one to hope that the centenary of Pasternak's birth will usher in new, truthful and penetrating pronouncements on this major writer and present an opportunity for assembling and publishing his correspondence in full.

EVGENY PASTERNAK
Oxford
May 1989

I

SECOND BIRTH

(1930–36)

I

The end of the Twenties was a historically oppressive, cruel time. Pasternak felt that it was the end of a period both in his art and in his life. He made no plans for the future and did his utmost to complete what he had started and assemble what he had in mind.

His books *My Sister, Life* and *Themes and Variations* were reissued in collected form under the title *Two Books* in 1927 and again in 1930. A volume of his poetry came out in 1927 as a separate book entitled *Nineteen Five*. His 1912–1916 poetry was reassembled and, together with poems he wrote later, comprised the 1929 collection *Over the Barriers*. In the summer of 1930 he completed writing *Spektorsky* and that winter he finished *Safe Conduct*. The first part of a new novel was put into shape and published under the title *A Tale*.*

In *Safe Conduct* Pasternak called a period of this sort "a poet's final year". He said of Mayakovsky† and Pushkin in this respect:

All of a sudden they finish off the projects they have not managed to complete. Frequently they add nothing to their state of incompletion apart from a newly acquired and only now acknowledged certainty that they are complete. And this certainty is passed on to posterity. . . .

How can one possibly feel so sad, when one feels so joyous? Is it not one's second birth? Or is it death?

---

* A chronology and bibliography will be found on pp. 247 and 251 respectively, but it is worth noting that A *Tale* was published in English under another title, *The Last Summer*, Peter Owen, London, 1959.

† A select index of persons mentioned in the text can be found on p. 253.

I

These quotations, full of tragic misunderstanding, round off the account given in *Safe Conduct* of the poet's final year and preface the concluding portrayal of Mayakovsky's last love (for Polonskaya) and of his death.

They faced Pasternak equally sharply in 1930, 1931 and at the beginning of 1932. The alternative path his fate might take is set out in his lyrical collection *Second Birth*, written and published at that time. Even before that – in 1928 – he had introduced into his poems a personification of the furtive approach of violent death:

> Powerful hunter, accurate shot,
> haunting banks where the soul's in spate,
> spare me the death of one who makes the hundred up,
> don't crumble me down to feed your whims.
>
> Let me escape the merely commonplace.
> Let darkness adorn me in willow and ice.
> Let morning flush me out of the reeds.
> Take aim. It's all over. Fire as I fly.
>
> And I thank you, O my despised ones,
> for this exalted and resounding end,
> and I kiss you all, your hands,
> homeland, fear, friends and family.

The same sense of menace, almost as an attribute of normal everyday life, is present in the acrostic of 1929 to Marina Tsvetayeva:*

> Any second something silly might slip out
> and bang go praise and slander both.
> And you, you the eternal trick end,
> what alternative had you in mind?

The real feeling of being stalked every day by death is conveyed with startling immediacy in the chapter from *Safe Conduct* devoted to Venice, which he wrote in the winter of 1929–30:

The lion's emblem was present in Venice in a great variety of forms. Thus the aperture for the insertion of secret denunciations – on the Censor's staircase, right next to the paintings of Veronese and Tintoretto – was fashioned in the shape of a lion's mouth. It

---

* The initial letters of the first words in each of the (full) fifteen lines of the acrostic make, in Russian, the two words MARINA TSVETAEVA (of which the following four lines account for AEVA).

2

is well known that the *bocca di leone* struck terror into the hearts of its contemporaries and that it gradually became a mark of ill-breeding in cases where the authorities themselves failed to express any regret, to mention the names of those who had mysteriously disappeared from view through the beautifully sculpted orifice.

The following passage, in which Pasternak expresses indignation at public indifference to the truth, was banned by the censor and deleted from the printed edition:

All around there are lion's muzzles – one visualizes them here, there and everywhere, nosing into one's vitals, sniffing it all out: lions' jaws, gnawing their way through one life after another in the secrecy of their den. From all around comes the lion's roar with its spurious assertion of immortality: the claim is entertained without fear of ridicule only because the lion is master of all that is immortal and has it securely tethered to its leonine leash. Everyone senses this; everyone puts up with it.

From the beginning of 1930 passages of reminiscence, valedictory overtones, constantly recur in Pasternak's work.

On 26 February he sent his sister Lydia the literary journals containing the first part of *Safe Conduct* and *A Tale*, remarking that, although the beginning of *Safe Conduct* related to 1927,

It was, after all, a different period. But it does contain one thing that is each year on the increase and which is killing me. I have started to overload my art with theoretical, valedictory excursions, like so many testamentary truths, in a sort of haunting presentiment of my imminent end – whether it be a total physical one or a partial and natural one, or, finally, an involuntary, figurative one. Does it not all come to the same thing? Do not get distressed at my moods but see whether it is all readable i.e. does not the informative commitment of which I am speaking so weigh down my text as to make it completely indigestible. These writings give me no such joy as did the pages of Luvers.* The reasons for it are, of course, neither personal nor family ones.

On 11 June he wrote to Olga Freidenberg:

* *The Childhood of Luvers.* The first two chapters of this unfinished novel were first published in book form in Moscow in 1924.

There is no reason for writing to you but one. I fear that if I do not write now I shall never have another opportunity to do so. So I am virtually taking my leave of you.

Do not be frightened, you do not have to take that literally. There is nothing seriously wrong with me and there is nothing directly threatening me. But I am ever more frequently haunted by a sense of the end, evoked in my case by the most decisive factor: contemplation of my own work. It has foundered in the past and I am powerless to shift it: I took no part in the creation of the present and I bear it no love.

In essence, he was talking of losing rapport with a milieu from which there came no lyrical response; of the dissolution of previous aesthetic values and of the lyrical poet having become an outcast, fit for nothing worthwhile.

6.III.30 Dearest Mother! . . . I am very tired. Not from these last years, or the difficulties of today's living conditions, but from my own life as a whole. It is not my work, or the circumstances of family life, or worry – in a word, it is not the way my life has turned out that has worn me down. I am worn down by the unchangeability of things, irrespective of what happens to my life. That is what I find sad and wearisome . . . that for virtually my entire life I have lacked an outlet for my talents and shall continue to do so.

    1.III.30

I fear that an utterly incommunicable heaviness and a barely superable darkness of spirit have so affected me that I have lost all touch with art . . . I wanted to say, and forgot: a sort of frustrated *biographical urge* – not my lyrical-youthful one, but a *petrifyingly insatiable one* – is ever more surely taking over everything I do. And that means art has had its say . . .

The phrase left pathetically hanging in the air on a sharply discordant note in his letter to his parents finds a harmonious solution, and is illuminated by other creative possibilities, in his declaratory poem "O had I known . . .":

> When a line comes from the heart,
> feeling thrusts a slave on stage;
> artifice resigns its part
> and earth itself breathes on the page.

Apposite to the work is Pasternak's idea of the lyric poet's destiny and his inalienable opportunities for self-expression which he set out in his letter of 29 September 1930 to Sergey Spassky:

> Present-day life has nothing to suggest to the lyric poet – neither a common language nor anything else. It merely suffers him: he is an extra-territorial element. That is why this aspect of creative activity has broken out of the aesthetic mould. The general tenor of communication used by the lyric poet is governed, not by his *degree of perceptivity* nor by the prevalence of any one kind of impression of *actuality* over any other, but is decided by he himself almost as a question of ethics. In other words, where in normal times we would consider it natural to say so-and-so and so-and-so, we now (each in his own manner) consider this our *duty*. And some see it one way, others another. The reasons for this lie outside us; there is nothing to be done about it for they are stronger than us and our efforts.

> Chopin never seeks the easy way,
> but improvises on the wing:
> inspiration works with chance and clay
> and builds the great predestined thing.

2

In *An Essay in Autobiography* Pasternak sombrely described the circumstances of Mayakovsky's last years as a time:

> when there was no more poetry, neither his own nor anyone else's, when Esenin hanged himself, when, to put it quite simply, literature ceased to exist (for, after all, the start of *Quiet Flows the Don* was also poetry, as were the early writings of Pilnyak and Babel, Fedin and Vsevolod Ivanov) . . .*

Pasternak saw the concrete historical-literary reason for the break in the chain in the unjust attitude taken to the writers known as Fellow-Travellers† which had developed into outright

---

* *An Essay in Autobiography*, p. 50.
† Poputchiki – the generic term given by Trotsky in *Literature and Revolution* (1923) to independent, non-Party, politically unaffiliated writers, free to write what they wanted short of criticizing the regime.

persecution, inaugurated by the reports of V.M. Friche ("On bourgeois tendencies in literature and the tastes of the critics") and
P.M. Kerzhentsev.

"I get very nervous and depressed," Pasternak wrote to Sergey
Spassky on 22 December 1928:

> almost to the point of being physically ill, at this recent and ever
> increasing talk about "the right wing danger" in literature. It would
> be easier if on the official side some definite steps were taken, to
> which one could react one way or the other. But not only are none
> being taken but none, it seems, are anticipated; the atmosphere,
> rendered tolerable over the years by force of habit, now reminds
> one, with renewed freshness of impact, of its own intolerability.

Pasternak goes on to say that it is natural for a conscientious person
to respond to official criticism by recognizing his mistakes on the
basis that "they misled us; it was not we who sang out of tune", but
that in the given situation to do so would be senseless in view of the
absurd injustice of such criticism. "Anything that carries a remote
echo of actual achievement is for the rubbish dump and that means,
in the first place, Leonov, Fedin and Vsevolod Ivanov", he wrote.

Fedin sent him his novel *Brothers* which amazed Pasternak by the
closeness of its artistic concepts to his own. He replied to the author
on 6 December 1928 with the idea of giving him support and
protecting him from unjust attacks of an inquisitorial nature.

> It has seemed to me that you, like the rest of us, chose to hold in
> check your descriptive talent, your sharpness and difference of
> style, and your own personal career in an epoch which obliterated
> detail and obliged us to live not in immutable circles and groups
> but in the semi-real chaos of a homogenous flux, but that you,
> like very few of us and perhaps better and more profoundly than
> that small handful, have managed spiritually to invest this (in fact
> compulsory) self-abnegation with sense and justification.

Three days later, on 9 December, Pasternak came out with an
official statement in the press in support of Fedin. It was published
in the journal *Chitatel i Pisatel** (Nos. 50–52, 1928).

> I do not know what classification is to be given in the sense of
> public rating to the branch of literature, in which pride of place

* *Reader and Writer* – Moscow illustrated weekly (1927–28) about books and
publishing.

6

belongs to Konstantin Fedin; and I do not know whether I have the right to suggest it, but I would be happy with any place in the same rank as being a position corresponding to my real ideological postulates and aspirations. I have named the author rather than the group because I consider deeds rather than intentions to be the cardinal consideration in our work.

BORIS PASTERNAK

Many of Pasternak's letters reflect his thoughts about "the Fellow-Travellers' involuntary act of self-abnegation and the distortion to which their historic role in the most recent past had been subjected." "We are perishing from our own preparedness" was a phrase he loved to repeat, as Tamara Ivanova,* who came to know Pasternak at this time, records in her memoirs.

His reproaches and regrets were, of course, primarily addressed to himself, in recollection of his own recent experiences:

When I wrote *Nineteen Five*, I knowingly compounded this piece of comparative vulgarity as part of a voluntary, idealistic compact with the time . . .

he wrote to Fedin; and in his letter to Pozner he set out the personal, biographical reasons for his compromise:

I was a witness to my own unmerited achievement of recognition. I am not conceited but this had to say something to my heart. I had to accommodate this nameless love in my life. And suddenly I came to recognize that it does not fit in. That this love would like to see me otherwise: *that it understands better than I do who I should be and how I am to repay it for its excessive devotion to me* . . .

Even the most tenuous of regrets on the score of "unintelligibility" (together with never-ending marks of respect) act on me like the unfounded jealousy of a person who has sacrificed everything for you. And I am not a wild animal; one must finally pay heed to such kind people, and . . . well, to hell with the truth, if it makes things about the house so difficult.

It was from the same standpoint of conscious limitation of their potential that Pasternak reacted to the tragedy of Mayakovsky and Aseyev.

---

* Wife of Vsevolod Ivanov.

His meeting with them in Aseyev's flat in the first few days of April 1928 is described in *An Essay in Autobiography*. Pasternak recalls the words uttered by Mayakovsky: "It's true . . . We really are different. You love lightning to be in the sky, and I – love it in an electric iron."* In V.A. Katanyan's opinion, the metaphor derives from the sight of a burn left by the iron on Aseyev's wife's dressing table.

Ignoring the demerits of this striking comparison – a lame one, since lightning in an iron means it is totally useless – it is clear that despite the sincere conviction of Mayakovsky and Aseyev in the rightness of their positions, Pasternak distinctly sensed in their words and poems the inner discord and the strain of the conscious abnegation to which they had submitted themselves.

On 4 April 1928, probably the day after the meeting in Aseyev's flat, Pasternak wrote to Mayakovsky to say:

> Our conversation was not hurtful to you or to me but is depressingly fruitless in terms of life, which is not overgenerous with the time or resources it puts at our disposal. It is sad. You keep making the mistake (and Aseyev repeats it after you) of thinking that my withdrawal [from LEF]† was a move elsewhere, and that I was exercising a preference for someone over someone else. . . . Perhaps I am at fault in relation to you for my limitations, my lack of willpower. Perhaps knowing, as I do, who you are I should have loved you more ardently and more effectually and retrieved you against your will from this insubstantial and semi-evanescent role of leader of a non-existent detachment standing on an imaginary position . . . In leaving LEF I broke with the last of those useless groupings but not with the aim of starting the whole sequence all over again. And you are doing your best not to understand this. B.P.

Nor did Aseyev want to understand it.

Pasternak considered Aseyev a splendid lyricist "with a rare form of poetic gift in its primordial, classic form". He recalled that among

---

* *An Essay in Autobiography*, pp. 48–49.

† LEF – "Left Wing Arts Front" (1922–29). A Moscow literary grouping of writers and painters, which was founded by Mayakovsky. Its journal LEF, of which only seven numbers appeared, existed from 1923–25, and its successor, *Novy LEF*, from 1927–28. Pasternak officially announced his withdrawal from the group in May 1927.

the young people at the start of the Twenties "while the rest of us were unable to give an intelligible account of ourselves and made a virtue of inarticulacy and a necessity of originality, only two, Aseyev and Tsvetayeva, could express themselves properly and write in a classical language and style."*

Pasternak admired Aseyev's "Oksana" in 1917 and praised "Steel Nightingale" in 1922. In Berlin, in 1922, he had fallen out with Khodasevich as a result of defending Aseyev, and in 1929 he defended Aseyev's role in the history of Russian literature in his letters to Pozner – who had ignored Aseyev in his review of the recent poetry. But at the same time Pasternak considered it necessary to point out that Aseyev's tragedy was that of having betrayed his innate poetic gift to please the spirit of the time and having taken the "all-too-easy" way out of the dilemma – the dilemma of "whether to suffer without illusions or thrive by deceiving ourselves and others."

Pasternak's attitude to Aseyev, who was violating his talents for the sake of temporary and ephemeral assignments, can be summed up in the one word "pity". When to this was added sudden alarm for Aseyev's life – in his periods of acute tuberculosis – Pasternak, forgetting the hurtful words thrown at him, and forgiving the accusations of betrayal, rushed to make his peace: "I was, naturally, bowled over by the news and went to see him, on a number of long visits, just as I did once before, that is 10 or 15 years ago," he wrote to Tikhonov on 14 July 1929.

The celebration of New Year 1930 had been officially cancelled as a bourgeois relic. Mayakovsky complied but, like many others, switched the traditional holiday back a day. The guests assembled in Gendrikov Lane on 30 December.

As on previous New Year's Eves, Pasternak turned up in the early hours of the morning, at the same time as Shklovsky; no one was in the mood for talking and the guests went their various ways. Pasternak left within a few minutes.

They soon met again, among the guests invited by Meyerhold. Evgeny Dolmatovsky remembers how Mayakovsky leapt on him for the "Akhmatova-like" quality of his semi-childish verse, but Pasternak intervened on his behalf, as he was still a mere child.

---

* *An Essay in Autobiography*, p. 53.

Pasternak was pained by RAPP's* harassment of his friends, who rapidly shifted position. He found it all the harder to bear because the critics left him alone, frequently naming him among "the greatest poets of our day". His customarily strict criteria therefore became particularly strict when it was a question of his own revolutionary poems.

In the 1940s he had compared his work on *Lieutenant Schmidt* to translation of Shakespeare; in *An Essay in Autobiography* he recalled that Mayakovsky did not like *Nineteen Five* or *Lieutenant Schmidt* and considered the writing of them a mistake. Compared to the widely ecstatic reception of *My Sister, Life*, which Pasternak called exaggerated, the reaction to *Nineteen Five* seemed to him equivocal; and its failure to deal with the realistic, substantive side of the book exasperated the author.

The critics gradually worked out a routine formula. It involved writing that, after abandoning his lyric poetry "which had fallen silent", Pasternak had descended from the philosophic heights into historical reality and from there had climbed up again to deal with a social theme. Or, as I. Sergievsky put it in *Molodaya Guardiya*† (No. 2, 1928), without once betraying his artistic conscience, Pasternak had mastered thematic material and come face to face with the present day:

"I can see from his last letters that he is very much on his own in his work," said Marina Tsvetayeva in a letter of 5 February 1928 to Leonid Pasternak:

> After all, the compliments of most of them relate to the *Nineteen Five* theme – in other words something like good marks for good conduct.

* RAPP (Russian Association of Proletarian Writers, founded 1925). Though few were proletarian in origin, the members of RAPP, such as Averbakh and Fadeyev asserted that the role of literature must be to serve the interests of the proletariat. At this time (1925), the Party Central Committee had proclaimed its neutrality as between competing literary groups – hence the survival of the Fellow-Travellers – but with the switch in 1928–9 from NEP to the Five Year Plan and to mass collectivization, the Party likewise discarded its literary liberalism. For a while (1929–32) RAPP was allowed to rule the roost, but in 1932 all separate literary groups, RAPP included, were disbanded and from early 1934 all writers, zealots and non-zealots alike, were marshalled into the conformist ranks of the new Union of Soviet Writers, an increasingly bureaucratic machine for imposing strict control under the banner of so-called Socialist Realism.

† *Young Guard* – a monthly journal, founded in 1922 and published by the Komsomol Central Committee.

Pasternak began to see these "good conduct awards" as a personally offensive act of indulgence towards him, viewed against the background of the campaign of political harassment of writers whose work seemed to him serious and whose fate evoked compassion. He was tortured by an awareness of the equivocal nature of his position and the degree of tolerance shown him by the critics, given the general dogmatism and the inquisitorial nature of the polemical line.

He sensed that he was living at odds with himself. He accused himself of odious compliance, and "impersonal submissiveness", as he called it, and saw the need at all costs to break out of the stalemate. Pasternak attributed to the same sense of self-discontent the "intensified autobiographicalism" of his most recent writings in which he appeared to defend himself against a charge of two-facedness. He replied to the words of genuine sympathy from the then editor of the journal *Zvezda*,* V. Sayanov, with the sharply defiant retort of someone driven to the brink:

> Your phrase that the editorial board considers me "one of the closest and most-needed collaborators of *Zvezda*" yet again reminds me of the falseness of my position which I find increasingly depressing year in year out, and for which I am not to blame. After all, I am not a wrecker. My books are not screened off behind a curtain, not interleaved with ricepaper. Everything in them is transparent? What then do you find topical and useful in them? Am I not an individual personality? My individuality never seemed to me a fortuitous accident which one could ignore, retaining just a tincture. But surely, is not this what people are combatting with such enthusiasm? And how is it possible to accord me such recognition when even the *Encyclopedia Britannica*† is unduly flattering about me in its article on Russian literature. If I did not have a family and I were not a morally average person, I would be duty bound, looking at what is happening around me, to come out in print with my objections to such benevolent criticism. It is all an abhorrent and excruciating riddle.

* *The Star* – the Leningrad monthly organ of Union of Soviet Writers, founded in 1924.

† i.e. how can Soviet criticism be so affirmative about him, when he is the "darling" of the capitalists (the dilemma recurred with *Doctor Zhivago*).

Pasternak's objective reasons were supplemented by "personal and, partly, family ones", of which frequent mention is made in the letters of the period. At that time everyone had to cope with unbelievable daily hardship, and Pasternak had been trying to refrain from complaining or attempting to secure for himself, as an exception, tolerable living conditions of which those around him also stood in need, passively and without daring to hope. At that time such efforts were regarded as demeaning. But by the end of 1928 he could stand it no longer and filled in a questionnaire sent him the previous year by the Board of the All-Russian Union of Writers, in which question No. 7 was "Living Conditions?". His answer ran:

Very poor. My father's old tied flat extremely overcrowded. 20 people (6 families) permanently domiciled. To this one needs to add frequent visits by relatives and friends proceeding along the 6 main independent access routes. Comparatively large studio (5 m^2 x 8.7 m^2), formerly my father's, devolved to me as result of space reallocations, is divided by partition. Because of location of stoves etc., room does not lend itself readily to being divided up: positioning of partition resulted in two narrow corridor-like rooms. Dining room is located in room where I work and full of noise and commotion all day long. Partitions have not been plastered so each year have been regarding stay in present conditions as temporary: circumstances and earnings have not permitted a move out of these conditions . . . Hemmed in on all sides by noise, can only concentrate for periods at a time by dint of extreme sublimated desperation, akin to self-oblivion. I urgently need change of flat. Wife is painter, in last year at VKhUTEMAS* and will need room to work in. I can easily, I think, meet and manage material expenditure contingent on minimum wishes formulated, once transferred to more tolerable working conditions.

The questionnaire bears the date of receipt by the Union of

* VKhUTEMAS (Higher Artistic Technical Studios 1920–26, when it was renamed VKhUTEIN): Polytechnic for Painters, Architects and Designers.

Writers "4 January 1929", plus the incoming number assigned to it, and is minuted "To be refused".

The room was separated from the unheated corridor by the partition. The corridor generated a lot of cold; the water in the bucket became encrusted with ice. The cold hit you as soon as you went out.

The flat fell quiet only at night. Pasternak used mostly to stay sitting at his writing desk – which stood slantwise beside the window – till a late hour and worked with the encouragement of cigarettes and hot tea. *Safe Conduct, Spektorsky, A Tale* were all written with a sensation of increasing fatigue and a disquieting awareness of not experiencing the happiness he had derived from his earlier works, and without which, as he considered, art loses its justification and its sense.

After a three month break Evgeniya Vladimirovna* resumed her Institute classes. Her fellow students in her year were strong personalities: Romadin, Chuikov, Maleina, Nissky, Sokolov-Skalya. She was due to hand in her diploma work by the end of 1929.

Her brother and sister brought her sick mother to Moscow from Leningrad. Her mother's long illness had started in the summer of 1924 when she had clambered on top of a tall wardrobe to pull out of a basket some small present for her grandson Zhenya.† Losing her balance, she had landed on her spine and hurt herself badly. This episode is indirectly echoed in *Doctor Zhivago* in the scene in which the wardrobe causes Anna Ivanovna Gromeko's death.‡ Aleksandra Veniaminovna Lurye loved her son-in-law and each time he came to see her was a red-letter day.

In the first week of November 1928 the Pasternaks were summoned by an alarming phone call. Evgeniya Vladimirovna set out immediately, but Boris Leonidovich was a bit delayed. The sick woman was fully conscious and talked cheerfully to the daughters and the son at her bedside. She already had no pulse. Pasternak came in, she smiled, tried to raise herself up to greet him and died.

On 14 November he wrote to his sister Josephine:

You will certainly have heard of the death of Zhenya's mother.

* Evgeniya Vladimirovna (née Lurye), Pasternak's first wife (1899–1965).

† The familiar form Zhenya is used for Evgeny (Pasternak's son by this first marriage and the author of this book) and for Evgeniya (Pasternak's first wife): the same applies to the diminutives Zhenechka and Zhenichka.

‡ *Doctor Zhivago*, Collins Harvill, 1958, republished 1988, p. 66.

The manner of her death, her last words and so forth brought out and reinforced at the last moment the likeness that there always was between her and Zhenya; and the latter's day-long tears, especially over the first twenty-four hours, underlined and still further strengthened this subtle link. Zhenya kept weeping, stroked and embraced the body, adjusted the pillow below it and, in between fits of tears and talking to visitors, set about making a furtive sketch of her mother. It was all done in haste, on the quiet, like a child – holding nothing back, everything – death and grief, the end and the continuation, fate and the immanent prospect – fused into one, it was all noble and evanescent beyond words.

She found it difficult to recover. On her return, after talking to the then famous Professor Kannabikh, she scraped her palette free of the old paint and set eagerly to work.

In the third part of *Doctor Zhivago* Pasternak incorporated features of what he had witnessed into the scenes of Anna Ivanovna Gromeko's illness and Tonya's inconsolable grief after her mother's death.

At the end of April, Evgeniya Vladimirovna was sent off to the "Kurpaty" Sanatorium in Gaspra, from where she returned restored to health and reinvigorated.

Their son Zhenya* was in his sixth year. It was time to deal with his education. They consulted friends and made enquiries. Within a matter of days the Pasternaks set off *à trois* for the former lodging house located at No. 10 Mertvy Lane (now Ostrovsky Street). There, in the room at the extreme end of the endless corridor which bisected the vast second-floor flat packed out with tenants and their belongings, they found Elizaveta Mikhailovna Stetsenko. She taught children French.

A greying lady of some fifty years or more, she gave an appearance of tallness. She was invariably dressed in a dark floor-length dress gathered tightly at the waist and done up to the chin with a stand-up collar secured by little buttons covered in the same material. She always sat upright and never leaned back against the back of the chair. She showed the same easy, unforced sprightliness in everything – her conversation, her ability to look, think and patiently endure. The same unemphatic, natural ease was readily apparent in others whose lot was similar to hers who could then

* The author.

14

still be encountered. The "diehards" was the term used for them, by now in a good-natured sense. All she could call her own was in the past: she now had to live in keeping with the grandeur of her loss, remaining, with unforced dignity, worthy of her memories and her dead husband's love. At the beginning of the war her only son, Georgy, a student at Petersburg University, had gone to the Front in East Prussia and been killed when the Russian cavalry had, on the orders of General Bezobrazov, attacked in dismounted formation German fortifications supported by heavy artillery and machine guns. Her husband, Dmitry Aleksandrovich Lopukhin, under whose command their son had been serving, had from a tragic sense of guilt fought with desperate courage, beyond the call of his age or rank. He was fatally wounded at the end of the war and suffered a long, painful death.

Elizaveta Mikhailovna had personally founded, equipped, and maintained throughout the war a large field hospital and had done unbroken service as senior theatre sister. She had raised the money to finance this by selling, on behalf of her husband and son, their estate in Orel which had been awarded a Bronze Medal at the World Exhibition in Paris for exemplary farm management.

On learning of the deaths of the Lopukhins, father and son, Ippolit Vasilyevich Stetsenko, a cavalry officer, who had been devotedly in love since his youth with the wife of his regimental commander, found Elizaveta Mikhailovna in the Caucasus, where she had earlier spent her childhood and her youth. She was the daughter of Mikhail (Mengli) Girey. Ippolit Vasilyevich persuaded Sergey Kirov to issue them permission to travel to Moscow. Elizaveta Mikhailovna decided to remain in Russia and agreed to become Ippolit Vasilyevich's wife.

When she spoke, she never raised her voice or her tone, inspiring trust and an unquestioning desire to be of service. Starting with French lessons, she soon took over Zhenya's entire upbringing. Until that spring, Pasternak had frequently written that he was worried about the boy being left to himself and going off somewhere with the neighbours for days at a time. Now he was able to feel reassured.

From March 1929, as had frequently been the case before, Pasternak experienced a dull ache in his lower jaw. X-rays revealed a cyst under his chin which had destroyed part of his jawbone. The operation was performed in the third week of June, lasted two hours and was extremely painful. On 9 July 1929, Pasternak wrote:

. . . I lost consciousness during it because the local anaesthetic did not work . . . and they were afraid to administer a general one for fear of severing the central facial nerve . . . Zhenya, poor lass, stood the other side of the door and they ran out to her and tried unsuccessfully to lead her away. But now, thank heaven, it is all behind us and it is only that one still thinks from time to time that, after all, these were doctors striving to cause as little pain as possible – so what must people who were being tortured have had to undergo? And what a good thing it is that our imagination is dulled and does not transmit a vivid picture of everything.

The wound took about a month to heal. During that time he was forbidden to speak. "My jaw affair is a long drawn out one, although it now causes me no pain. Zhenya is looking after me devotedly, does my errands for me and allows no one near me. There are always flowers on my table and Yulia Bentsionovna cooks for us and generally looks after me."

Pasternak was at that time translating Rilke's "Requiem for a Lady Friend".

On 8 July he insisted that Evgeniya Vladimirovna, her son and Elizaveta Mikhailovna leave for Ognevsky Ovrag near Kiev where Dmitry Petrovich Konchalovsky had a large timber house. Konchalovsky's wife, Zinaida Ivanovna (née Ilovaiskaya) let rooms during the summer and ran a sort of pension. The Pasternaks occupied a large room – a sort of attic below the roof – on the upper floor. On 17 July Boris Pasternak joined them there. His writing desk stood in the corner by the entrance where there was a steep, wooden staircase. To enter the room one had to go behind Pasternak's back, and this bothered him. He detected in his conversations with his host a note of incomprehension and disapproval for his work and his views. Dmitry Petrovich was a specialist on Ancient Rome. His historical forecasts and appraisals were gloomy.

Elizaveta Mikhailovna used to talk to Pasternak about the past. Her fate had been determined not by any prognostications about the future but by her own faith and loyalty. Pasternak found this sympathetic and understandable. In the autumn he wrote jokingly in a copy of his book *Over the Barriers*: "To dear, dear, dear Elizaveta Mikhailovna, the clearest and wisest of women, from the dullard taught – in part – by her, in memory of summer 1929."

She was a living witness to court life at the beginning of the century and belonged to the progressively-minded aristocracy, which saw the urgent need for democratic reform, but kept being constantly reminded of the Tsar's inability to understand the country's needs or to respond to them in accord with history. Pasternak's conversations with Elizaveta Mikhailovna helped him to give in the third part of *Safe Conduct* a succinct portrayal of the aura of doom of that period and of the historic atmosphere absorbed by his generation on the eve of the World War.

On her return to Moscow, Evgeniya Vladimirovna plunged headlong into painting a large-scale composition on an industrial subject for her diploma work. On 15 December Pasternak wrote to his father:

> It is a very difficult and worrying time for Zhenya. In three days time she has to submit her diploma work for painting. She has chosen as her subject a foundry shop at a metallurgical factory (like something by Menzel, but with the range of colour of your first oils – "On The Bridge", for example). She has been working at the factory itself, where the movement made things difficult and the days were dark, but she had nowhere to put her easel at home. The work is not finished; there are some successful bits among large areas of rough daub. We will see what comes of it, but at home there is no space to turn in and working conditions are ghastly."

By the end of 1929 she had successfully graduated from the Institute and was dreaming of doing serious work on her own.

4

Back in 1922 the pianist Genrikh Gustavovich Neigaus,* who had been invited to become a Professor at the Conservatoire, and the philosopher Valentin Ferdinandovich Asmus, had both moved to Moscow. They had become friends in Kiev after the Civil War and used to arrange joint musical and literary evenings.

In 1928 Neigaus, with his wife, Zinaida Nikolayevna, and their two sons who had been born in Moscow, Adrian and Stanislav, were living in Trubnikovsky Lane, while Asmus and his wife,

---

* Neigaus has been and is variously rendered as Neuhaus, Neigauz, etc.

Irina Sergeyevna, and their daughter Masha were on Zubovsky Boulevard. Their family friendship became still closer as the years went by; they shared wide-ranging interests in literature and philosophy. Asmus became friendly with a number of writers and appeared in print as a literary critic.

Pasternak's poems sent Zinaida Neigaus into raptures. In her memoirs which, in 1964, as Zinaida Pasternak, she dictated to Zoya Maslennikova, we read that one day:

> Irina Sergeyevna popped in to us full of the joys of life and announced that she had made Pasternak's acquaintance. Her manner of achieving this was original: having recognized Pasternak, whose face was not that ordinary, from his portrait, she went up to him and introduced herself. She told him that she and her husband were ardent admirers of his poetry and thereupon invited him to come and visit them . . . I was convinced that Pasternak would not come and asked Genrikh Gustavovich to go along without me, and stayed at home with the children. In the event Pasternak did turn up and stayed with them the entire evening.

Pasternak wrote on 16 January 1929 as of a recent event that "having attended one of his concerts he got to meet one of our best pianists here, Genrikh Neigaus". The circumstances of their newly-formed friendship, founded on the mutual admiration of Boris Pasternak and Genrikh Neigaus, the motive force of which was the energy of Irina Sergeyevna Asmus, who had fallen in love with Pasternak, are graphically reconstructed in the memoirs of Nikolay Vilyam-Vilmont. *

Pasternak wrote to his parents:

> 6.III.30 . . . The only bright spot in our existence is the various concert performances given by my latest friend (i.e. my friend of this last year), Genrikh Neigaus, after which we – some of his friends – have got into the habit of spending the rest of the evening in one or other's place. The libations provided are copious but the snacks, which for technical reasons are almost impossible to come by, modest. The last time he played with Koenemann on two pianos and it was curious to learn that even a difference in touch can convert the pianos of the same firm into instruments of incommensurably discrete timbre. Without once diverging in

---

* Unpublished.

rhythm they all the while diverged in the music, and even Zhenya and Irina, eyes closed, could tell Neigaus' entries from the way he would suddenly inject a wave of powerful sonority, with a fantastic feeling of rhythm and temperament, into the briskly athletic finger sequence. After that (without Koenemann, of course) we stayed together till 6 a.m., drinking, eating, playing the piano and reading poetry and dancing the foxtrot in Shura and Irina's room; Fedichka* was moved in with Zhenya.

None of this pleased Evgeniya Vladimirovna. She was accused of unfounded jealousy and failure to understand. By the spring she was again having lung trouble. The doctors advised her to go to Europe for treatment. She sought to persuade her husband to apply for the necessary permission and for all three of them to go. Pasternak put off taking a decision and persisted in his doubts.

> 9.IV.30 . . . I have long been thinking of going abroad for a year and a half or so, and each year I give up the idea . . . But given the present determination to go abroad at some point nevertheless, and in view of our state of general exhaustion, which is the most important thing of all, one cannot go on indefinitely evading the question; one cannot fail sooner or later to come to a decision. And so I have given my word to Zhenya that when the current chapter of *Safe Conduct* is finished I will give this plan my final consideration and get down to doing something about it.
>
> By the way, an acquaintance of mine, Ir. Serg. Asmus, showed rare insight in devising a way to help me write this chapter on Marburg, Cohen, Ida V[ysotskaya] and Venice. In Zhenya's presence, she commissioned me to do it for her by a fixed date, the day of her birthday and – of even greater help to me – asked Zhenya to do her portrait, took her out for walks etc. So Zhenya and I made a pact; on the seventh I would give a reading of my chapter and as from the eighth I would start applying for a passport.

Further on in his letter, Pasternak asks his parents about an entry visa for his wife and son, as he himself was proposing to arrive six months later after finishing the next, planned, part of *Safe Conduct*.

* Fedor (Fedya, Fedichka), the son of Aleksandr Leonidovich (younger brother of Pasternak) and Irina Nikolayevna Pasternak.

There must be no element of chance in it, either in its length or in the scope of the subjects it deals with. There is a finite amount which has to be written nowhere else but here and the working out of which cannot be done abroad. This is specifically the part which sifts through the bases of my conceptions, the most up-to-date ones, the most – from a superficial, localized view – controversial etc. To write about them in other, easier conditions would be ignoble; and it would introduce into the text an element which is not there.

On 14 April Mayakovsky shot himself. The last part of *Safe Conduct*, the force and persuasiveness of which were intended to make an impact on the fate of the generation whose dramatic figurehead was Mayakovsky, lost its essential relevance. A year later Pasternak rounded off *Safe Conduct* with a sort of necrology describing the strange phenomenon he called "the poet's final year", one which, he believed, repeats itself from century to century.

Pasternak was subsequently to declare that "the book came out at a third of its planned length."

Once he had begun the formalities to be allowed a trip abroad, Pasternak soon found that he would not be given permission. As a last resort, he decided to ask Gorky's help and wrote to him on 31 April:

I have been hard put to work of late, especially this winter when the metropolis found itself in such an absurd and totally unjustified position of privilege vis-à-vis what was happening in the countryside, and town-dwellers were being invited to pay visits to the victims and congratulate them on the shocks and misfortunes they had suffered. Up to this winter it was my understanding that, however much I was drawn to the West, I would move nowhere until I finished what I had started. I dangled this prospect before myself as a promised reward, and it was the one thing that kept me going.

But now I feel there is no point in deluding myself. None of this will come about; I overestimated my powers of endurance and perhaps my strength. I shall not manage anything worthwhile and deferment will not help. Something has burst inside me; I do not know when, but I felt it recently. I have decided against delaying. Perhaps the journey will cure me, if my full spiritual demise has not yet already set in.

I made various attempts and the first few steps convinced me

20

that without your intercession on my behalf I shall not get an exit permit. Please help me – that is what I'm asking."

Gorky's reply was received on 19 June:

I will not carry out your request and very much advise you against pursuing your application for permission to travel abroad – wait a while! The fact is that Anatoly Kamensky recently came out here and is now writing nasty little stories for *Rul** and giving the most vulgar "lectures". I am sure that his conduct – in conjunction with similar behaviour by Vl. Azov – will for a certain time create complications for writers wishing to go abroad. It has always been the case that decent people are called on to pay for the acts of scoundrels, and now it has become your turn.
I wish you all the best.

A. Peshkov

Pasternak did not start to challenge the justice of the theoretical formulation propounded by Gorky or to express doubt in its reasonableness. On 20 June he wrote to his sister Lydia: "I have met with refusal from all sides, and now I have had a reply from G., in which he advises me most cordially to wait, i.e. refuses to support me in my efforts. So, one has to wave goodbye to this matter for the time being. In the autumn I will renew my efforts on behalf of Zhenya and Zhenichka, since the main obstacle is evidently me."

5

The passages quoted from Pasternak's letters have been given in no particular order and without observing their chronological sequence but they all in varying degree mirror his state of emotional exhaustion and his presentiment of the end. It is easy to imagine Pasternak's grief and loss at Mayakovsky's suicide. This loss vastly intensified the gloom to which Pasternak had been prone during the past year and confirmed to him that there was no way out of it.

Pasternak saw the same message in yet another recent shock – the arrest and execution by firing squad of Vladimir Sillov, "the sole honest, vital and honourable" one "of the LEF people in

* *The Helm* – Russian émigré journal published in Berlin.

their present make-up", as he wrote on 1 March 1930 to Nikolay Chukovsky. Pasternak called Sillov:

an example of the new ethics, towards the (unsuccessful and merely verbalized) implantation of which LEF contributed by dint of its violation of the consciences of some and the talents of others.

"There was only one person," he considered:

who for a brief moment, lent verisimilitude to an impossible and imposed myth, and that was V.S.* I will be more specific. There was only one place I knew in Moscow, a visit to which inspired some doubt in me as to the correctness of my impressions. That was the Sillovs' room in the Proletkult hostel on Vozdvizhenka.

"It was an event in my own life – not just a nearby occurrence. I shall never put it from my mind." The reason for Sillov's arrest was the private diary he had been keeping – it contained criticism of Stalin. He had hidden it away but it was discovered by those "who nose into one's vitals".

On 26 March Pasternak wrote to his father:

He was 28 years old. People say he kept a diary: not a routine, everyday diary but the diary of a supporter of the revolution, and that he thought too much . . . As soon as I heard about it I went to see his wife, whose close friend I had once been: the scars on her arm from her first attempt to throw herself out of the window on to the street below were just beginning to heal.

In Pasternak's eyes the rapid way in which events succeeded one another had special, symbolic meaning. On 14 April 1930, when he learnt of what had happened, he called Olga Sillova to meet him at the very spot. "Something told me," he wrote in *Safe Conduct*, "that the shock would give her an outlet for her own grief." Memoirists have recalled Pasternak shedding tears over the dead man: "He walked around the room, without looking to see who was there, and whenever he bumped into someone he fell on their chest – and his whole face was drenched in tears."

In taking his last leave of Mayakovsky that same day, he was saying goodbye to his youth and youthful enthusiasms, to all that had once filled his life and given it a sense of justification, goodbye to

* Vladimir Sillov.

what he used to call "superheatedly conceptualizing, ultra-receptive art".

The romantic notion of the role of the poet "harnessing himself to life's criteria and paying with his life for doing so" had again been substantiated and personified in Mayakovsky's fate.

Notes of this tragic theme are to be heard in the poems of *Second Birth*. Principally, of course, in the section "Death of a Poet". The poem is a direct response to what he experienced: strength of feeling has been transmuted into strength of communication and of release; in other words, into artistic strength. Pasternak has borrowed from Lermontov not only the title but also the combination of a lament for the dead with a diatribe addressed to Mayakovsky's following who had stoked the "conflagration"; "people of fictitious reputations and bogus, unjustified pretensions", as Pasternak called them in *Safe Conduct*, and from whose influence he had always wanted to rescue Mayakovsky. Like Lermontov's poem, "Death of a Poet" too was printed without its concluding words of wrath.

The title and the last twelve lines were removed from the published edition, probably at the insistence of Vyacheslav Polonsky, the recently reappointed editor of *Novy Mir*.† But even the surviving last lines of "Extract", as the poem was called in the journal, offended and provoked Aseyev:

> Mount Etna to the smaller hills:
> the sound of your shot to the cowards.

The "circular ripples" of gratuitous explanations and pitiful alibis provoked by the pistol shot were as alien and unintelligible to Pasternak as the attribution of the outcome of the Battle of Borodino to Napoleon's catching a cold. The sifting of detail and the elucidation of imagined hidden reasons had the effect of turning the epilogue to the tragedy into a farce.

> But friends made gossiping a minor art,
> forgetting Life, and I, were stood apart.

> What else? You swept them to the wall like trash,
> or worse, so now you live in their report,
> in which your power is dust, your powder, ash.
> Sordid details mesmerise their sort.

* *New World* – Moscow literary and political monthly journal, organ of Union of Soviet Writers, founded 1925.

23

Tittle-tattle, gossip – it's a dam
in case this tragedy should break its banks
and inundate their puny, pea-brained ranks.
For them, a funeral means a plate of ham.

6

In the absence of any possibility of going to Germany, the Pasternaks
were left without firm summer plans. It was the year of forced
collectivization and people were afraid of having trouble with food
shortages.

On 6 January 1930, there appeared in print the decree of the
Federation of Soviet Writers Associations providing for the formation of writers' shock brigades, to be despatched to the collective
and State farms. Zoya Maslennikova recorded Pasternak's account
of one such visit.

> "What I saw there [he said] cannot be described in words. It
> was such inhuman, such unimaginable distress, such terrible
> misfortune that it seemed almost to verge on the abstract; it
> exceeded the bounds of one's comprehension. I fell ill."

A similar impression is given in the letter to Gorky, asking for help
with getting abroad; and on 9 January 1930 Pasternak wrote to his
sister Lydia:

> Everyone is living under great stress, but that which people living
> in the town have to undergo in their daily life is simply a bed
> of roses compared with what is happening in the countryside.
> Measures of the most far-embracing, epoch-making kind are
> being taken in the countryside and one has to be blind not to see
> what unprecedented prospects this may create for the State, but
> in my opinion, one has also to be a man of the soil to be in a fit
> position to talk about it, i.e. one has to experience these surgical
> transformations in terms of one's own flesh and blood; to sing
> hymns to it from the sidelines is even more immoral than to
> sing hymns about a war from the rear. The air is full of it.

It is worth noting that it was Andrey Platonov's impressions of
his visits to the countryside during the collectivization period that
caused him, between December 1929 and April 1930, to write his

novel *The Foundation Pit*. His tale became the strongest expression of the horror which defied comprehension and found an outlet on an abstract-cosmic plane. Pasternak knew Platonov, had a high opinion of him and loved him. They frequently met at the Pilnyaks.

The painter and musician Anna Ivanovna Troyanovskaya had been inviting the Pasternaks to stay in her summer cottage "Bugry" near Maloyaroslavets. It was a traditional refuge for people from the arts world. In the 1918–21 famine years, the composer Medtner lived there and subsequently the painter, Falk. Petr Petrovich Konchalovsky soon after bought "Bugry" from Anna Troyanovskaya and settled down there.

Preparations for the journey were made, then deferred. The uncertainty created confusion and difficulty.

The Asmuses and the Neigauses had lived near Kiev for many years. Irina Sergeyevna decided once again to help by taking the initiative. Zinaida Nikolayevna recalled:

> They asked me, as the one who was keen on travel, to go and rent dachas for all of them. We settled on Irpen. We got together enough money to cover the advance payment and I set off. I took four dachas: for us, for the Asmuses, for Boris Leonidovich Pasternak, and for his brother, Aleksandr Leonidovich and his wife Irina Nikolayevna . . .
>
> As usual, one had to look for a piano for Genrikh Gustavovich in Kiev and have it transported by cart to Irpen. The dachas of the A.L. and I.N. Pasternaks and ours were next to one another and I had deliberately taken those for B.L. Pasternak and his wife and the Asmuses a bit further off . . .

Zinaida Nikolayevna returned to Moscow and with her customary strength of purpose got everyone ready for the journey within a few days. They travelled complete with kitchenware, linen and mattresses all done up in bundles. That spring the Pasternaks had acquired a domestic servant, Elena Petrovna Kuzmina, a wonderfully warm-hearted person who subsequently became a devoted helpmate to them – and to Elizaveta Mikhailovna, who also made the journey to Irpen. Pasternak stayed on in Moscow in order, as in past years, to tidy up the flat, finish writing one or two things and get the rest into some sort of shape so that he could resume his work on them in the summer. He also wanted to get in some money, if possible, and to await the answer from Gorky.

On 11 June he wrote to Olga Freidenberg inviting her to be their guest at Irpen:

Some new acquaintances persuaded us into spending the summer near Kiev and have rented a dacha for us. Zhenya and Zhenichka and his governess have been there since the end of May. Apparently it was not the wisest of ideas. The first impressions of Zhenya and Shura's wife (his family has also settled down in the same area) have verged on despair; it seemed pointless to have gone so far and with such difficulty. But the general opinion is that food supplies will be easier in the Ukraine than in the north.

On 22 June Pasternak arrived in Irpen. The summer dacha settlement, with its fenced off plots and neatly drilled roadways, had grown up in a large clearing in the forest. There was no river nearby; it was a fair distance – across a field overgrown with savory and wormwood, with a church on top of the hill – to the forest proper. There were meadows and copses left untouched within the settlement. The dachas were of a substantial size, winter ones. On the Pasternak's site grew an enormous, spreading oak tree which Evgeniya Vladimirovna spent many sessions getting down on a large canvas.

Genrikh Gustavovich was playing Chopin and Brahms in Kiev. His 15 August concert on the stage of the former merchants' open-air club was the main event of the summer. They all went off together to Kiev to attend it and came back to Irpen the following morning. That evening and the playing of Chopin's E minor Concerto formed the subject of the poem "Ballade", dedicated to Genrikh Neigaus.

> A blow, another blow. A race of notes.
> And then, there, like a sick eagle
> stretched on its thermal, turning,
> returning, Chopin's sad theme.
>
> Far below, the monkey-puzzle's
> exuberance, but sombre, as if it found,
> reaching for roots in ravines,
> Podol by night, the Dnieper at rest.

Irina Nikolayevna Pasternak, whose cottage stood on the same plot as the Neigauses', had a visit from her sisters. Her brother, Nikolay Nikolayevich Vilyam-Vilmont, whose wife had died in

June, came to stay with her for the second half of the season.

People frequently came out to see them from Kiev. In the evenings they would have their supper in the open air, in one of the copses. They talked, recited poetry and had philosophical discussions.

They were troubled times. The "dekulakization" campaign was in progress in the villages and people came to the house where the Pasternaks were living "to confiscate the valuables".

It all combined to heighten and give greater colour to his impressions. Pasternak, with a feeling of fortune being on his side, finished *Spektorsky* and read Romain Rolland, with whom he had just started to correspond. Mariya Pavlovna Kudashova, who had shortly before gone to see Rolland in Switzerland and become his wife, had been known to Pasternak since 1915. She was then a young student and under her maiden name of Maya Cuvilliés had published her French verses in the second "Centrifuge" miscellany.*

The summer was magnificent – wonderful friends, wonderful surroundings . . .

Pasternak wrote in his letter of 20 October 1930 to Olga Freidenberg.

And my work, to which I had said goodbye in my letter to you this spring, has somehow suddenly revived in the sun: it has been a long, long time since I have done so much work as I did in Irpen. Naturally, our world there was one of complete loss of contact and isolation, like the solitude of Hamsun's world of famine, but it was a robust, balanced world.

The two ballads "Summer" and "Sometime in a concert hall . . ." written at the end of August when they were all still in Irpen contain vivid details of their summer days, the approach of autumn and their departure.

We understood our banquet's prototype:
symposia, Plato, plague on the streets.

It was the hundredth anniversary of Pushkin's visit to Boldino in 1830 when he had written this particular "Small Tragedy".

* "Centrifuge" – a Futurist group with its own publishing house (1914), which published a series of poetry almanacs (the reference here is to the second one, of 1916).

Pasternak and Asmus called to mind the Platonic dialogue in his "Feast",* the theme of which is that love of the beautiful is the path to growth of the soul and the way to immortality – in particular, to the immortality of the artist. Irina Sergeyevna, to whom Pasternak dedicated his "Summer", took a fervent part in these discussions.

Mayakovsky's recent death dominated their thoughts. Invariably it was the subject of their reminiscences and surmises, of their perusal and analysis of his poems. L. Vysheslavtsev relates that Pasternak discovered in Mayakovsky's works, from his earliest poems onwards, numerous prophecies and presentiments of his own death and could recite them from memory.

Zinaida Nikolayevna Neigaus was a person of few words. She had to look after the family and her two sons, the elder of whom was in his fifth year and the younger was then three. Genrikh Gustavovich took a peculiar pride in repeating that his practical abilities were limited to being able to fasten a safety pin – Zina did everything else. The word was that in Kiev, which suffered much during the Civil War years, it was she who fetched in wood for the Conservatoire, saw to the heating of the auditorium, swept it out and produced the piano for Neigaus' concert – which he gave with enormous success.

On a visit to his brother, who was in the cottage next door to the Neigaus', Pasternak found Zinaida at her domestic chores – washing the linen for starching and ironing later, scrubbing the floors and getting the cooking done. He rushed over to help with fetching water from the well and collecting kindling for the stove. She turned down his offers, saying she was used to doing it all herself.

The time for departure was growing nearer. They did not all leave immediately. Zinaida Nikolayevna remembers that at the end there remained just the two families – hers and Boris Pasternak's. The horses which were to take them to the station were due to arrive in the early morning. They got their things together the previous evening. When she had finished her own packing, she went to see whether the Pasternaks were ready. Evgenia Vladimirovna was carefully assembling the paintings she had done that summer and Boris was busy putting things away in the suitcases

* One of the short pieces Pushkin wrote during that summer, "Feast in the Time of Plague", was evoked by the plague in the Moscow area which had caused the city to be put out of bounds and so prevented Pushkin's return to the city. Boldino was some eighty miles east of Moscow.

with the painstaking care he had learnt in childhood. There was little time left. Zinaida rushed in to help, and swiftly finished off their packing without further ado or fuss. Pasternak was lost in admiration.

> Was it that I wanted life a little sweeter?
> No, it wasn't that. It was only this:
> I had to break out of the crystal ball
> where deeds were dreams and dreams were deeds.

> Would I have found the strength to act
> without the dream I dreamed in Irpen?
> Which showed me what largesse a life could hold,
> the night we packed our things to go.

That is the opening of the first poem (not included in the book) in the spring 1931 cycle from Pasternak's collection *Second Birth*, as set out in the author's handwritten version retained by Zinaida Nikolayevna. There is a later handwritten entry in the margin: "A marginal version. Worry about Zina (vis-à-vis Garrik)* and Zhenichka and Zhenya,† Kodzhory, August 1931. (Zina and Adik‡ are down below in the meadow)."

7

They returned to Moscow on 22 September 1930 in the evening. Six days later Pasternak took the manuscript of Spektorsky to the publishing house. Two ballads, dedicated to the Neigauses, husband and wife, were handed to *Krasnaya Nov*;§ and *Novy Mir* received "Introduction to Spektorsky" and "Death of a Poet".

The next task was to complete the third and final part of *Safe Conduct*, devoted to his relations with Mayakovsky and to the latter's death.

Pasternak's openness of character did not allow him to make a secret of his attraction to Zinaida Neigaus. According to her memoirs, he came to see them within a day or so of their return

---

* A familiar form for Genrikh (Neigaus).
† i.e. little Evgeny and Evgeniya.
‡ Adrian Neigaus, Zinaida's elder son by her first marriage.
§ *Red Virgin Soil* – Moscow literary monthly (1921–42).

from Irpen. He brought the ballads dedicated to them and, saying that he still did not know how his life was going to work out, confessed to Genrikh Neigaus his feelings for his wife. Neigaus reacted with understanding and sympathy: he himself had a second family in which his daughter, Militsa, of the same age as his younger son, was growing up.

On returning home, Pasternak told his wife Evgeniya everything. She reacted to his confession with indignation and with pain and considered it impossible for them to continue to live together.

"I left my family," Pasternak wrote to Spassky on 15 February 1931:

> lived for a while with one lot of friends (finishing *Safe Conduct* in their flat) and am now with another (in Pilnyak's flat), in his study. I may not say anything because the person whom I love is not free, and she is the wife of a dear friend whom I shall not stop loving. But all the same it fails to be a drama because it has more joy to it than guilt and shame.

Genrikh Neigaus was away on a concert tour in Siberia at this time. Pasternak frequently visited Zinaida in Trubnikovsky Lane. He recalled these visits four months later:

> Window. Lectern. Carpets, like the echo
> alert in a glen, hoarding every note
> they've ever heard. Things said without words.
> Playing could be congenial to a writer here. [. . .]

> Window. Night. Frost glints in the tree-fork
> like the tendons tensed at my temples. Window.
> Blue the forest's stave of branching notes.
> And the yard. My friend lived here. Ages since

> my eyes sought out Siberia, but my friend
> was a town on his own, was an Omsk or a Tomsk,
> was a circle of ceasefire, a circle of comrades,
> concerns and particular traits.

During the first year of their friendship and of his admiration for Neigaus' piano-playing Pasternak presented him with the manuscript score of his 1909 sonata. Neigaus said that maybe one day he would play it as an encore. He recalled having once played to Pasternak his own youthful compositions which he had been forced to drop at the age of sixteen. "Garry, why don't you compose?

You would have such a faithful only-friend!" exclaimed Pasternak.

Pasternak and Zinaida considered 21 January 1931, the day of the death of Feliks Blumenfeld, the famous composer and conductor who was also Neigaus' uncle and teacher, the day of their betrothal. Recalling Blumenfeld's funeral and the concert given in his memory, Pasternak wrote:

A great musician is dead,
your uncle, your idol,
but loss leaves warmth behind
and majesty, a setting sun. [. . .]

Like an elephant lugging beams
or toppling timber, the chorus
burst the confines of the hall,
like Samson shattering brick.

It was fit and proper there,
but set free from its service
it flew through the opened space
and seemed our song of betrothal.

Pasternak wrote out a fair copy of the second and third parts of *Safe Conduct* in the morocco-bound album which Marina Tsvetayeva had sent him in 1926. She had blanked out the inscription "To my dearest mother, for collecting poetic gold dust. Alya. 26 September 1925." Pasternak ended his manuscript entry with an epilogue addressed to Rilke in which he recalls 1926 when he then "lived for, and belonged to" his family. Reproaching himself with being unable to make others happy, he wrote:

I was guilty of launching out on something for which I was insufficiently equipped and I involved another's life in this venture and at the same time brought a third life into being.

A smile made a round loaf of the chin of the young painter, suffusing her cheeks and eyes in light . . . One wanted to bathe in her face. And since she always needed this illumination to be beautiful she had to have happiness in order to please.

People will say that all faces are like that. Not so. I know others. I know a face that smites and slashes regardless of whether in sorrow or joy and it becomes all the more beautiful the more often one encounters it in situations where another kind of beauty would pall. Whether this woman soars aloft or falls headlong,

31

her startling attraction remains unchanged. There is little on earth she needs as much as the earth needs her because she is femininity itself, extracted from the quarry of creation as a rough-hewn block of granite pride . . .

Pasternak meant to round off his "Prologue" with a scene from the start of the revolution – the summer of 1917 in *My Sister, Life*. When preparing *Safe Conduct* for publication, he decided it was otiose and added as an afterthought: "NB: I had been meaning to finish the prologue. It remains unfinished because it is null and void and not for publication."

The image of the young painter is lit up with the tenderness of a final parting in the poem which opens the April 1931 cycle:

> Years from now, a bit of Brahms
> in the concert hall will leave me
> unable to breathe, eyeballs drowning,
> when I recall six hearts as one,
>
> walks, bathing, a flower bed, a forehead
> gone like a dream, artistic and noble,
> the slow, gentle, wide smile, lit like a lamp,
> the way she looked, her smile, her brow.

It took all winter to go through the procedure necessary to get permission for Evgeniya Vladimirovna to seek treatment in Germany in such a way as to enable her son to stay with his grandmother and grandfather in the meanwhile. By the spring Pasternak succeeded, with Romain Rolland's help, in obtaining a foreign passport. Their journey was scheduled for the beginning of May. The question of the publication of *Spektorsky* by GIKhL,* which caused doubts at in-house editorial conferences, was due to be decided in March. The author's presentation of the book and its discussion was fixed for 14 March. The critics were united in their opinion of its artistic inadequacy, its structural weakness, and the absence of thematic connection between chapters. Viktor Shklovsky spoke out in defence of it as a cohesive whole, Anatoly Tarasenkov's article "Boris Pasternak" published in *Zvezda* (No. 5, 1931), evinced an inability to read and understand the subject matter of the poem: it confused the two heroines – Mariya Ilyina and Olga Bukhteyeva – with one another. On 28 March 1931, two weeks after giving a

---

* Main Publishing House for Artistic Literature.

public reading of *Spektorsky* in GIKhL, Pasternak gave another reading on the club premises of the Federation of Soviet Writers Associations.

"He came out on to the stage, looking handsome and really very young," recalled Aleksandr Gladkov:

> He gave a shy, welcoming smile, showing his white teeth, and launched into unneeded explanatory remarks, jumping from one to the other, and then – suddenly sensing himself lost – broke off, said something like "Well, you'll see for yourselves," gave another smile and started to intone: "Accustomed as I am to picking out from life's sweet loaf the raisins of Sonority . . ." Even now, thirty odd years later, I can recapture all his intonations and . . . I still hear his thick, low voice with its nasal timbre resounding in my ears.

Spektorsky was published by GIKhL in the first half of July. It had a print-run of 6000 copies.*

Pilnyak had returned from America in April 1931. His house was a meeting point for the literary public and politicians-turned-journalists. Pasternak read the poems he had written and the concluding chapters of *Safe Conduct*. Issue No. 4 of *Novy Mir* came out at this point with Pasternak's "To Boris Pilnyak": the title had not survived the printing and had had to be changed to the anonymous "To A Friend". The poem ended in the four lines:

> Crassly, in the great Soviet era,
> when passionate conviction commands its place,
> the poet's position has been left unfilled:
> filled, the place is fraught with danger.

Pasternak's answer to the puzzlement which these words aroused was: "To my friend – Pilnyak. The sense of the line 'filled, the place is fraught with danger' is that it is dangerous when it is not empty (when it is occupied). B.P. 21.V.31." This is undoubtedly an echo of Mayakovsky's death.

In his analysis of these poems, the leading RAPP critic, A. P. Selivanovsky, drew conclusions about Pasternak experiencing a profound crisis in his creative approach and his conceptual outlook, and charged that "the line of Pasternak's poetry today and the line of socialist art are at variance."

---

* Given Pasternak's standing at the time, this was a modest print-run.

The anniversary of Mayakovsky's death on 14 April 1931 was marked in *Literaturnaya Gazeta* by the appearance of a number of memorial items about him which included the chapters from *Safe Conduct* devoted to Pasternak's first encounter with Mayakovsky in spring 1914.

At an evening meeting in memory of Mayakovsky in Moscow University, Pasternak added to what he had said by going on to insist on the difference between the poet and other types of creative people – intellectuals, prose-writers, painters:

> If one were to assemble everything written by a poet, however great a master he might be, it would never measure up to the role he played because of all the arts poetry is the most arbitrary phenomenon. [*It is closest of all to sign language, code-writing and other signalling systems.*] It is an indicator to the existence of certain values in which we see a reflection of what we call – in inverted commas (a grammatical mark of respect to our time) – "immortality" and this in essence is the single most valuable hallmark of our race. [*The physiological roots of culture are planted in man himself.*] The most thoroughbred expression of these formal qualities is the poet who dedicates his life to recalling the existence of these qualities and offers himself up on the altar of his theme. [*Author's italics.*]

This was what first struck people about Mayakovsky; and the tragic content of his role from the outset, combined with his conscious acceptance of self-immolation, were equally evident features of his. Esenin's tragic properties are secondary ones: he "borrowed the note of tragedy, the note of suicide from Mayakovsky." Pasternak noted that Mayakovsky was a "prophet of the first order" in his life, a harbinger and urgent communicator of the future, and concluded by saying of Mayakovsky's revolutionary-mindedness: "He dreamed of revolution before it even happened." His "penchant for revolution was rough-hewn of a quite special, and, I am not at all afraid to say, of an individualistic type, capable of competing on terms with the official manner of address of our revolution." It may be that his revolutionaryism "will some day, to our greater credit, be proclaimed our common manner of address, which we have as yet not attained."

On 27 April Pasternak recited poems from *Second Birth* at a joint literary evening held by *Novy Mir*.

8

Three days later, in the middle of preparations to leave Pilnyak's flat and move to Volkhonka, with the aim of helping Evgeniya Vladimirovna to get ready to go abroad and seeing her off, Pasternak wrote to Zinaida Neigaus at her Trubnikovsky Lane address. The letter carried overtones – from the April cycle of *Second Birth* – of the simplicity and openness of attitude towards life and their times with which the image of Zinaida Nikolayevna was ever after connected in his mind.

30 April 1931

My dear one, my great, wonderful one, my inimitable one!

Today is the thirtieth and it's now morning. I feel I want to fix it in my memory. Everyone has left and I am alone in the house with Aida [the dog] in Boris'* flat. There were guests yesterday and this morning the dining table still has its two leaves extended on either side, with a long white table cloth laid over it, gleaming sunnily beneath the silver and the green glassware, with two jugs filled with stocks on top of it. The door on to the balcony has been open and there too was sun and glass and greenery.

In an hour I shall go to see Zhenya and spend some part of the day with her – rather more than has been the case these last few months when I have looked in on her rarely and only for a minute or so.

I shall then start the process of saying goodbye to her. I did not know that it would be so easy. That it would be like a clear, peaceful, spring day, surrounded by poems evoked by something as immense, as scarcely credible, as really apparent as you, gazing so openly and so straightforwardly at these times of ours – with such faith in the earth and all that is around, and in its meaning.

I did not know that prior to our parting I was to become like you in all things – my cup filled to overflowing with you, you who render everything into total joy – everything that falls under your influence, within your penumbra.

* i.e. Pilnyak's flat.

I did not know that I would be spared the experiences that parting entails – the emotional flux and the casual ease of indifference or of innate coldness; that this would be an unclouded, bright parting from someone dear to me, radiant with life, and gracious, in a world at peace with itself, endlessly at peace, true to itself, and filled with your presence.

But I am sitting down to write this here because this house inspires me to do so. I shall soon be leaving. Let us fix in our minds this morning and this atmosphere and the quiet of this house in the absence of O.S. and E.I.,* who fill it up with their absence in town; just as my gratitude to them and amazement at them – those wonderful women, who have become, even if they have not consented to it, my mother and my sister – fill the house with my thoughts of them.

And this is all your doing, yours, yours!

I will see you tomorrow. My evening engagement has been switched to the 4th. Baranov, the Head of the Airforce of the Republic, will be the main speaker, but I am to start. Do you remember, Garry's phrase: "Liszt and the airship"?† An odd pairing.

All yours – my gentle, gentle
true love.

Yesterday there was a lot of drinking. Voronsky kissed me and said I would soon become the Black Saviour of our day – the pock-marked, horrific image of Our Lord, the forbidden image used by the sectarians.‡ I had recited something or other, some unpoetical but very "anti" poem§ which I had written down the previous morning.

Pasternak's pressing urge to fix "the morning and the atmosphere" in their minds, which was the basic reason for the letter, took shape in his poem "The early part of April the 30th". In an

* Olga Sergeyevna and Elena Ivanovna, Pilnyak's wife and mother.

† Joint cultural-educational evenings were then often held. One such must have been a piano recital by Neigaus, preceded by a talk by Baranov on air defence. The latter must subsequently have spoken again in conjunction with a poetry reading by Pasternak.

‡ Ikon of the Black Saviour. A reference to the ikon associated with the Khlysty (Flagellants) sect, founded in Russia in the seventeenth century, of which traces remain in the Urals, North Caucasus and the Ukraine.

§ i.e. – inferentially – anti-establishment.

earlier version the first verses convey in a more explicit form the presentiment of the future and the festive spirit of its anticipation:

The early part of April the 30th
took a turn before lunch. Since then,
the tramlines' necklaces have lost their heat,
turntables G and B have cooled.

Like tumbled fruit under cheesecloth,
the town merges and emerges from a muslin haze.
Pygmified, the people pass below.
Boulevards are dusk within the dusk.

The day is summoned home: sunset waves
its sumptuous ambassadorial passport.
Coolness opens, like a rose relaxed.
Everywhere the tang of turpentines.

Pasternak spent a lot of time working at this poem. On 14 June he wrote to Zinaida Nikolayevna:

I am frittering away my talents and my time on the poem (the First of May one) I had already done and read to you and the Asmus's; I replace the odd word only to return again, in the majority of cases, to the original draft version.

It is impossible to say firmly what poem Pasternak wrote the previous morning, 28 April, and read aloud in Voronsky's presence. It is tempting to think it was "Not yesterday, but more than a century ago", which had been sent to Polonsky from Kodzhory in August 1931 together with the first of May poem. But what is one to make of the words "unpoetical, but very 'anti'"? As is known, Pasternak considered poems on topical themes a frivolous genre, unfailingly popular with the public, and a form of "emotional titillation". He perceived their tantalizing ambivalence and considered them an unworthy occupation for an artist. His own distrust of facile writing caused him to be ruthless with such things and invariably consign them to the wastepaper basket. At times he would derive pleasure and success from reciting such impromptu verses to his friends, but he never kept them or had them printed. A poem described by him as "unpoetical, but very 'anti'" is, therefore, probably not going to be found among his books. It was almost unthinkable during the constant changes and political manoeuvres from one side to another to be able to write something

37

profound and likely to retain its significance and veracity. Yet to remain silent meant remaining a puzzle, an incomprehensible exception.

The reality of those days, on which the artist might draw for his inspiration and his live model, took the form of ideas and plans. Orientation towards the future and faith in the possibility of constructing it – without retaining any natural link with the past and without any real basis for it in the present – were the unfailing subjects of all conversations, debates and discussions. Pasternak, with his realistic perception of wider issues, did not find this enough. He was not able to ignore the contingent difficulties and contradictions and realized that many years would elapse:

> Until the gathered ferment of the years
> breaks into being and gives out a cry,
> yet, like the scent of sodden cyclamen,
> it cannot fail to make its presence felt.

His poem "Not yesterday, but more than a century ago" noted the direct parallelism with previous historical examples of seeking to achieve the transformation of Russia by a strong, ruling will, to which Pushkin's "Stanzas" had been devoted in 1826. Liberal democratic critics had at the time considered Pushkin's poem, addressed to the Tsar, a betrayal of the ideals of the Decembrists and an act of compromise vis-à-vis the regime. Drawing on "the century-old prototype", Pasternak discerned a basis for hope in "the active growth of general moral forces" and the reestablishment of "life's shattered unity", as he wrote to Medvedev in 1929. The poem, which is addressed to Stalin, voices an appeal to boldness and magnanimity.

> Not yesterday, but more than a century ago.
> Yet the old cravings are still powerful.
> We want the glorious. We want the good.
> We want to see things free from fear.
>
> Unlike some fancy fop, the spendthrift
> of his bright, brief span, we yearn
> for labour shared by everyone,
> for the common discipline of law. [. . .]
>
> So: take consolation from this parallel,
> go forward without flinching,

as long as you're alive, and not a relic,
not someone that we grieve about.

It was probably the excessive public optimism voiced in the poem
which induced the author in 1934 to omit it from the re-issue of
Second Birth. Like other "civic" poems, "In the early part of April
the 30th" and "When I get fed up with the froth", it too was not
included in the 1933 one-volume edition of his poetry. Aleksey
Kruchenykh called Pasternak "Saturn, eating his own children" for
excluding from the book what Kruchenykh considered his best
poems.

On 5 May 1931 Evgeniya Vladimirovna Pasternak and her son
left for Berlin. The expectation was that after her course of treatment
for tuberculosis she would travel to Paris and study painting pro-
fessionally under Falk, who had been her teacher at VKhUTEMAS.
On the eve of their departure, Pasternak went to stay in their
Volkhonka flat, saw them off at the railway station, and followed
this up with a letter:

My dear friend, Zhenechka,
    You are now on your way. Tomorrow I shall expect a telegram.
Of course, I will be worrying, and this time even more than
usual.

He goes on to say that his close relationship with Zinaida Neigaus
is not an obstacle to their emotional togetherness, that the Neigauses, too, realize this; and that she must not give way to despair:

It is so easy to surrender oneself to a morbid, frenetic grief, as
everyone knows: it is sterile, it does not enrich one, does not
explode into a burst of creativity: "kill" – that is the only maxim
it can yield and of which it is capable. But these are burnt offerings
made out of weakness. One must not draw up rules for one's
heart in line with them . . .

In the hope that Evgeniya would, after recuperating, get down to
serious work and find her own professional future, he concluded:

I stuck your spare photograph (for the passport) on to the first
page of Rilke's best book (*Buch der Bilder*), and am keeping it
constantly by me.

The same note of reassurance and parting is struck in other poems
written at the time:

Don't fret, don't weep, don't overtax
your strength, don't take yourself to task.
You flourish in me, rooted in my being,
like a prop, like a friend, like potential.

With my faith in the future, I'm not afraid
of coming across as a pedlar of phrases.
We're not one life, we're not a fusion of souls,
we're cutting back our intertwined deception. [. . .]

Safe journey. Safe journey. Our ties
and desires live under different roofs.
Like a plant set straight by sunlight,
you'll see the whole world differently.

9

To give herself an opportunity to take a look at herself and discover
her own feelings, Zinaida Nikolayevna and her elder son left for
Kiev on 12 May. Pasternak paid her a visit there but returned on
27 May so as to be able the next day – following up an initiative of
Gorky's – to accompany a brigade of *Izvestiya* writers on a visit to
the model factories of the first Five Year Plan in Chelyabinsk,
Magnitogorsk and Kuznetsk. The brigade consisted of Vyacheslav
Polonsky, Fedor Gladkov, Aleksandr Malyshkin, Pasternak and the
illustrator, Svarog – who was good at playing the guitar and proved
a pleasant and entertaining companion on the journey. Pasternak
always had difficulty with public occasions and public speeches,
which tended to spill over into "a chain of banquets". He restricted
his voyage to ten days (28 May to 7 June) and visited only Chelyabinsk. People remember him giving readings of his poetry in the
regional public library, in the commune for young people, and on
the premises of the editorial board of the Chelyabinsk Tractor
Factory's newspaper.

Pasternak set out his impressions of the building of the Chelyabinsk Tractor Factory in a letter of 3 June to Zinaida Nikolayevna:

They really are putting up enormous constructions. The vast
areas allocated to the project which are gradually being filled up
with sections of the buildings give an idea of the Cyclopean scale

of design and of the productive capacity which will result when the factories are built. Although it has already been said a thousand times before, all the same, the comparison with the Petrine scale of construction inevitably recurs. Such is the construction work in Chelyabinsk, i.e. on such a limitless scale, that the eye can hardly take in the dimensions of the building site on the sandy-clay plateau stretching beyond the city and parallel to it . . .

Pasternak, unlike Mayakovsky who loved "planned vastness" and "the stretch of ten-league strides", was not able to comfort himself with tales of the future. He was unhappy with his inability to visualize the projected tasks and he was irritated by the inappropriate, stilted and unrealistic officialese in which they were defined and these prospects adumbrated:

> run-of-the-mill human stupidity nowhere emerged to such a degree of bovine standardization as in the circumstances of this journey. That alone made it worthwhile. It always seemed to me that the sterility of the clichés of industrial pep-talk is a distorted echo of some other language which in situ can be the vehicle for the truth. I have become convinced of the opposite. It was worth making the journey for that alone. I am now clear that there is nothing ennobling or revelatory behind it all; that behind the vacuity and banality which always put me off there is nothing but organized mediocrity; and that it is no use looking for anything else; and if I was not afraid of something which was alien to me then, I am now quite beyond all hesitation on that score.

Pasternak saw the trip as useful because it enabled him to realize the artificiality of language of the public activist – intellectuals whose speech was modelled "on the people", and who, in their turn, became models copied by genuine sons of the people who copied this copy as best they could, some "in a pseudo-bookish way, others in a hyper-imaginative way". These impressions were later incorporated into the description of Petr Terentyev's way of speech in the 1936 drafts for a prose novel.

On the other hand "the sterility of city speech" was likened by Pasternak to a second-hand adaptation of the language of military communication, stripped of its original purpose. A few months later Pasternak wrote in his cycle, "Waves":*

* A cycle contained in *Second Birth* (1932).

Towering, timeless, in the mist:
if only we could see our time
the way we see the mountain range,
looming, soaring, sheer.

Its foot, by day, by night,
would always be a stride ahead.
My prophecies a squall of rain,
footling underneath those heights.

No need for anyone to nag.
Unknown to everyone,
I'd cease to be a journeyman
and live the life of poetry.

The priority of real tasks which evoke an immediate and direct response is here contrasted with the secondary nature of intangible logical propositions. Back in 1925, in response to the Party's Central Committee decree on literature, Pasternak had written of the impermanency of axioms not grounded in the immanent realities of life which "spoke to the artist without his knowing it or willing it and even contrary to his will".

In Moscow a letter from his Georgian friend, Paolo Yashvili, awaited Pasternak. It set out plans for a summer excursion to Tiflis and spoke of great opportunities – the sort Andrey Bely had had, for living for several months in the mountains or beside the sea working and getting into print.

Pasternak was very excited by the invitation, the more so in that his brother's family was preparing to move from Volkhonka to a new house on Gogolevsky Boulevard built, with the help of Aleksandr Leonidovich, for Moscow architects. Zinaida Nikolayevna was living in Kiev with friends and was beginning to find it irksome. Pasternak had not succeeded in finding her a place in a holiday home for the summer. Genrikh Neigaus and, later, Irina Asmus, who had both reacted painfully to Pasternak's close relationship with Zinaida Nikolayevna, had been visiting Kiev. In order to extract the "poisoned arrows" of the hurtful words which Zinaida and Irina had exchanged, Pasternak sent Zinaida on 27 July his recently-written poem "Like pollen whirling in the air . . ." and a long letter assuring her that the crisis which had cost Mayakovsky his life had, in his case, been transmuted, thanks to his meeting with her, into a second birth. He wrote that the chapter in

Safe Conduct dealing with Mayakovsky's meeting with Veronika Polonskaya had been written with himself and her in mind and

> that the readiness to live no more than a year giving full expression to all that life means and then die is something one cannot find within oneself as an act of will, but has to be given one by another person – a rare person, as rare as a wonder of nature.

Pasternak was held back in Moscow by his efforts to establish his claim to the room vacated by his brother, to get his publishing affairs in order and – without much success – to get some money.

In his poems "Like pollen whirling in the air . . ." and "There will be no one at home . . .", dated "Moscow 31.VI.",* the signs of these concerns give way to anticipation of how, in the autumn, on his return home, he will resume work:

> Wet white flakes fall like flywheels,
> each a glitter rapidly rocking.
> Roofs and snow and snow and roofs
> and only this and nothing else. [. . .]

> But the door curtain stirs.
> An unforeseen intrusion.
> Footsteps measure off silence.
> In you'll walk, like whatever will be.

The "side version" which has survived in his writing finishes off:

> Snow will settle and see the blue,
> the sparkle, the softness, the silence.
> For us, too, forgiveness will come into focus.
> We will believe, go on living, and wait.

In the fourth section of *Second Birth* these two poems are linked with two others, written in Kiev in the first days of June. "You are here, we breathe the same air" and "Chopin never seeks the easy way".

Within a few days, the three of them – together with Adik Neigaus – set off for Vladikavkaz and from there to Tiflis by the Georgian Military Highway.

* Both poems mentioned here appear in *Second Birth* (1932).

10

If one thinks of Boris Pasternak's subsequent life as a sequel to *Second Birth*, one must metaphorically see Georgia, where he first arrived on 13 March 1931 travelling over the Krestovy Pass to Mlety, as the land which became his "second homeland".

Both aspects of the comparison are, of course, in large measure a poetic declaration. The biographical backing for both propositions, however, largely coincides.

In all, Pasternak paid four brief visits to Georgia. The last, a year before his death in the spring of 1959. Standing on the step of the train departing for Moscow as it was gathering speed, he shouted back to Nina Tabidze: "Nina! Look for me in your house. I am still there!"

In *An Essay in Autobiography*, Pasternak says:

> Over the decades since the publication of *Safe Conduct*, I have several times thought that if it were to be reissued, I would add a chapter about the Caucasus and the two Georgian poets. But time has gone by and there has seemed no need for other additions. The only lacuna has been this missing chapter.*

Then follow the concluding pages of the essay, written with all the power at Pasternak's command. The images of his friends, Paolo Yashvili and Titsian Tabidze, who died tragic deaths in 1937, are sketched in with loving care against the backcloth of Georgia, as he remembered it in the summer of 1931.

The first mention of this additional chapter for *Safe Conduct* and the associations in it, which remained alive in Pasternak's memory for nearly a quarter of a century and had been set out in highly summarized form in the essay, are contained in the letter he wrote to Paolo Yashvili from Lake Shartash, near Sverdlovsk, where Pasternak and Zinaida Nikolayevna, the two boys and a Neigaus cousin, Natalya Feliksovna Blumenfeld, had been found accommodation for the summer through the Union of Writers.

> It is wonderful that almost before we settled in, we started to relive again the summer we spent with you. To do so with such

* *An Essay in Autobiography*, p. 56.

44

total recapture, such sense of immediacy – it is the first time it has happened to us. We did not try to make comparisons. We did not compare the landscapes, did not compare the people. We simply – as if fellow conspirators – uttered as one person the name of Kodzhory and then in a continuous litany started to recite – Tiflis, Okrokhany, Kobulety, Tsagveri and Bakuriani and all the other places and associations. Because it is not only the south and the Caucasus – in other words an unfathomable and always startling beauty; not only Titsian and Shanshiashvili, Nadiradze and Mitsishvili, Gaprindashvili and Leonidze – that is to say wonderful people by any standards who need no comparison to demonstrate their incomparability. It is something more, something moreover that has now become rare throughout the world. Because (leaving aside her magical originality) it is in a wider sense a land miraculously preserved from any break in her continuity, a land remaining close to the soil and not wafted away into the realm of complete abstraction, a land with an immediate pictorial impact, where reality prevails day in, day out, however great her present privations.

It is in this light that we have now been visualizing Georgia and reliving with a sense of amazement what we experienced when we were with you – as if confronted with the unbelievable and the legendary . . . But first of all we needed to find ourselves here, cast into this organism which has no spiritual rites, which wishes – for no particular reason – to graft these requirements on to itself, in a mechanical way, having no notion of what they are about, getting others to do it and at enormous cost . . . – this we needed in order to understand it all; in order, amid our yearnings for Russian culture, to recall Tiflis with gratitude and to yearn for it too with precisely the same yearning. And now it is clear to me. This city, together with everyone I met in it and with everything which I went to find in it, and which I took there with me, will be the same for me as was Chopin, Scriabin, Marburg, Venice and Rilke; will be one of the chapters in *Safe Conduct*, itself a life-long task, one of its – as you know – few chapters; one of these chapters and, in terms of undertaking them, the next to come . . . This cycle of recollections is already taking me over; it is, as Titsian would say, already painting me . . . Whatever I might now intend, I cannot omit Georgia from my next work. And all of it (exactly what is hard to foresee) will revolve around your amazing

45

homeland, just as the story of one part of my life is centred on Mayakovsky.

Pasternak's paradoxical assertion that poetry serves as a preparation for prose, just as a painter's sketches serve him as preparation for painting a picture, was repeatedly confirmed by his own literary experience. The Georgian theme was initially developed by him in his poems of 1931 and 1936 and in his translations from the Georgian, i.e. giving a Russian language interpretation of modern Georgian poetry of the nineteenth and twentieth centuries.

When Pasternak arrived in Tiflis on 14 July 1931, the first person he met that evening was Paolo Yashvili, in whose house the members of the "Blue Horns"* group had gathered. If Paolo was the head of the group – and his position, especially in the future, was to be in some ways a reminder of Mayakovsky's tragically ambivalent position as leader of LEF – then the heart and soul of the group was Titsian Tabidze. That same evening Pasternak met Titsian and his wife, Nina Aleksandrovna, for the first time.

They spent the next few days travelling around the outlying areas, with visits to Mtskheta and Dzhvari. The city was spread out along a valley and dominated by the surrounding mountains: it seemed strikingly vulnerable. The view served as a living illustration to its glorious history.

This became the theme of the poem "It was evening. All around the restive . . ."

> On the slope, the four of us
> looked down as one. Tiflis stirred
> far below, like the hilt of a sword
> and gave us a glimpse of enamel work. [. . .]
>
> There, tribute money was paid,
> life seized up for a century,
> Tamburlaine fought out of the mountains
> to where the steaming sulphur springs.

The ruins of the Dzhvari Monastery, described by Lermontov, captured Pasternak's imagination. Simon Chikovani writes in his article entitled "The sacred ties of brotherhood" that the Georgian

---

* The "Blue Horns" were a group of Georgian Symbolist poets. The group was criticized at the Congress of Soviet Writers in 1934 as being made up merely of Fellow-Travellers.

theme first came to Pasternak "because of his love for Lermontov", artistically transformed through the prism of Vrubel's art. May one add that he must have derived an equally early, childhood impression from the illustrations for Lermontov's *Mtsyri* done by Leonid Pasternak in the same Kushnerev-Pryanishnikov edition of 1891. The actual profundity of these impressions is spelt out in Pasternak's ironic reply of 23 June 1946 to I.S. Burkov:

> You have solved the riddle. Lermontov, specifically in the Pryanishnikov illustrated edition which came out when I was no more than five years old, exercised almost as much influence on me as the New Testament and the Prophets.

In the original published version of the poem, "When clambering in the Caucasus . . ." the Lermontov theme was openly stated. The entire visit to Mtskheta is an allegory derived from the content of his poems and recollections of his death – an ambivalent one, as captured, on the one hand, in the distorting mirror of society's account of it, and on the other, in the real recollections of him preserved in the natural landscape of the area.

> The ruined gateposts slouch
> like superannuated knights.
> Dzhvari, the cloisters of Mtsyri
> have scaled such heights
> we find ourselves shivering.
> But an even greater surprise
> sends a shudder right to the bone:
> the meeting of waters should never have happened.
> But it does, to satisfy lines
> in the exercise book of an army cadet.

The comparison has been dropped from the final text as printed in the book, as was also the case with a number of themes which seemed to the author unhappily phrased on re-reading. There remained the comparison between the mountains of the Caucasus and those of Southern Germany, the background against which he had pictured Evgeniya Vladimirovna. The poem hints at his alarm on her behalf – she to whom he had been sending endless, unanswered letters, pervaded by his feelings of guilt and pity:

> Tossing in the turbulence of life,
> caught in the currents, the tug of the days,

I could sooner cut water with scissors
as cut out a shape for my life.

Don't be afraid of dreams, or torture yourself.
Let it be. I love and think and know. Look:
even the river's transparent stuff
can't imagine its separate lives.

Pasternak spent August in Kodzhory in room No. 8 at the Kurort Hotel.

"The house in Kodzhory stood on the corner of the main street at the bend," we read in *An Essay in Autobiography*:

> The road climbs past its facade, curves around it and carries on past its rear wall. All passers-by, on foot or otherwise, can be seen from the building twice.*

The group of old buildings on the corner by the main road in Kodzhory is still there today. They now look very different after repair and reconstruction. Among them is the building which housed the former hotel. The old, semi-ruined highway – now little used – veers away from the new road and bends round it from behind.

It was here that Pasternak started the manuscript of his new book of poems. He opened one of his notebooks with the poem "Was it that I wanted life a little sweeter" followed by a line of music from Brahms' Intermezzo op. 117 No. 3; then came two of the June poems composed in Moscow and two in Kiev. These were followed by two of the Kodzhory poems with the author's signature at the end.

His cycle of civic poems, including "The early part of April the 30th" and "Not yesterday, but more than a century ago" was supplemented by the poem "O Future! The cloud's tattered edge". Under the title of "A Civic Triad" the cycle was sent to *Novy Mir*. Only the first two were published: the text of the third remained among Vladimir Lidin's papers up to 1960 and was unknown. It was probably left out of the book as being too intimate. It is composed in the form of a remembrance of the original sin of Adam and Eve in the Garden of Paradise:

> I have already been through all this.
> I have been treacherous. I know.
> I know what betrayal tastes like.

* *An Essay in Autobiography*, p. 59.

48

The summer concentrates. Heat and no cloud.
Heat in the ferns. Silence.
Not a fly, not an animal stirs. No bird moves.
Summer bakes.

In September, after visits to Abastumani, Borzhomi and Bakuriani, where Leonidze was then living, Paolo Yashvili took Pasternak
to the sea, to Kobulety. At that time Kobulety was a small seaside
spot with a park of conifers stretching along an amazingly large
beach of coloured pebbles, mostly of a handsome grey-brown
colour. A cluster of some twenty old estate houses formed its centre.
There was Dzyubenko's the Chemists, the market and the post
office. Beyond, in the direction of its northern headland, from
which there is a view of Poti, there stood the hotel, the Kursaal
with its restaurant, and a few imposing summer cottages which had
previously belonged to retired generals. By 1931 they had been
taken over by the government and they had their own, separate
restaurant.

Simon Chikovani recalled:

Paolo Yashvili brought along Boris Leonidovich and Zinaida
Nikolayevna and her son Adik Neigaus from her first marriage
and settled them into the hotel where I and Beso Zhgenti were
staying.
    . . . Pasternak, who was already then in my eyes a great lyric
poet, turned out to be an exceptionally charming person of an
enchantingly poetic nature. He immediately astounded me – who
had spent my whole life trying to learn to swim – by starting to
undress on the way down to the beach, before we had even
reached the sea, and once there boldly struck out into the far
distance. Imagine the effect on me, who then used to consider
anyone able to swim little short of a hero! Paolo, Beso, Zinaida
Nikolayevna, Adik and I sat down by the sea and stayed waiting
for a hotel room to be vacated; when Pasternak, who had had his
swim, learned that there was still no room available, he said: "It's
a case of waiting for the tide to turn," adding after a moment's
thought: "That's how old sayings become metaphors . . ." We
had a meal together in the so-called Kursaal, and meanwhile
rooms on the second floor, immediately over ours, became free.
The Pasternaks were assigned to eat in the official restaurant and
Beso and I continued to take our meals in the Kursaal. But it was
difficult to get anything to eat. Boris Leonidovich realized this

immediately and started coming back from his restaurant with the odd crust of bread for Beso and me and – failing to find us in, would leave it on the windowsill for us. It became a drill. Shalva Karivelishvili and Elena Beriashvili lived not far from us and for a whole month we were almost inseparable. Paolo returned to Tiflis but we stayed on in the hotel. Pasternak, as I remember, used to work in the mornings. At dawn we would already hear his characteristic droning and mumbling coming down to us from the floor above. It meant that Boris Leonidovich was reading aloud his most recent verses, checking their musicality by ear. He was working at some new, large composition – as it turned out, at "Waves", shortly to attain fame as a poem . . . We returned together to Tiflis. He asked us to wake him up when we reached the Tsipa Tunnel as he wanted to catch a sight of the surroundings there; but he stayed awake and it was I who had to be woken up by him. We got no more sleep till we arrived at our destination. In Tiflis we parted at the station, having barely time to say goodbye, and it was a long while after that before we met again.

Pasternak left Tiflis on 16 October. The day before, a non-working day, he had taken a manuscript, entitled "New Verses", to the Zakkniga* Publishing House and left it with an employee, Garegin Bebutov, whom he happened to come across. The manuscript had a note attached: "Will Zakkniga not take a collection of new poems of 800–1000 lines in length off me? . . . I am leaving you the immediately available part of the collection (600 lines) under cover with a note. I leave tomorrow for Moscow . . ." The next morning Bebutov brought the contract to the railway station. Pasternak signed it, saying that on arrival in Moscow he would tidy up the drafts of the other poems and send them off soon afterwards. Three poems under the general heading "Tiflis" were soon published in the fortnightly *Tempi* (Tiflis, No. 10 for 1931). These were "It was evening. The fun had started . . .", "When clambering in the Caucasus" and "The early part of April the 30th" – in their earlier versions.

The poetical declaration of *Safe Conduct*, in other words, its basic programme and the plan of its creative development for subsequent

* TransCaucasian Books – a publishing house cum bookseller set up in Tiflis in 1924 under local Party auspices. Renamed Zakgiz in 1933.

years was already contained in the original brief version of "Waves", left with Bebutov and not published.

In the full text of the declaration, which came out in issue No. 1 of *Krasnaya Nov* for 1932 and later formed the first section of the book, the same concepts acquired finality and universality. The cycle opens with the undertaking to give a truthful account of the experience of existence, shouldered by the artist:

> Everything is here: things I've lived through,
> things I've lived by, things I wish for,
> things which uphold me,
> things as they really are.

Further on, this undertaking is repeated and modulated. The inclusiveness and the discreteness of the tasks is conveyed by their juxtaposition in terms of meaning and rhythm with the waves brought in by the surf.

> Their darkness is not to be gauged,
> not to be numbered, its meaning not yet complete,
> but all things are arrayed in its ferment,
> as the sea's own song is salt from the foam.

Those elements, which had previously seemed self-sufficient, have to submit to the scene's requirement for the integrity and pellucid clarity to be found in the seashore and the horizon at Kobulety. The original runs:

> A line of thread eight versts* long
> and also a straight thread of foam
> contain this attempt
> to tamper with straightness . . . [. . .]
>
> Straight as inborn gifts
> we treat as luck.

which becomes in the final text:

> The big beach is eight versts wide
> and so all-seeing it takes in everything
> you can take out to it
> like a passing whim.

---

* A Russian unit of length roughly equal to two thirds of a mile; eight versts is approximately five miles.

The big beach is pebble, bare,
unblinkered, staring at everything,
sharp as the clear lens of the eye,
the low, optically perfect sky.

Such aims were far removed from his earlier aim, based on historically favourable conditions for artistic approximation. They demanded hard, back-breaking work, the location for which was
readily but sadly visualized by him as being in their Moscow flat at
wintertime, shorn of partitions and still further compacted:

I want to be home in the flat
whose space floods me with sadness.
I'll enter, take off my coat, assume
a self in the light from the street.

I'll pass through plaster and lathe,
pass through partitions like light,
as image leads to image,
as theme suggests theme.

The task is lifelong, growing
with every day: let us call it
the sedentary life; even so
I feel a pang of regret. [. . .]

The heart unlocks itself again.
I will hear you, Moscow,
crawling, smoking, growing, building,
will hear and put it into words.

The original version ran:

crawling, smoking, Moscow,
coming to an end.

which in a dialectic sense is, as is well known, one and the same
thing.

The determination to live purposively and to bear fruit in tranquillity was justified by reference to future immortality:

And I'll accept you, like a harness,
for the sake of future high spirits.
So that you'll learn me by rote like poetry,
and know me by heart, like a true story.

52

The question of the possibility of carrying out these intentions, based on an exact understanding of history, was a tragic one:

In the work of great poets
there are signs of such ordinariness
that, once get to know them,
they leave you unable to utter a word.

Once recognize the thing you share
with everything, what the future holds,
and there is no choice: you succumb
to the simple like some rare heresy.

But unless you keep it secret,
you will not be spared.
Though people need it most,
complication is what they comprehend.

In Goethe's *Faust* this age-old, pagan, and still humanly unencompassed experience is expressed thus:

The few who went to the heart of things
and laid the laws of life before the world
were crucified or else consumed by fire,
as you were, I think, already told.

In Pasternak's original manuscript version of the translation, we read (in place of the last line) "at the will of the populace, from the very earliest days."

The compositional nucleus of "Waves" (poems 4–9 and, in part, 10) consists of a philosophically and lyrically inspired account of a journey from Vladikavkaz along the Georgian Military Highway. The rough drafts of these parts of the cycle were probably done in Kobulety and worked up after Pasternak's arrival in Moscow.

Use of scenic detail en route gave many artists the chance of finding a natural solution to the problems of large-scale composition. External factors – topographic ones, it would seem – dictate the thematic framework. Fidelity to nature is the justification for innovation and profundity of treatment. Of the authors who achieved supreme excellence in this genre, Pasternak had long since known and loved Heinrich Heine. One of Pasternak's closest associates was Nikolay Tikhonov who had travelled the same

Tiflis-Vladikavkaz route in the opposite direction and described it in his book *The Highway*.

Pasternak felt that he had not exhausted the theme of Georgia in his *Second Birth* and that many of the concepts put forward in it were in need of substantial elaboration. His two 1936 poetic cycles, "The Artist" and "Summer Notebooks", served this purpose.

11

The winter of 1931–32 was a monstrously difficult one for Pasternak. Evgeniya Vladimirovna and her son returned from Germany in time for New Year. The pain of the family split was compounded by their having nowhere to go where they could avoid bumping into one another and by there being nowhere for Pasternak to live. Letters from people involved and the recollections of eyewitnesses create a picture of suffering which verged on insanity and suicide.

The final verses of *Second Birth* were being completed:

> When I get fed up with the froth
> of perennial two-faced flatterers,
> I long, as you need to nod off in sunshine,
> to recall how the face of life once looked . . . [. . .]

> And these are the years of the 5 Year Plan.
> Winter again and the fourth year here.
> Like the reflection in Svetlan's lamps,
> two women are burnish among his burdens.

> I tell them we belong to the future
> like everyone alive in these times.
> And if we're lame, so what? The new man
> Has ridden over us, driving the Plan.

In his letter of 11 February 1932 Pasternak told his sister that he had recently finished a lyrical work that was very important to him:

What degenerative power one's lot in life can exert on one; how confining is the effect of finding oneself in public ownership, in a state of warmly consented bondage. For herein too lies the age-old cruelty of unhappy Russia: when she favours someone with her love, the person chosen has to be forever in her sight.

He has, as it were, to perform in the arena for her; to reward her love with a Roman spectacle. And if no one has escaped this outcome, what is there for me to say, I to whom she almost finds difficulty in extending her love, as Germany did to Heine . . . I told you of my debt to fate . . .

O the way of the world . . .
If only I'd known when I started
that lines can choke in their blood,
haemorrhage in the throat and kill. [. . .]

But old age is the coliseum
which permits no empty rhetoric,
no rehearsal for the actor –
requiring only certain death.

In 1934, when family tragedies receded into the background and everything more or less settled down, Pasternak presented his *Second Birth* to Elizaveta Mikhailovna Stetsenko, with an inscription which could be considered a brief summary of what he had been through:

To dear Elizaveta Mikhailovna, with deepest love, B.P.
There is no cause for going on about this little book; it shows too many traces of *how not to act* in life or in the less responsible field of art. But it serves as a constant reminder to me that we have survived safe and sound thanks to you: that the author would not still be alive if it were not for your presence.
It would never have entered my mind to present you with a copy of this book. It would be an impertinence to remind you in so casual a manner – you whose devoted efforts served to buttress the rhymes. But you did express en passant a wish to glance through it.
When I write something worthwhile, a real, human book (and – not just bits of verse!!) I shall ask your permission to dedicate it to you.
My debt to you cannot be measured. You know that yourself, but that is not the point, nor would it have distressed me. The sadder thing is that I cannot find words sufficient to give you an idea of my gratitude to you.
8.XI.34   Yours, B.

In the spring of 1932, at the insistence of Gorky and with the help of Ivan Evdokimov who relinquished part of the living space allocated him, a small, as yet undecorated two-room flat on the first floor of the side-wing of "Herzen House" (Flat 7, No. 25 Tverskoy Boulevard) was partitioned off for Pasternak's use. (It now forms one of the rooms of the main office at the Literary Institute.) On 24 May he wrote to his sister:

> I moved in here yesterday. There are two rooms with a still unfinished bathroom, and the electricity not installed – a temporary flatlet made available to me, Zina and her children by the All-Russian Union of Writers.

When Pasternak left the Volkhonka flat, he destroyed all his papers. He said subsequently that he had then burnt the manuscript of the novel as well, of which the completed first section had been published in 1922 as his *Childhood of Luvers* tale. He had made several attempts to finish this prose work which he had described as the rough draft for a novel, but had been distracted by other, urgent work which brought in earnings faster and which made fewer demands on his time and energy.

The prose project now related to a theme, on which he had made a start with his 1929 *A Tale* and which would include the Civil War in the Urals.

At the beginning of June, Pasternak and family travelled to the Urals at the invitation of the Sverdlovsk Party Regional Committee and the board of the All-Russian Union of Soviet Writers. They spent about a month at the hotel in Sverdlovsk and then at the Party Committee's summer residence at Lake Shartash, of which Zinaida Nikolayevna has given a detailed account in her memoirs. *

His hopes that it would give him an opportunity to do some work were disappointed; nor did he succeed in doing any local travel or seeing places he felt he needed to see. The difference between the living standards of the privileged sector to which the Regional Party Committee assigned their guest, the starving families of the kulaks deported here, the penury of the surrounding villages and the general destruction, reduced Pasternak to profound despair verging on nervous collapse. By the beginning of August he could no longer put up with it and returned to Moscow.

His state of severe depression at what he had seen was evident in a note dated 21 September 1932 appended to a collection of his

* Unpublished.

poems which was under preparation in the Federatsiya publishing house:

What I value above all in the Revolution is its moral meaning. I would distantly compare its effect with that produced by Tolstoy, carried to the infinite. He who has been morally crushed at the very outset beneath its incriminatory excesses, has had occasion again and again to feel himself once more crushed beneath them – if one takes the widest and severest interpretation of the spirit of the revolution. It was always incumbent on each individual to recall the existence of that spirit and not forget it, for life issued no reminder. The Revolution is so unbelievably harsh towards the hundreds of thousands and the millions: yet so gentle towards those with qualifications and those with assured positions.

The small flat on Tverskoy Boulevard was cramped and the repair work was not completed until September. Evgeniya Vladimirovna agreed to swap flats.

The Volkhonka rooms were in a fearful state. Before he had had time to get them in order, and while the window frames had their panes missing or broken (as a result of the demolition of the Cathedral of Christ the Saviour); and with the ceiling leaking on rainy days, Pasternak received a visit from D. P. Svyatopolk-Mirsky, the critic and literary historian recently arrived from England.

The day after the visit Pasternak left for Leningrad, where evening meetings at which he was to read his poems had been arranged for 11, 12, and 13 October. Zinaida Nikolayevna was meanwhile making the Volkhonka rooms spick and span. On his return, Pasternak wrote to Olga Freidenberg:

I found the flat unrecognizable! In four days Zina managed to call the glazier and get hold of some glass – all the rest she did herself, with her own hands: she improvised curtains that pull aside on cords, repaired and re-upholstered two completely useless spring mattresses (making a couch out of one of them), polished the floors, and so on and so forth. She made a wonderful job of my room; it defies description, because you would have to have seen it before to know what it was like!

Zinaida Nikolayevna was proud of being a good mistress of the house, in the full sense of the word. The main thing was for her husband to be able to work without worries to distract him. He, for his part, always felt it his duty to be her material support.

In spring 1932, Pasternak wrote to his sister:

I am happy, Josephine dear. But I love Zina too much; as she does me – excessively. One can live a month or two months in that way but this is our second year living together. In order to exist, to work, to plan things, one has to be able to subordinate one's feelings to some sort of reassuring general schedule, whatever the reason for having one – be it cold egotistical calculation or in the cold sense of doing one's allotted duty to the best of one's ability.

Things have been unbearably difficult for Zina, four times more complicated than in the past: she has spent the last year and a half, and especially the last winter, forever scampering from one household chore to another, collapsing one moment with lung inflammation and the next from the effect of her operations, and she still never stops working. I find I have to earn an excessive amount. I have to be able to concentrate in order to do so. But we behave like smoke up a non-existent chimney – stifling my writing beneath a blanketing fog of happiness to the point where all sense of direction is lost; and we shall probably perish from suffocation. One cannot live in this way and we shall not be able to manage . . .

She is very handsome and was one of the select beauties here.

The letter goes on to say that when her father, a fifty-year old Quartermaster General, had married for the second time, his bride was an eighteen year old. Zina was the daughter of this marriage. Her father died when she was ten. There had been a hospitable summer residence with relatives, officer cadets and university students galore. It emerged that the mother's widow's pension was not enough to support her and all the children from both marriages. They moved to Petersburg and Zina was sent to study at the Smolny Institute. At fifteen she fell in love with her forty-five year old cousin, who had a family of his own. At first he used to arrange meetings with her, a student at the Institute, in private rooms, but then he rented a secret flat for their rendezvous. For three years, while still a virtual child, she was his mistress; and she divided up these three years between her secret and her lessons.

"She seems to me terribly part of my kith and kin, and awfully, awfully close to my heart," wrote Pasternak:

And she is close to me, not in the sense that Papa, for example, would think apropos of me. She is close not along the lines of the Maupassant story, not in terms of the jealous pity felt by any major figure of artistic temperament for the lot of a young girl, a future beauty – that is a complex axiom, which would take a long time to explore; of course, I am subject to that. But one cannot be a great memorable landmark of the age, one cannot be a great poet solely as a result of a combination of favourable circumstances; solely by virtue of one's resources of innate talent put to good effect; solely from the experience one has derived from life. For an absolute requirement is a total break with all logic of this sort, the advent of almost some sort of calamity to enable the elements of the outside world and of uncertainty to irrupt on to the scene.

Zina is intimately close to me in having fully paid as a woman and a human being for the right – which others are given gratuitously, but which she, unlike the majority of intelligent women, scarcely uses: the right to pass judgement on life and the soul and its history and its sufferings. And she is close to me for not using this right. She is just as foolish, as stupid, as elemental as I. Just as pure and holy in her consummated depravity, just as sombre.

This became the outline for the character of the heroine of his new creative venture. From inertia* Pasternak gave her the name of Evgeniya Vikentyevna Luvers, née Istomina.

In a dedicatory inscription in 1934 to Elizaveta Mikhailovna, referring to his new prose work, he promises to write "a worthwhile, genuinely human book." To judge from his letter of 8 December, he must have started "intensified work" on it in the first few days of December 1932. The circumstances and difficulties of this initial stage are set out in his letter of 4 March 1933 to Gorky:

I have been unable to work for some time, Aleksey Maksimovich, because I consider it to be prose work and I cannot put it together. As soon as the opening of something I intend doing has taken on a shape, my material circumstances (not necessarily disastrous but, nevertheless, still genuine) have caused me to get it into print. That is why all I have published is fragments, and there is nothing to look back at. All these last years I have long been

* i.e. Pasternak simply carried over the name of his earlier heroine in *The Childhood of Luvers*.

dreaming of a prose work which would set the seal of finality on my unfinished work, like a lid on a box, and round off the story of all my plots and dramatis personae.

It is only just recently, this last month or two, that I have sat down to do this and found myself believing in it and wanting very much to see it through. But it will take me a long time to write it, not in the sense of having to sit figuring it out or struggling with the style, but in respect of the plot: it is very diffuse and gets broader as I fill it in . . . In short – fortunately (for the project) – it cannot be published in sections until it is finished as a whole and it will take not less than a year to write. And, to make matters worse, there is one more thing: as I fill it in (and not before) I shall have to go out and visit the various places (or sectors of life, if you like) included in it.

Pasternak did not succeed in getting down to do the work, as he had hoped. The contract for the collected edition was torn up. *Safe Conduct* was not reissued. He had to resort to translation to earn money. His work at prose writing continued with lengthy breaks up to the war. The manuscripts of this, together with work by Leonid Osipovich, were packed up together and put in a large trunk at the beginning of the war, and taken to Vsevolod Ivanov's next-door dacha – which had someone to look after it – in Peredelkino, where it was totally consumed by fire in the winter of 1941–42.

Individual extracts were published in newspapers and weeklies in 1936–39. At the end of the Fifties, when going through the papers of the deceased editor of *Znamya*,* Vsevolod Vishnevsky, his secretary M. A. Milman came across the typescript of the opening of a novel about Patrick Zhivult which Pasternak had given to the journal in 1936. It incorporates all the excerpts published during the author's lifetime and was printed in issue No.6 of *Novy Mir* for 1980.

Of the relationship of the hero to Istomina – who changed the course of his life and destroyed his family, Pasternak wrote:

Istomina's outward appearance gave me no rest. There was nothing extraordinary about this. Her looks would have captivated anyone. But the madness which we call force of attraction was to take possession of me later. At the start I experienced the effect of other forces.

* *The Banner* – a Moscow literary monthly of the Union of Soviet Writers, founded in Moscow in 1931.

. . . Istomina was the only one among us with an openly broken life. She was the one who most corresponded to my sense of the end. Without knowing the details of her personal background, I thought to detect in her the print of time, the mark of man in confinement, imprisoned with all the immortality of his talents inside a nasty cage of circumstantial bondage. And my yearning for her in person was overshadowed by a yearning to be beside her in that self-same cage.

Resuming work on prose writing after the war, despite all the differences in plan and tasks he had in mind for it, Pasternak retained the youthfulness of his heroine and the same basic traits of character. She became the "girl from a different world", Larisa Fedorovna Gishar (or Guichard), or in her married name, Antipova.

The image of the cage and bondage undoubtedly goes back to the "first impression of a woman" in the person of the horse woman from Dahomey* in 1901. It links up with the names of the successive heroines: Luvers (English 'louvres' – grille, venetian blinds); and Guichard (French "guichet" – peephole in a prison window). In the original rough draft of *Doctor Zhivago* Rodion Gishar took on the surname of Reshetnikov (Russian "resheto" – sieve or grille).

12

The period of roughly eight years during which the books *A Tale, Safe Conduct* and *Second Birth*, and the three revolutionary episodes from *Spektorsky* were completed and published, and work started on translation of Georgian poetry, was also that of Pasternak's most active participation in the public side of literary life.

The passing of the years has caused the events which determined the feelings of Pasternak's contemporaries to fade in colour. Their words and deeds are now difficult to understand. The emotive passage in his *An Essay in Autobiography*, about how glad Pasternak was to escape the artificially exaggerated role designated for him at that time, mostly arouses incomprehension. It begins with his recalling sending a personal letter to Stalin to thank him for his minute of 4 December 1935 on Lili Brik's letter about the increasing

* In 1901, at the Moscow Zoo, Pasternak was taken to see a spirited riding display by a troupe of horsewomen from Dahomey.

tendency to suppress mention of Mayakovsky's role – a minute to the effect that "Mayakovsky was and remains the best poet of talent of our Soviet epoch."

Pasternak knew of Lili Brik's efforts on Mayakovsky's behalf and had helped with them. He was delighted with this ruling as being a successful outcome to his own affair; and, as he wrote:

> I thanked the author of these words in a personal letter because they rescued me from the over-inflation of my significance, to which I had started to become subject in the middle of the Thirties, at the time of the Writers Congress. I love my life and am happy with it. I do not need any extra gilding for it. I cannot conceive of a life that has no secrecy, no privacy, a life lived in the crystalline glitter of a display window.*

His contemporaries frequently speak of his "humbler than thou" attitude, of his appearance or pose of being a child and a poet remote from reality. This sort of misunderstanding arose because they themselves, for various reasons, were infinitely more remote from reality in their credulous optimism or pre-packaged pessimism.

Pasternak realized the fruitlessness of a predetermined approach. In some instances consciously, in most thanks to an artist's saving intuition, his seemingly mistaken and misconceived words and deeds – to which he readily admitted – were paradoxically faithful to life's basic truths. To stay faithful was painfully difficult for him; at times involving mortal risk, even though he fought shy of extremes, never made excessive demands of his time and age and sought as far as he was able to meet it halfway.

"I was then," Pasternak recalled in his letter to V. F. Asmus of 3 March 1953:

> "eighteen years younger – Mayakovsky had not yet been deified; they went along with me, would send me abroad and would print whatever stuff or nonsense I might utter; I really was not suffering from any form of illness; but I was incorrigibly miserable and gradually fading away like someone in a fairy tale bewitched by an evil spirit. I felt I wanted to achieve by upright means and genuinely something for the benefit of those around me – who were trying to help me on my way – but this something could only be accomplished by counterfeiting it. The task was an irresoluble one: it was like squaring the circle.

* *An Essay in Autobiography*, pp. 50–51.

62

"I was struggling," Pasternak wrote in the same letter, "to carry out a resolve that could not be carried out which obscured my entire horizon and blocked my every path – I was taking leave of my senses and fading away."

The overwhelming majority of Soviet bibliographical works relating to Pasternak which came out during his lifetime appeared in these years. There were several editions of his books and of his collected poems; of these, the first volume of his Collected Works was originally due to have been the most comprehensive. Three books of prose were printed: *Safe Conduct*, *A Tale* and *Aerial Ways* (1933). Almost everything collected in them had already been published in monthlies, weeklies and newspapers. The critics kept him closely in their sights, gradually becoming more uniformly tendentious. The substantive analyses offered by N. L. Stepanov and Ivan Rozanov, following previous articles by Nikolay Aseyev, Valery Bryusov, Mikhail Kuzmin, Yakov Chernyak, Marina Tsvetayeva, Osip Mandelstam, Konstantin Loks and Yury Tynyanov, gave place to equivocal reviews of a didactic-assessorial kind.

This was, in effect, a variation on the device developed by Aseyev in his article "Organizing Our Speech" and by Mayakovsky who had suggested using Pasternak's artistic innovations to help develop an extensive informational language for use in telegrams and press announcements. With few exceptions, everyone recognized his artistic mastery. At the same time, they unanimously reproached him with a conceptual overview that was not consonant with the times; and flatly demanded that he restructure his subject matter and his ideological standpoint. There were threateningly hostile articles and speeches questioning the effectiveness of his re-education. The contributions aimed at giving him support and encouragement were characterized by a certainty that he was sincerely trying to reform himself, making undoubted headway and would any moment now be ready to fulfil all demands made upon him by the times.

Pasternak made speeches at literary evenings, recited his poems and took part in discussion about them. The Press came out with his reactions to political events and his answers to various kinds of questionnaires. After his election on 11 September 1928 to the Council of the Federation of Associations of Soviet Writers of the USSR and, in autumn 1934, to the Board of the Union of Soviet Writers, he took part, of his own volition, in their informal discussions, and plenary and thematic sessions. His advice of that time to young authors and the grateful responses he received are recalled in their memoirs.

The shorthand records of his speeches at the First Writers' Congress (Pravda 3.VIII.1934) and the III Plenum of the Board of the Union of Soviet Writers in Minsk (*Literaturnaya Gazeta* 24.II.1936), revised by Pasternak, have been printed among his public works. Attempts to publish – without detailed footnotes – texts of his speeches, unrevised by the author, from among a large number of surviving shorthand records and protocols of meetings proved unsuccessful. The shorthand writers had grown accustomed to the oratorical style of other speakers and to the finite range of subjects under discussion, and could not follow the thread of Pasternak's thoughts. In 1957 G. Bebutov found the stenographic record of Pasternak's speech at the All-Union Translators Conference and sent it to the author. Pasternak replied:

I was not too pleased with the old stenographic record you sent me. I always speak badly, jumping ahead, without any apparent connection and without ending my sentences. In the record taken by the stenographers this comes to look so foolish as to resemble farce.

By contrast, the magnetic tape recordings of Pasternak made in 1947 and 1957 retain the logic and the liveliness of the original.

The principal public events in the field of literary activity at that time were the "creative discussions". The All-Russian Union of Soviet Writers announced a discussion "On Political Lyric Poetry" for 10 December 1931. Aseyev gave the main speech. He stated that poetry was in a catastrophic state of collapse. Aseyev spoke out sharply against those who had challenged Mayakovsky and who had been, as he put it, the reason for his death, and against all who ignored the importance of contemporary political tasks. He went on to affirm the need to perfect language and to seek new poetic forms. The task, as he saw it, was to master a perfected technique of verse composition and teach it to the young people.

Pasternak arrived late for the speech; he could guess its content beforehand without difficulty. He was invited to speak immediately after Aseyev. He started by upholding the artist's right to creative freedom and self-appraisal, as formulated by Pushkin. If society needed art, as people affirmed, one must understand that art, as distinct from a craft, did not consist solely of technology, and show confidence in the artist and exercise restraint.

When he read *Vechernaya Moskva*'s* account of the start of the discussion the next day, Pasternak saw that he had been deliberately misunderstood and, on 13 December, he asked to be allowed to speak to give additional clarification.

Reconstructed from the text of the stenographic records of both speeches, what he said was:†

I wish to say that when one talks of art, one needs to visualize what one means by it. *It is a field of activity* which the Revolution handed over to us with all its problems alive and kicking, and which we encounter in our midst. *One cannot talk of it as if it were a drainpipe, or a construction job and so bring the question down to technique, to rhythm. This is not the case.* These are difficult fields, with different ranges of problems. Art has been relegated to one side as being the most problematic element of what there remained to us from the past; as the most problematic of games. This involves a degree of trust. *What is it justified by?* By the fact that the artist is the summation of all that is vitalizing and continuous in man. Thus, if there is a presupposition that man will grow, that he will develop in one or other period, then this postulate has to be truest of art; and this is the basis for trusting in art . . .

Art differs from crafts in that it is itself responsible for assigning itself a task; it is present within the epoch as a living organism; and it differs from a craft – which does not know what it wants – because a craft does everything that another wishes it to do. Our quandary arises for this very reason – and important people are guilty of this error – that we all say: one needs to do so-and-so and so-and-so, and it is not clear who it is who needs to do it. In art this word "needs" is up to the artist himself . . . I, for example, will say that it is quite clear that I have a line of succession which must be preserved.

People keep talking about literature being a craft. Does this mean that people are fated to be born either craftsmen or geniuses? No – it is a question of teaching oneself . . . A young beginner

* *Evening Moscow* – the sole Moscow evening paper.
† In this, and subsequent quotations from stenographic records the text in italics indicates those passages which have been substantially reconstructed by the author.

has no technique; he is trying out artistic forms of expression for the first time . . . He will in any case be experimenting with rhythm . . . It is precisely then that the beginner may acquire that sharpness of style which in the case of the formalists is there for life in the shape of childhood survivals that never change. *One needs energy and audacity to make progress. Failing that, disaster will ensue.* To talk about the technique of writing poetry is to talk about the technique of achieving disaster. *The incursion of craft into poetry shows that* someone has no audacity, that he is, as it were, using or writing with someone else's voice, not his own. He is not, as an artist, accepting a risk. One has to remember that one needs to accept taking risks; nothing on earth exists without risktaking . . . *If I exist together with everyone else and go forward to confront difficulties* this means I want to exist, and for an artist that is sufficient. He rallies to the defence of his creative outlook so as to be able to surmount creative barriers . . . We have a dictatorship of the proletariat, not a dictatorship of mediocrities. These are different concepts . . . The age exists for the people, and I am a man of this age and I am aware of it. *Only in this sense can one speak of "restructuring" as distinct from a collectively-imposed thesis.*

And in conclusion: One must not exploit the situation for parasitical ends. Yet previous speakers kept referring back to the contributions of their predecessors. Kruchenykh asked Aseyev what sort of form our Union should take. In my view, the right answer is: it depends on the function – thus, for example, the form a policeman's hat takes is a helmet.

Criticism of what Pasternak said came in a speech by A. Selivanovsky, a leading RAPP critic, in Aseyev's concluding speech and in a newspaper report by D. Kalm, together with a threat:

If anyone else had uttered such reactionary thoughts as those which distinctly obtruded through his "halo of misapprehension" [B. Pasternak's expression] in Pasternak's speech, he would have been shouted down. There are many people who applaud Pasternak on such occasions and thereby help disorient the poet himself! . . .

It would be a good thing for B. Pasternak to start thinking about who is applauding him and why . . .

The publication of *Safe Conduct* a month before the discussion had itself brought the critics' hostile attentions down on Pasternak. Ya. Elsberg, A. Selivanovsky and N. Oruzheinikov had come out – from a RAPP standpoint – in condemnation of his literary aesthetics and his general outlook as a whole. Following the discussion, Anatoly Tarasenkov published in *Literaturnaya Gazeta* for 18 December 1931 an article entitled "Idealism's Safe Conduct". On 4 January 1932 the same newspaper printed a poll it had conducted among the writers' community. A lasting impression was left by R. Miller-Budnitskaya's article "On the 'philosophy of art' of B. Pasternak and R. M. Rilke" (*Zvezda* No. 5, 1932), in which the author of *Safe Conduct* was accused of subjective idealism and neo-Kantianism. This determined the book's subsequent fate. On 4 March 1933 Pasternak wrote to Gorky:

> Ever since 1929 GIKhL (at the time in question it was called *Zemlya i Fabrika*)* has been getting my prose work together and was due to publish it these last few days. It was intimated to them that they should themselves suggest I renounce the appearance of *Safe Conduct* as part of the book on the grounds that it had been ill received in literary quarters and it would be uncomradely of me to spurn their disapproval. There is evidently nothing to be done about it: the GIKhL management exhausted all possibilities of winning over to my side the influential protagonists of a ban, and got nowhere; and I gave up long since.

His one-volume selected prose works, *Aerial Ways*,† (GIKhL 1933), came out without *Safe Conduct*. The latter was not published – in the manuscript version entrusted to the publishing house – until 1982.

Any pronouncement by Pasternak became a target for criticism. On 6 April 1932 Pasternak gave a reading of his "Waves" at the 13th literary ten-day meeting of the Federation of Soviet Writers' Associations as part of his report on his own creative activity. The discussion was so intense that its closure had to be put off till 11 April.

Extreme positions were taken by Mate Zalka, who accused Pasternak of standing "on the other side of the barricades" of class warfare, and also by Aleksey Surkov, who said:

* Land and Factory – Moscow-Leningrad publishing house for popular classic literature (1922–30).

† This contained "Aerial Ways", "The Mark of Apelles", "Letters from Tula" and "The Childhood of Luvers".

There are two general criteria which will give us straight away an idea of poetry's class allegiance. Is Pasternak's poetry idealist or materialist? It is the poetry of a subjective idealist. For him the world is not outside us but inside us.

Vsevolod Vishnevsky unexpectedly took Pasternak's side. He all but shouted in response to Mate Zalka:

Everything he puts his hand to is part of his great, exhilarating art, originating in man's inner being, and I am certain that if we find ourselves alongside him in a difficult moment, somewhere out at sea, he will be on our side; and if we should say to him: "Help us with your art", I am sure he will not refuse; and if the time comes for us to march to the Carpathians or the Alps, you, Comrade Pasternak, will help us.

Paolo Yashvili said apropos of Mate Zalka's renewed attack:

. . . this is not a comradely approach, not a comradely form of discussion but an attempt to intimidate, and I do not know how you propose to intimidate Comrade Vishnevsky – both you and he hold the Order of the Red Banner, and I think there is no point your seeking to intimidate one another, but please do not try and put the wind up us – the third parties.

Pasternak felt crushed by what had transpired. When he was invited to give his opinion at the end, he said that the artist must take a more profound view of actuality than was assumed in such a discussion:

When a great artist (like Tolstoy) sees the reality all around him, viewing it in terms of the meagre resources and rights at his disposal, he becomes ridiculous in his own eyes. But when he succumbs to a mood of that sort, then it is time for him to give up art and do hard labour instead. Many speakers here have been using metaphorical comparisons – rifle-fire, barricades. For me those are not metaphors. I dislike them – from the Tolstoyan point of view. If you feel this attitude is nonsense, just the fruits of enlightenment, then you need to give it all up; and there are people who do indeed give up art for a period of time. Maybe this is how Narbut came to give up poetry; how Churylin acted at one stage: it is a generally familiar occurrence, except that it does not occur in the case of grey mediocrities – they experience no such misgivings . . . I do not understand how one can take the attitude to art that it is some sort of worldly rule-of-thumb – you have got such-and-such, so you would be better off if you did so-and-so.

Art . . . is suffering, and from this something results.

Sergey Bobrov, who had once adored literary debates and scandals, wrote down on his return from the discussion of 11 April 1932:

The almost unbearable picture of Pasternak's harassment has been torturing me all day . . . It is monstrous. A succession of stupid old fogies got up to speak and almost threatened to take an axe to Borya.

When he made his speech at the end his face was frighteningly grey, he got all muddled up and did not know what to say – indeed what was there to be said? The spectacle of someone trampled into the dust.

Pasternak later wrote in a dedicatory note addressed to Aleksey Kruchenykh apropos of the photograph of him taken at that time:

Was very tired after reading poems at Writers Federation meeting. Taken during interval. Tired and dishevelled.

The Second RAPP Production Conference took place between 16 and 18 April. At it Averbakh criticized Selivanovsky for his tolerant attitude towards Pasternak, and E. Troshchenko enunciated that: "If yesterday Pasternak might still have been a Fellow-Traveller, today, in our conditions of class warfare, he ceases to be a Fellow-Traveller and turns into a bourgeois disease carrier."

Pasternak's position seemed hopeless. The following day, 24 April, *Pravda* unexpectedly carried a Central Committee Decree of 23 April 1932 "Concerning the Restructuring of Literary-Artistic Organizations" which announced the abolition of RAPP.* Priority was given to the task of uniting literary forces and literary trends, and a Committee for the preparation and organization of the Union of Writers (*Orgkomitet*) was set up.

Pasternak made no comment at the time on this reform which radically altered his position. Not until March 1936, when V. Kirpotin and A. Gidash hinted in the course of the discussion on formalism that he was insufficiently deferential towards the people

---

* See footnote on p. 10.

and the Party, did Pasternak say, in reply, that he would have suffered a thousand deaths at the hands of the critics at that time and only the Party's intervention had saved him from a tragic end.

In any case, the 1932 development concerned only a change in tone and the elimination of the physical consequences of the RAPP accusations. In effect, the formulas then adopted always served the purposes of Pasternak's critics and needed no additions until 1956. There was a standard kit of brief quotations developed for use against him. It included: "What millenium is it out there, my friends?" – supposedly illustrating Pasternak's escapism; "Filled the poet's place is fraught with danger" – implies his refusal of loyal poetic cooperation. There could be a dozen or so examples of this kind, depending on the length of the article in question. Exceptions to this rule, for example the analysis of Pasternak's poetics done by V. Trenin and Nikolay Khardzhiev for *Literaturnaya Gazeta* or an article by B. Bukhshtab, were simply not accepted for publication.

Pasternak saw this and understood. He sedulously avoided providing forewords for his books or making opening speeches at literary evenings; he dissuaded people from writing books or reviews about him. If these were inescapable, he politely praised the authors of what appeared in print – Tarasenkov, for example, who, together with Aleksey Selivanovsky and Kornely Zelinsky, showed the greatest interest in him at that time.

> What to do? Vague from the first,
> the rumour that singled him out
> turns to a memory in the man's lifetime. [. . .]
>
> He parched for freedom and peace.
> But the years were a drift of clouds
> which came passing over his workplace,
> by now his locksmith's bench left stooped.

– Pasternak wrote as his summing up of what he had observed at the end of 1936.

13

Maksim Gorky came back from abroad to help with the organization of the Union of Soviet Writers. As *Orgkomitet* chairman, he devised a scheme for sending writers' brigades on visits to regions and Republics to study the state of literature on the spot and to help with preparations for the Congress and the presentation of reports.

In the summer of 1933 Pasternak signed a contract for a small book of Georgian translations. Until then he had translated only from European languages and decided himself which poems were congenial to him and what degree of perfection he could achieve in their translation. Now he was coming up against an unknown tongue. Since 1931 he had put in some work on Georgian; this gave him some knowledge of the alphabet and the grammar, and the ability to read after a fashion and understand and make a speech at table, but any real knowledge of the language, essential for recreating in Russian verses in harmony with the original, demanded much time and energy. The dates stipulated in the contract obliged him to resort to interlinear cribs. Pasternak had written down some poems by Tabidze and Yashvili from the readings given by the authors back in 1931. These translations were now – in October 1933 – offered in finished form to the monthly journal *Literatura i Iskusstvo Zakavkazya.**

In the hope of digging out new authorial interlinear cribs, Pasternak joined the writers' brigade which set out for Tiflis on 14 November 1933.

The pleasure of meeting friends, the journey through Georgia, the jokes of Nikolay Tikhonov, with whom he shared a room in the Hotel Orient, and the charming company of the Leonidze family could not blot out the aching sense of frustration at time wasted, which – as he wrote to his wife – was aroused in him by "the organized official chit-chat" of meetings and discussion sessions spiced with lavish banquets. With the prior permission of Petr Pavlenko, the head of the brigade, he left for home on 29 November before the end of the visit.

At the beginning of the following year, 1934, his Georgian translations started to appear in the monthlies: *30 Dnei* (No. 1), *Molodaya Gvardiya* (No. 2), *Novy Mir* (No. 3), *Krasnaya Nov* (No. 6); they were printed several times in *Literaturnaya Gazeta* and *Izvestiya*. The collection *Georgian Poets in the translations of B. Pasternak and N. Tikhonov* came out in 1935, in Tiflis; Sovetsky Pisatel† in Moscow published his *The Snake Eater* (1934) and *Georgian Lyrics* (1935).

The process of enrolling writers as members of the Writers'

---

* *TransCaucasian Literature and Art.*
† Soviet Writer – Moscow literary publishing house, founded 1934.

Union began on the run-up to the First Writers' Congress, and Pasternak was one of the first to be accepted for enrolment. Examination of forthcoming reports, prior run-throughs of events and discussions were all in train. On 13 May, Aseyev presented a report on poetical mastery, which was patently hostile to Pasternak. Aseyev had been the representative for poets and poetry on the commission for the enrolment of members into the Writers' Union and played a leading part in the Union's *Orgkomitet*. Aseyev said that "Pasternak, hiding behind the heights of his own intellect, is busying himself with the obscurantist glorification of the past at the expense of the present." In the classification proposed by Aseyev, Pasternak was assigned to the most negative category, "premeditated rejection of topicality".

Discussion of the report was arranged for 22–23 May, the dates of the All-Union Conference of Poets. Pasternak spoke on the first day. The newspaper account has it that Pasternak, taking issue with N. N. Aseyev in connection with his recent report, "pointed out that form plays a negative role within the general domain of art, if people begin to idolize it . . . If rhymes could be built up with the aid of petrol or olive oil rather than words, the position of LEF and its followers would be utterly otiose." He went on to say that in art as distinct from history "our age has not yet got a name" and that all talk about poetic intonation "belongs to the realm of pure fantasy". In his report, Aseyev had awarded poets marks. Pasternak said that this smacked of "the first day at school" and called on poets to preserve their sense of comradeship, thus reminding Aseyev of their former friendship.

Eighteen months previously, Pasternak had written in Kruchenykh's scrap album, into which a photograph of Aseyev had been glued:

> Splendid photo. Get me a copy, Alesha. Why this eternal tension between me and Kolya?
>
> He did so much for me that maybe it was he who created me – and now has grounds for repenting of having done so. How much I too regret all of this! But it is just trivia in this time of ours when there are a few who eat their fill (I too among them) amid a universal famine. Everything pales beside this ignominy. I cannot now discern any shadings against this contrast, but Kolya manages to do so.

13.XII.1932.Moscow   B.P.

It was on 13 May 1934 at the height of the pre-Congress discussion that Osip Mandelstam was arrested. Pasternak turned to Bukharin for help on his behalf. At the same time as the case was resubmitted for re-examination, Stalin telephoned Pasternak. This was within a few days of 20 June. The contents of their conversation were passed on to Akhmatova and Nadezhda Mandelstam, and written down by them immediately after the event with reasonable accuracy.* The conversation was not about interceding on Mandelstam's behalf: Stalin immediately said that all would be well with him. Stalin, as interrogator, was seeking to find out how widely known were the verses for which Mandelstam had been arrested, and Pasternak, to whom they had been read by the author himself, sensed the trap opening up dangerous lines of enquiry into his friendship with Mandelstam, Mandelstam's literary supremacy, and the reasons why the writers' organization had not been interceding on his behalf. Pasternak hastened to switch from this subject to what he considered the fundamental question – the right to dispose of people's life and death. Fortunately for his interlocutor, Stalin broke off this conversation.† Mandelstam had his exile to Cherdyn commuted to a "minus" restriction.‡ He settled in Voronezh. At the beginning of 1936 Pasternak, together with Akhmatova, visited the prosecutor's office in the hope of alleviating the conditions of his stay in Voronezh, and sent him money there.

The Writers' Congress was put off several times. Gorky was trying to obtain concessions and plenary powers; preparatory conferences were being held; changes were being rung on the

* See *Hope Against Hope* by Nadezhda Mandelstam, Collins Harvill, London, 1971, pp. 145–49.

† An interesting account in *Novy Mir* (No. 6, 1988) by Evgeny Pasternak and B. M. Borisov contains new and unpublished details of a subsequent demarche to Stalin by Pasternak and Akhmatova (in the form of two letters in a single envelope handed in personally by the latter at the Kremlin) in autumn 1935 asking in terms for Stalin's help on behalf of her just arrested (second) husband, Nikolai Punin, and her son, Lev Gumilev. They were both released the following day. Pasternak must have considered this part of his interrupted dialogue with Stalin and it led him, for a brief while, to see this as one sign of a "lessening of the terror".

‡ A non-specified form of administrative exile, often imposed following a term in camp or prison. The "minus" was part of a serial entry in a Soviet internal passport indicating the number of towns in which residence was prohibited. This could range from Moscow and Leningrad (minus two) to those plus republican capitals (minus seventeen), extending further to so-called "closed cities", et seq. Cherdyn, just west of the Urals was outside the "magic" circle of Russian cities, while Voronezh was, as it were, within the pale.

rapporteurs and guests still being invited – everything was being done to ensure that the Congress be the basis for the further existence of the Union of Soviet Writers and a triumph for Soviet literature.

The opening of the Congress was finally fixed for 17 August 1934. The attitude towards Pasternak taken there and the role set aside for him in the discussions that developed was a total surprise for him and for his opponents, of whom Aleksy Surkov took pride of place.

Pasternak was named in Nikolay Bukharin's report "On poetry, poetics and the tasks of poetical art in the USSR", along with Tikhonov, Selvinsky, and, in part, Aseyev, as a poet "of major calibre" with a decisive influence on young poets.

Bukharin rejected the style of Mayakovsky's "agitational" literature as "too elementary" an example to be worthy of imitation and spoke of the need of modern poetry for overviews, the monumental approach and a different conception of reality. He affirmed that the characteristic of genuine poetry was profundity of thought – thought not expressed directly, not lying on the surface, but emanating from the poet's language, evoking other pictures, other images and feelings in the reader's mind. He illustrated his argument with quotations from Pasternak, mainly from *My Sister, Life*. Commenting on Pasternak's "egocentricity", into which his images sometimes lapsed, Bukharin considered that his "sealing himself inside the mother-of-pearl shell of his personal experiences" was a form of protest against the old world with which he had already broken at the time of the Imperialist War.* "Such is Boris Pasternak," concluded Bukharin, "one of the most remarkable masters of verse of our time, who has not only strung a whole row of lyrical pearls on to the necklace of his talent, but has produced a whole number of revolutionary works marked by deep sincerity."

The subject of Pasternak was also raised in the next report to the Congress delivered by Tikhonov who said that "in *The High Malady* Pasternak produced the best lines on Lenin to date" and contrasted them with the "hyperbole" of Mayakovsky's poem "Vladimir Ilyich Lenin". Gorky also spoke of the harmfulness of Mayakovsky's hyperbole.

All these propositions were challenged by Surkov who did not agree that the time of Mayakoky's "agitational" verse was over and done with; and argued that "for a large group of people who are

* i.e. the First World War.

growing up in our literature, B.L. Pasternak's art is not a suitable compass point by which to chart their growth."

In 1958, recalling his meetings with Gorky, Pasternak told Zoya Maslennikova:

> At the First Writers Congress we sat next to each other on the presidium. Gorky made a joke of it when my name came up at the rostrum, poked me with his elbow and enquired: "Well, how are you going to answer this one?" And had a little good-natured fun at my expense. It did not then occur to me that I was seeing him for the last time.

Pasternak presided over the seventh session of the Congress, on the evening of 21 August, and delivered a speech at the twenty-first on 29 August. He openly distanced himself from the polemical free-for-all and drew a distinction between empty internal literary disputes and real life, which was intruding upon the proceedings of the Congress. He had discerned in the speeches made by the workers' delegations the language of organic fact in all its primal intensity, in other words, poetry's source, its point of departure.

> Poetry is prose – prose not in the sense of the entirety of all prose works, whosesoever they be, but prose itself, prose's voice, prose in action and not in a belles-lettres rendering. Poetry is the language of organic fact i.e. fact with vital consequences. And, of course, like everything in this world, it can be good or bad depending on whether we preserve it in an undistorted form or contrive to spoil it. But however that may be, poetry is just this – pure prose in its primal intensity . . .
> There are norms of conduct which facilitate an artist's work. One should profit from them. One such is: if good fortune should favour one of us, we become well off, but may the soul-destroying burden of riches pass us by. "Do not cut yourself off from the masses," the Party says in such cases. I have no right to use the sayings of the Party. I would say, in just the same sense as it uses: "Do not sacrifice your personality for the sake of position." With all the enormous warmth with which the people and the State surround us, the danger of becoming a socialist functionary is too great. Stay away from these proffered favours, for the sake of the basic sources from which they derive – in the name of our great and real, and productive love for the fatherland and its very greatest men of today; and remain at a proper

distance, a distance dictated by the pressure of one's affairs and by one's concern. Anyone who is unaware of this changes from wolf into lapdog . . .

The text of the speech, with some brief cuts, was published in the Press and since then has been reprinted several times.

The Congress was accompanied by a festival of literature in Gorky Park, by meetings of delegates and delegations, literary evenings and public speeches.

Pasternak's name was frequently mentioned in the speeches of Soviet and foreign participants: he was the centre of attention; and he figures in numerous memoirs dealing with that period. "And the way they greeted Pasternak! – the whole auditorium got up to applaud, and how splendidly he spoke, weightily, subtly and eloquently," according to N. Smirnov's account of the impressions of Vladimir Zazubrin. But Pasternak had placed great hopes in the Congress and was disappointed by its results. E. Mindlin recalls: "What Pasternak considered the most essential for the fate of Russian literature did not come up for discussion at the Congress. 'I am mortally dejected,' he repeated several times. 'You understand, simply mortally so.'" Pasternak complained of this in a letter of 27 September 1934 to Spassky:

[the Congress] astounded me and might have astounded you by the immediacy with which it rushed from hot to cold and kept switching from some pleasant surprise into some long familiar and deadening deduction. In musical terms it was a case of adding two false notes to the known musical frame of three true ones to produce a discord, but this time the entire symphony was played in this key and that, of course, was something new.

Pasternak sought to return as soon as possible to Odoyevo, where he had been spending the summer in the modest writers' rest house on the high bank of the Upa together with Zinaida Nikolayevna and Stasik.* He left on 31 August, after the speech given by A. I. Stetsky, Head of the Department of Culture of the Central Committee, without waiting for the closing sessions or the elections to the board and its first organizational plenum, which he, as a unanimously selected member of it, was obliged to attend.

---

* Familiar form of Stanislav Neigaus, Zinaida's younger son by her first marriage.

14

On 26 October Pasternak gave the opening speech at a Lermontov evening held in the Writers' Club. Its basic points were noted down by Anatoly Tarasenkov:

> Lermontov was born when Pushkin was sixteen years old. Pushkin had done all the prepatory work for Lermontov, as constructor, as founder, and as a realist writer. We do not see the eighteenth century with our own eyes, so that we can believe in varying theories about it. Pushkin, who created for us the nineteenth century pattern we know, has obscured the eighteenth century from our gaze. The nineteenth century has bequeathed to us vital evidence of itself. Lermontov took over where Pushkin left off and later on this became the intimate, everyday intonations of Lev Tolstoy's *Childhood, Boyhood and Youth*.

A quarter of a century later Pasternak repeated this thought in a letter written in English to his English translator, Eugene Kayden, and dwelt additionally on the tragic exactitude characteristic of Lermontov's style, calling him the progenitor of "our present-day subjective-cum-biographical realism in poetry and prose."

On 30 October 1934, Pasternak complained to Olga Freidenberg:

> It's a mad life – not a free moment. I've been intending to write to you for ages and have wanted even more to hear from you. Most of all should I like to forget everything and run off somewhere for a year or two. I want more than anything to work, to write at last and for the first time something worthwhile in prose – dull, boring, modest but with breadth and vitality. Well, it can't be done. I'm the victim of telephone debauchery, always being prevailed on to do something as if I were society's kept woman. I resist. I refuse. I waste my time and strength on these refusals. It is sad and shameful.

There was his participation in the Writers' Union board meetings, the presentation of their work reports by the poets, the visit to a young writers' school in Maleyevka and the preparations for a series of Georgian literature evenings. Despite it all, he tried to keep up his prose writing; in a letter to his father on 25 December he wrote:

As for me, I have at last come to my senses. All I wrote to date ceases to exist. That world is no more and I have nothing in hand to show to the new one. It would be bad if I failed to realize this. But I have the good fortune to be alive and seeing straight, so that now I am rapidly reconverting myself into a Dickens-type prose writer and, after that – if the energy supply lasts out – into a Pushkin-type poet. Don't imagine I'm thinking of comparing myself to them. I'm naming them to give you an idea of the inner transformation I am undergoing. I could say the same thing in another respect too. I have become a small particle of my time and age and of my State, and its interests have become my interests.

In retrospect Pasternak saw his attempts of that time to write a conceivably printable novel about the fates of a generation as an endeavour to square the circle. How could one conceivably write of historic truth and the interests of society in the year of Kirov's murder and the start of the preparation of Stalin's terror?

In the winter of 1941–42 he explained to Gladkov that there was nothing he could rely on and he found "the changing attitude towards the Imperialist War caused by political relativities" a constant hindrance.

On 11 January 1935 Pasternak drew an advance payment from Litfond* for his prose work; and the same day sent his wife in Abramtsevo a letter apologizing to her for the slow progress he was making with his exacting task:

The main trouble with my work is that it is stuck at a point which required my doing background reading (into the history of the Civil War etc.) and I started on that . . . The various lines of argument which I wanted to pursue took time to come together; linkages in time started emerging: the plot filled out and the project took on a sort of spatial dimension. It then became possible to tell the tale properly as our elders used to do. Do you know how many years they took over it? How long, for example, did it take to write *War and Peace* or Gogol spend writing *Dead Souls*? I shall be taking a long time over mine; and the wider it spreads and the greater the degree of definition it lends to what I have already written – that is, the more the finished chunks oust the

* Literary Fund – organization set up in 1934 under Union of Writers to look after the welfare of Soviet writers, and administer its housing resources.

more generalized and approximative earlier versions – the nearer it will take me to the future possibility of making a new approach to my poetry writing, not in the sense of injecting absolutely novel elements into this presumptive poetry but in that of giving it a greater resultant clarity, inconceivable of attainment in terms of one's accumulated experience without making a break in the pattern.

Anatoly Tarasenkov recorded in his diary Pasternak's detailed account – relating to January 1935 – of the inception of his "generalist prose":

> You are quite right to call it generalist . . . It is very important to me. It progresses slowly but surely. The raw material for it is the present day. I want to attain Pushkin's succinctness. I want to bed it down with concrete facts. Facts and more facts . . . Take Dostoyevsky – he has no special descriptive passages setting the scene, but the Petersburg landscape is there in all he writes, even though his works are overloaded with straight facts. When we lost Chekhov, we lost the art of prose writing . . . It is very difficult for me to write a proper prose work – apart from my own poetical legacy, there is the additional pressure of the very strong poetical tradition of the twentieth century on our entire literature. My work will be an attempt to round off my as yet incomplete prose works. It will be a continuation of *The Childhood of Luvers*. It will be a house, with its rooms, its streets and all their endless ramifications . . . I need facts from life – facts are of intrinsic value. Even if it is a failure – and I know in advance that it will be a flop – I must write it in any case . . .

V. Nezval recalls that when he met Pasternak at the Congress, he quoted to him a line by Lautréamont: "As perfect as the chance encounter of a raincoat and a sewing machine on the operating table." Pasternak gave him a barely perceptible smile and said:

> We used to spend a lot of time over images like that. I want to write a book in prose about how bad things got for me – keeping it as simple and realistic as possible. You know, sometimes you do have to make yourself go into reverse. Keeping it quite simple.

On 10 January 1935 Pasternak made the preparations for, and chaired, an evening devoted to the memory of Andrey Bely. At the beginning of February the Georgians arrived. They left Moscow for

Leningrad after the conference on "The Poets of Soviet Georgia", at which Aleksandr Shcherbakov delivered the opening speech and where, on 3 February, Pasternak read his translations from the Georgian.

Korney Chukovsky's diary mentions a literary evening in the Mayakovsky Club on 9 February.

They were staying in the Oktyabrskaya Hotel. In Zinaida Nikolayevna's memoirs this journey to Leningrad and their conversations at the time are connected with the beginning of Boris Pasternak's insomnia and nervous exhaustion.

Public interest in him was active and genuine. It led to misunderstandings which were fraught with risk and liable to result in reprimands. On 17 February, *Literaturnaya Gazeta* announced a meeting of the presidium of the board of the Union of Soviet Writers. The meeting had been summoned to discuss and approve the outline reports to be presented at the Board's second plenum devoted to "The state and the tasks of Soviet literary criticism". The newspaper account reported that in his speech at the meeting "Comrade Pasternak outlined the concept of a critic's honour in purely abstract terms, for which he was reprimanded by Shcherbakov." Pasternak had in effect attempted to say that critics should be governed by their conscience in the absolute sense of that word. He was not present at the plenum itself.

His letter of 10 March to Titsian Tabidze conveys a tangible impression of an impending inner crisis: he complains of the onset of a "grey, enfeebling emptiness" which is preventing him working. "What will happen to my work if this is repeated tomorrow?"

In April he was obliged, together with his wife, to go to the Uzkoye Rest House. There was talk of his needing treatment in hospital for "a severe attack of neglected neurasthenia". He intended continuing work on his prose writing and, so as to enjoy the necessary quietness and solitude, went back to Uzkoye, this time by himself. His family went to stay in a summer cottage in Zagoryanka.

The clouds of Fascism were gathering over Europe and Pasternak was appalled by its inhuman manifestations; he saw it as "a reactionary footnote to the history of Russia" and "a distorting mirror"*
of revolutionary Russia.

A meeting of the International Writers Congress was summoned

---

* Institute of World Literature of USSR Academy of Science (IMLI), Stock No. 41, Schedule 1, No. 199, folios 76–78 (Shorthand Record).

in Paris in support of the anti-Fascist forces. Pasternak was not included on the Soviet delegation, but on the eve of the opening Ilya Ehrenburg reported to Moscow that two writers with a European reputation should be despatched immediately to Paris to attend the Congress. They were Pasternak and Babel.

A car was sent to fetch Pasternak. He tried to refuse on the grounds of illness, but the official who had come to get him relayed the words of Poskrebyshev that this was an order and not subject to questioning.

The following day, 21 June, when the Congress had already opened, Pasternak – clad in a brand new suit, made up for him within the previous twenty-four hours, and an overcoat – left for Paris, together with Babel. Pasternak sent a telegram to his parents that he would be spending a whole day in Berlin, but they were in Munich and only his sister, Josephine, and her husband were able to come.

In Paris, Ehrenburg read through a school exercise book in which Pasternak had written down in French the text of his proposed speech, which he had prepared en route. Ilya Grigoryevich related that it was phrased in nineteenth century French and as such quite unsuitable for delivery. He tore up the exercise book and requested Pasternak simply to say a few words about poetry. Ehrenburg wrote in his book that the draft speech was largely devoted to Pasternak's illness, but he considered that this subject led into the thought – crucial to Pasternak – that culture does not need unions and organizations to protect it; that what is needed is to show concern for people's life and freedom, thereby allowing culture to regenerate and consolidate itself by its own efforts, as a derivative effect, as a product of this climate.

Pasternak appeared on the stage on 25 July, the penultimate day of the Congress, and was met with applause. "André Malraux interpreted Pasternak's speech," wrote Ehrenburg, "and then read his poem 'Thus they begin . . .' [in its French version]. The Congress responded with a prolonged ovation. Pasternak realized what Malraux's words meant: 'You have before you one of the greatest poets of our time.'"

Tikhonov later said that he and Marina Tsvetayeva had managed to piece together from the disjointed sentences of the shorthand record a text which was printed in the Congress report.

He also recalled that the Salle de la Mutualité where the meetings were held was guarded by a progressive citizens' brigade under the leadership of Tsvetayeva's husband, Sergey Efron. She herself attended the sessions and used to read Pasternak her poems during the debates. Pasternak formally presented her to the Soviet delegation. Tikhonov immediately enchanted her – which one can judge from her letter to him, written soon after her departure for Favières on 6 July 1936.

Pasternak and Tsvetayeva saw each other frequently. She would show him Paris, and take him on visits to the suburbs. Tsvetayeva left Paris on 28 June, without waiting for the departure of the Soviet delegation. She wrote to Teskova of her disappointment in Pasternak, of their "non-meeting". She wrote to Tikhonov too on the same lines.

The possibility was discussed of allowing Pasternak to stay on in Paris for a while for treatment, but this plan was turned down and on 4 July, with part of the delegation, headed by Shcherbakov, he left for London, from where he sailed two days later for Leningrad on a Soviet steamer.

In Leningrad he stayed with the Freidenbergs. He was feeling a little better. He went out with Anna Akhmatova for walks round the city. Zinaida Nikolayevna was alarmed by the news from those back from Paris that Pasternak had stayed on in Leningrad and by a letter from him requesting her not to come there. She telephoned the Freidenbergs and the following day arrived herself. The two of them moved into the Evropeiskaya Hotel where they stayed for a few days until they got his luggage back from the Customs, after which, on 17 July, they returned to Moscow.

The Zagoryanka summer cottage now gave way to the sanatorium at Bolshevo, where Pasternak stayed till the end of August.

On 21 December 1935, Pasternak attended the discussion of Tvardovsky's *The Land of Muravia* and made a speech, warmly and unequivocally in favour of the poem and its author. On 4 January 1936 he spoke at the First All-Union Conference of Translators. The critics did not overlook him.

15

At that time, Aleksey Surkov was preparing the third plenum of the board of the Union of Soviet Writers devoted to Soviet poetry and problems of its development. He wrote to Gorky about the need to revise the erroneous assessments given to poets at the First Congress. His report on "Creative Work" raised questions about Soviet poetry as a whole and the need to create positive images and optimistic works. Poetry, it was proclaimed, was oriented towards the people. The following classification of poets was proposed:

1. Soviet by passport but not in spirit: Klyuev, Klychkov, Mandelstam.

2. Growing into socialism, coming towards the revolution. On its far right flank, this group has the presence of the "transient visitor" to our epoch – Boris Pasternak; on its left that of the defunct Mayakovsky, Tikhonov and Bagritsky. In the cases of Lugovskoy and Selvinsky, this transition is characterized by the desire that others effect it for them . . .

A third group was to have comprised those who had grown up within the revolution, but no specific names are put forward for inclusion in Surkov's letter to Gorky.

During the two and a half months' run up to the plenum, this categorization was, apparently, somewhat toned down. Nevertheless, Pasternak was presented with fairly harsh demands to "carry out a thorough review of the philosophical basis of his creative work" in Surkov's reports presented in Minsk on 13 February 1936."

Pasternak's speech of 15 February to the plenum was printed in *Literaturnaya Gazeta* (24 February 1936) under the heading "On modesty and boldness". He praised Surkov's report and accepted without reservation the demands made of him. At the same time he said that his response had to be freely given – in other words, accepting the attendant risks and possibilities of a tragic outcome, so that for some time to come his writing would deteriorate:

This will be bad in many respects: on the artistic side, this switch from one position to another has to be done within a space where there are few images and no landmarks, a space converted into a no-man's-land by publicity campaigns and distractions. It will be bad in respect of the aims which it pursues because, Comrades, I shall not be using a common language to speak to the themes which unite us; I shall not be repeating your words, Comrades – I shall be challenging you and as you are in the majority, once again our dispute will be to the death and the outcome will be in your favour. And though I am not allowing any hopes to influence my decision, I have no choice: this is how I must live and I cannot do otherwise.

In Pasternak's speech, Tolstoyan distrust of "highsounding" phrases spilled over into a warning against the then incipient practice of "literary junketing", of "bombastic banality" as an obligatory ritual. These habits, representing "the crude tastes of mediocrities", were beginning to take hold in the name of the revolution. This phenomenon lay behind Pasternak's true assertion that the real active participants in the spiritual world are the men of genius. As he paradoxically put it:

the man of genius is akin to the man in the street: not only that, but he is, moreover, the rarest and most outstanding specimen of that breed – its immortal embodiment. The two are both, quantitatively speaking, polarities of mankind seen as a homogeneous, exemplary whole; the middle ground is not, however, unoccupied. Between them is a distorting layer of mediocrity made up of "people who are someone" striving to be special, to order others around, to make suggestions, to sit in judgement and to offer advice.

Pasternak devoted part of his speech to defending himself against "the perversion of public recitals of poetry into music hall performances, now being taken to quite absurd lengths", and he upheld his right to the degree of privacy required by a productive existence. He developed further his description of the speeches at the First Writers Congress as a mixture of truth and falsehood, on which he had briefly touched in an earlier letter to Spassky. On this occasion he said, in criticism of this dualistic approach:

Many false propositions have become articles of dogma through having been advanced in conjunction with some irrefutable and even sacrosanct tenet, so that some of the manna from these absolute truths falls on to assertions which are far from being incumbent on all.

For example, Bezymensky started off with things like the revolution, the masses and Soviet society and then, on a demagogic note, switched to the offensive, accusing me – as if it were something non-Soviet – of failing to "travel around reading verse" (his expression). And so what . . . if I refrain from doing so out of respect for our times which have sufficiently grown up to require authentic and more serious forms of poetry.

Of particular importance was Pasternak's call for audacity and an independent spirit from each member of the writers' corporation as being an "atom in the make-up of the body public":

> For many things we have ourselves to blame... We keep loading ourselves down with various additional chains which no one needs and nobody has asked for. People want results from us and we spend all the time swearing to be loyal... Art without risk-taking and spiritual self-sacrifice is inconceivable... don't wait for directives on that score.

However Pasternak did not stop there. His public actions at that time were unthinkable and simply suicidal, judged by the norms of socialist conduct then in force.*

In the context of the press campaign, of which Stalin was the initiator – and there were transparent hints to this effect in the press – Pasternak's words about writers having a moral duty to the country's history appeared a direct challenge. And this, as the events of late 1936 were to show, was how they were indeed taken by the Union of Writers.

Articles carrying official backing then started appearing in the press, calling for "the restructuring of the entire arts front under the sign of the struggle in favour of art for the millions, against formalism and crude naturalism". The first such appeared in *Pravda* for 28 January 1936 headed "Cacophony instead of music" on the subject of Shostakovich's opera *Lady Macbeth of Mtsensk*: it was a crude, illiterate defamation of the work of one of the best modern composers. It gave the signal for a whole series of similar articles in the same and other newspapers which made immediate haste to seek out and unmask "formalists" in all fields of creative activity: the cinema, painting and architecture. The artists' unions were thrown into absolute panic; it rapidly took the form of self-flagellation and mutual obloquy, officially designated "the discussion about formalism".

---

* His private ones, too, showed similar disconcern for his own wellbeing. Pasternak was virtually the only person to express to Bukharin his support at the time of the latter's persecution: first in a telegram in late 1936 (when the net was being pulled tighter) and then – even more astoundingly – in late January 1937 in a personal letter written weeks after Bukharin's trial, the major showpiece of the Great Terror. (See Pasternak and Borisov, "Materials for a Creative History of Boris Pasternak's Novel *Doctor Zhivago*", *Novy Mir*, No. 6, 1988.)

Aleksandr Gladkov has recalled that when these events were at their height, Meyerhold, who had been on the receiving end of attacks ever since 1929, was invited to a personal meeting with Stalin at which he could pass on his requests and complaints. Meyerhold turned to Pasternak for advice. Pasternak spoke out sharply against such spurious proposals which made the independent artist dependent on casual, false and vague undertakings. He strongly advised declining the meeting.

Meanwhile the campaign spread to take in literature. An article in *Komsomolskaya Pravda* for 23 February 1936, "A frank conversation about the works of Boris Pasternak", attracted little attention and was not meant to evoke public reaction. An article by Zaslavsky, "The dreams and sounds of Marietta Shaginyan", *in Pravda*, and another, "On the protagonists of formalism", in *Komsomolskaya Pravda* were of a different complexion. On 10 March *Pravda* published a new editorial article on Bulgakov's play *Molière* – "Surface glitter and bogus content".

The same day, 10 March 1936, the Moscow Writers Organization inaugurated a discussion on formalism with an opening report by V. Stavsky. Pasternak did not attend this session and his work attracted no basic criticism, but he learnt that among those now accused of formalism were writers whom he valued and considered to be real literary figures worthy of respect. On the eve of the following session he approached Anatoly Tarasenkov and nervously asked his advice: "Should one come out in public and take a risk in doing so?" Tarasenkov said that he ought to speak. B. Zaks and E. Krekshin, who were also present, retorted that he should not; and Zaks subsequently regarded Tarasenko's advice as verging on a deliberate provocation.

On 13 March Pasternak arrived at the Moscow Writers' meeting and asked for the floor in order to state in public his disagreement with the line taken by *Pravda*. He said that he did not understand why the question had been put: it had in any case been examined at discussions before and after the Congress. The critics were, no doubt, failing to measure up to their job of understanding the tasks set by history and were, instead, busy probing around to find passages which might bear a resemblance to formalism. One should not confuse the youthful formalist days of this generation, which were already all in the past and had been surmounted by the artists who had developed their own personalities and their own outlook on art, with artistic originality and brilliance.

Just suppose tomorrow they suddenly start saying – "maybe the people are guilty of formalism – go and have a look." And we start rummaging into their sayings and come up with: "Don't use my nose for pecking at rowan berries", "You can tell a thief by his hat"*, or "Don't stick your pig's snout into my kitchen garden." This is what gives language its colour. They can say why do you make it so complicated – "the thief's hat is on fire" – when one can say quite simply, "If you've committed a theft, don't think you're going to get away with it, because you're not." What will become of us, and not only of us but of mankind, if we have enquiries of this sort?

Pasternak once more appealed to the conscience of the critics:

Doubtless there are many among us whose hearts sink at what they read each day, and think – who's for the high jump today? Just imagine, Comrade critics, supposing we all became critics and started criticizing the air we breathe – what would happen then?

Pasternak asked that they appreciate the difference between he who creates – the artist – and he who judges – the critic.

May one, for example, say to a woman who is half out of her mind with worry and grief how dare she give birth to a little girl when she was supposed to produce a little boy? No, one cannot.

But may one say to the doctor who attended her, how dare he attend her without having washed his hands, so causing a blood infection? That one can say.

I would suggest the following as a principle: if you have to yell at people in your articles, is it not possible to yell individually? Then things would at least become a little more distinct, because when all yell together, one can distinguish nothing. Perhaps, you could actually give up yelling – that would be really splendid, or maybe those who write these articles could even stop and think and then, perhaps, we could understand at least something of what you are saying.

You demand not only that writers paint the entire picture and open it up, but also that they avoid floweriness. Why are we, the

* The old saying "You can tell a thief by his hat" figures in a story by Tolstoy describing how a public speaker caused the (unidentified) thief in the crowd to give himself away by saying that the thief's hat was "smouldering" . . . whereupon the guilty person clutched involuntarily at his headgear.

unfortunate readers of your articles, not within our rights to demand that you make them intelligible?

And what does stick out are these labels – formalism, naturalism – naturalism, formalism. I do not believe that you write in these terms because reason tells you to do so; that everyone who does so talks the same way at home, with his family, etc. It's just not true . . . One fails to sense any love for art in all this. This applies both to our milieu and to the milieu of the critics.

In our milieu this comes out during our discussions; and you applaud. People have been picking over individual sentences from Pilnyak, from Leonov . . . There's nothing particularly odd about them . . . After all, here we are in the Union of Writers – and if you agree with me you should be taking it to heart – certainly not expressing your delight.

People have referred to floweriness – what do we do with Gogol then? . . . We say that we need to do such-and-such but fail to notice what has been done. And serious adult writers come along and are spoken to as if they were young boys. It is all deeply deplorable.*

Pasternak's speech evoked many harsh responses, especially from Kirpotin, Gidash and Surkov. It was indeed only to be expected. His contribution was, in effect, the one and only protest against a political campaign staged against a background of mass self-denunciation and admission of error. The text was not published. *Komsomolskaya Pravda* printed a tendentious selection of quotations from it, together with a harshly critical editorial summing-up. *Literaturnaya Gazeta* of 15 March in an article entitled "Once more on the subject of self-criticism", said:

Pasternak is invited to reflect on where the path of individualism, professional arrogance and pretentious superiority is leading him.

On 16 March he spoke for the second time. He gave a detailed clarification of all the points in his first speech so as to clear up possible omissions without in any way losing his dignity; and he introduced an element of humour and tried to disperse the feeling of tension. Nevertheless he again fell serious at the end of his speech and said:

* See footnote on p. 80.

88

In my opinion our art has become somewhat soulless because we have overstepped the mark with our idealization of what is public . . . We take it all somewhat idealistically . . . I am talking not about the varnishing of reality, the embellishment of facts . . . these phenomena have long since been identified; I am talking of the inner essence, the inner fermentation of art.

In my opinion, we have, quite wrongly, let the tragic spirit escape from our art. I cannot accept even a landscape that has no element of the tragic in its make-up. I cannot accept that the vegetable world has no element of the tragic to it. And what is one to say of the human world? How can it have happened that we parted company with what, if not the fundamental, is one of the main aspects of art?

I search for the reason for this and find it in one completely inevitable misunderstanding. We started as historians. As historians we were obliged to deny that the tragic had a role in our days because we had declared mankind's entire existence up to the Socialist Revolution to be tragic. And it is natural that if mankind in its previous state of being fought its fight in the name of the present state of affairs, it was bound to arrive at this present state, which, by contrast, is considered not to be tragic.

Why do we not rename this "previous" state, call it say "a state of bestiality" and thus retain the tragic for ourselves. The tragic element is present in joy; it is man's dignity and his seriousness of purpose, his attainment of full growth, his ability while being still part of nature to overcome it . . .

At this point there were cries from the audience: "Quite wrong!" and noise, and Pasternak ended on an amicable, urbane note of apology.

One of the most tragic epochs in history was guilty of a great lie in renouncing the right to the tragic feeling:

> since petit-bourgeois optimists were rooted out
> and grief became a badge of shame.

In his letter of 1 October 1936 to Olga Freidenberg, Pasternak briefly summed up:

. . . It began with the article about Shostakovich and then took in the theatre and literature (with the same sort of insolent, sickeningly unoriginal, parrot-like, arbitrary attacks on Meyerhold, Marietta Shaginyan, Bulgakov and others). Then it spread to the artists and to the best of them, such as Vladimir Lebedev.

When the Writers Union held an open discussion of these articles, I was foolish enough to attend it. On hearing what complete and utter nonentities said about the Pilnyaks, the Fedins and the Leonovs (referring to them almost exclusively in the plural), I could not restrain myself and made an attempt to attack precisely this aspect of our whole literary scene, calling everything by its real name. I was met first of all by blank astonishment on the part of administrators and even officials, who could not understand why I should venture to the defence of my colleagues when no one had harmed me or even thought of doing so. I was given such a rebuff that, later (again on official instigation) friends from the Union – good friends, some even close ones – were lined up to come and enquire after my health. No one could believe that I was feeling fine and was sleeping and able to work. That, too, they took for rebelliousness.

. . . There is yet one more factor, inconceivable because at first glance it contradicts common sense. There are certain miserable, completely cowed nonentities who are driven by the force of their own mediocrity to hail as the style and spirit of the times that inarticulate, quivering obsequiousness to which they are condemned by the absence of a choice – that is, by the poverty of their intellectual resources. When such people hear someone asserting that the greatness of the Revolution lies precisely in a person's being able at a time of revolution – especially at a time of revolution – to speak out freely and think daringly, they are ready to proclaim such a view of events as being virtually counter-revolutionary.

II

PEREDELKINO

(1936–45)

I

"When they sent me to Paris I was, as it happened, ill . . ." Pasternak wrote to his parents on 1 October 1937:

> the reasons were in the atmosphere and . . . on general grounds. I was worn down by what they were doing to me – do you remember? – and I was depressed by the feeling of not belonging to myself and offended by the need to exist in the form of an inflated and incommensurable legend . . . And therefore in my anguish of that time, I felt death's breath on me (it is difficult to explain, but the process of observing that my life, albeit simply my own, brought into being by you and nurtured with your values of truth and modesty, had become, through no fault of mine, a theatrical performance, even this, my life – this act of observation was mortally wounding).

This "inner hell" ended with the commencement of work: "This is the same winter prose," he wrote in August 1935 from Bolshevo to Zinaida Nikolayevna: "again, as always, in my own way, in the spirit and the style of *Safe Conduct* and 'Waves'."

On his eventual return to Moscow Pasternak started to look through and rework his old translations of Heinrich von Kleist. In the spring of 1936 he offered to Vsevolod Vishnevsky for the journal *Znamya* a new version of *Prince Friedrich of Homburg*.

In November–December he started once more to write poems. One of them had as its subject the funeral of the twenty-eight-year-old Komsomol poet, Nikolai Dementyev, who had committed suicide on 28 October 1935.

His own recent thoughts of death and his benumbed sense of the approaching end which had pursued him in the summer months found expression in his words that "salvation and grace" are to be found not in suicide but in a forbearing and fruitful existence.

The beauty and spirituality of the darkening firmament, of the branches bespangled with frost, contrasts in the poem with the wordless anguish of the "silent witnesses" at the funeral ceremony:

> As the Kama leaves the Zakama behind,*
> filled with tears, my eyes look out
> from this room and its wreaths
> to the blackness beyond.
>
> Unobserved, with the stealth
> of a thief, I will make my departure,
> out of this civic ceremonial
> into the darkened courtyard.

was the wording of the original variant.

The poem was called "The Funeral of a Comrade". Pasternak read it at an evening in the Trade Union House on 28 February 1936. In a version, curtailed at the insistence of the editors, and without a title, it became part of the selection "Some Poems" which appeared in the April issue of the journal *Znamya*.

Another poem was evoked by the publication in Prague of a collection of Pasternak's verse, translated by the Czech poet, Josef Hora. Pasternak responded with a rapturous letter to Hora on 15 November 1936:

> My Dear Friend, how am I to thank you. Although I do not know Czech, yet even if the languages were not so close to one another, the magic force of these off-prints would be bound to reach me by some other channel, thus obviating my non-comprehension. Your taste, evident in the choice of poems, the sight itself of the print, the fact that this thing of joy has been conceived in Prague, the birthplace of Rilke who means so much to me, and many, many other things would in any case have had a stupendous effect on me . . . After many, many years you are the first – as twenty years ago – to have compelled me to re-experience the thrilling miracle of poetic reincarnation, and whatever the means (were it even by witchcraft) you employed to achieve this, the extent of my astonished gratitude must be intelligible to you.

---

* "Zakamye", meaning literally the hinterland of the Kama river, is a term coined by Pasternak.

Recently, a book of mine came out in Prague,
bringing back a time when I was certain
of the "order"* to be delivered to the door
from nearby waning glows of kerosene,
and the lamplit paper
of my different trade.

Pasternak told the Austrian writer, Fritz Brügel, who had visited him at that time, about the origin of this poem:

Hora's translations stirred me deeply. When I started to record in my diary this feeling of being profoundly stirred, the result was the quite unaccustomed and unexpected one for me of an entry in verse . . . There is much in Hora's verse which sounds like phrases from ancient Russian annals recounting how the Varangians† of old came to our country to blaze a trail to the land of the Greeks.

Then, suddenly, an edition from Prague.
As if, on impulse, the rivers reversed
and made the journey back from Greece
to the Varangians, just to call
at their old addresses for half an hour.

This poem was added at the last moment to the cycle being printed in *Znamya* to compensate for editorial cuts, and in the selection it became the first part of the poem which had previously begun with the line "Poet, do not accept on trust . . ."

At the request of the chief editor of *Izvestiya*, Nikolay Bukharin, to whom Pasternak was much indebted, in particular for interceding on behalf of Mandelstam, two poems were written for New Year 1936. In a 1956 commentary, Pasternak called them "a sincere attempt, one of the most intense (the last one in that period), to live in terms of the thoughts of that time and in tune with it."‡

The crystal clarity of the first poem, "I understand all that lives . . ." was combined in the second with the contraposition, fundamental to Pasternak's stance, of the creative man to the man of action – "the talent for deed".

Pasternak drew justification for his "contrariness", his fear of the

---

* i.e. Groceries.
† i.e. Vikings.
‡ The two *Izvestiya* poems were not included in subsequent collections, though the first part of the first poem was included in his *On Early Trains* (1943) under the title "The Artist".

"glittering lustre of the display window" and of the "over-inflation of one's own importance", from the moral experience of artists close to him. The opposing of "peace and freedom" to action expressed in deeds tended to evoke memories of the poems of Pushkin's latter days and of Blok's deathbed speech. It is probable that the poems were written in response to Stalin's minute on Lili Brik's letter: by recognizing Mayakovsky, Stalin spared Pasternak the hopes entertained for him that he might replace Mayakovsky and take over the latter's assignments.

In his speech at the Minsk plenary meeting, Pasternak delivered a pitiless verdict on his new poetic experiments:

> For a certain time, I shall, from my own previous point of view, be writing badly – up to the moment when I come to terms with the novelty of the themes and concepts with which I want to deal . . . I have had two such poems published in a January issue of *Izvestiya*; they were written in hot haste, any old how, with an unlaboured ease admissible for pure lyricism, but inadmissible for subjects of the sort which require artistic forethought; and yet, this has to be the case – I am not able to change matters; for some time I shall be writing like a hack: forgive me.

This was said in full awareness of the inevitability of the new coming of age, with sacrificial preparedness to draw a line under the path already travelled and to start anew, putting his faith solely in the disinterested elemental truths of existence and historical evolution.

In introducing this poem into the book, the second part, dedicated to "the talent for deed", was dropped. This second part forms the opening of the cycle which has acquired the title "The Artist" and stands among Pasternak's determinative, epochal, and confessional poems:

> I like the mulishness of a writer
> at the top of his bent. He's forgotten
> to phrase-monger, forgotten his audience,
> would like to forget his previous books.

Twenty years later, this concept expanded into the disturbing "It's vulgar to be famous":

> But who is he? On what battlefield
> did he acquire this late-won experience?
> With whom were his combats fought?

With his own self, with his own self.

This "battlefield" is directly linked with the words "Old age is like Rome" from the 1932 poem and with Hamlet entering onto the stage in 1946.*

> He parched for freedom and peace.
> But the years were a drift of clouds
> which came passing over his workplace,
> by now his locksmith's bench left stooped.

"What an impossible life this is!" he wrote on 25 April 1936 to his sister Lydia in England, where she had gone to settle on getting married.

Its absurdities here, which are becoming barriers for the artist, are legendary. But such is and such must be the revolution, as it becomes more and more the event of the century, and emerges more and more evidently into the mainstream amid the thick of the peoples. Is there time therein for personal destiny, for deserving case histories? But history has now brandished something intractable and of major significance, and this exalts. And it suffices to remember this to stop looking over one's shoulder and attempting to draw up a balance sheet.

These thoughts also found reflection in an article by Pasternak printed in *Izvestiya* on 15 June 1936, three years after the promulgation of the Draft USSR Constitution. The article was entitled "A New Coming of Age", in the sense of history starting afresh after all the metamorphoses of the previous two decades. The emergent possibility of arriving at a perception of, and creatively giving spiritual expression to, past experience in terms of the real present and not of some imaginary future was what Pasternak called freedom.

Never (and herein lies the root of the blind accusation of me and a number of artists of apoliticism) – never have I understood freedom as a release from obligation, as a dispensation, as a favour. I have never visualized freedom as an object which can

---

* "Hamlet" – the first poem in the Zhivago sequence begins:
  Every bit of me is here on stage.
  At the door, I pause and try
  to work out from a distant echo
  what will happen in my time.

be obtained or wheedled from someone by demands and tears. There is no power in the world which could give me freedom if I do not possess it in embryo and if I fail to grasp it myself – coming not from god or someone in authority over me, but from the air and from the future, from the earth and from my own self, using my virtues and fortitude and creative talents to the full, without regard for weaknesses or ulterior calculations. That is how I also visualize socialist freedom to myself.

2

From the spring of 1933 there was constant talk of the parents returning to Moscow. With Hitler coming to power, it became impossible for them as Soviet subjects to remain in Germany.

The Soviet organization responsible for exhibitions assumed charge of arranging the export from Berlin of Leonid Pasternak's pictures; and promises were received about the possibility of publishing a monograph on his work and providing him with a flat; their vagueness, however, prompted doubt in Boris Pasternak who was seeing to these affairs. There was discussion about a hotel room where they could live for a time while awaiting a flat. Knowing how difficult things were in Moscow with housing space and how many years he himself had been unable to move out from the cramped quarters of an overpopulated communal flat, Pasternak took a realistic view of the actuality of cloudy undertakings of this sort.

In the autumn of 1935 *Literaturnaya Gazeta* announced the building of a writers' house in Lavrushinsky Lane. It was proposed to move people in to the first fifty flats by the end of the year and to finish their construction in the first half of 1936. Boris Pasternak was listed among the writers in acute need of housing.

But things dragged on, and on 13 May 1936, Pasternak, finally believing in the possibility, informed his parents:

Your presence would lend meaning to a whole number of material easements which are projected for me and which I have not yet fully grasped. As from this summer I shall evidently be receiving a dacha on its own in a writers' settlement near Moscow, and then in the autumn (in exchange for Volkhonka) a flat too. I had not spoken of this before because I spent all of the last four years receiving promises on these lines and I do not believe in any assurance. And it is precisely in response to this inner tendency that I keep saying to you: make the move, and once there we shall see; let us see together.

But by the autumn Pasternak had still not received the flat. On 24 November he announced: "I paid in the money for the flat and it is now secured for you," but he was not able to move into it till a year later – in December 1937.

Construction of the dacha settlement in Peredelkino was proceeding simultaneously. Pasternak wrote on 1 October 1936 to Olga Freidenberg to tell her how

construction of these writers' dachas was nearing completion. They were far from being made available free of charge, so one had to decide whether to take it on, make journeys there to watch over its completion, and go to a lot of trouble to get the money together. A decision had to be taken on the new town flat in terms of money and in principle – also during those months, for construction of the house was nearing completion and allocation of the flats had begun. All these options were so evidently beyond my budget and so far (at least three times) in excess of my requirements that at any other moment I would have renounced all of them or at least half of them and thereby economized on time, strength, peace of mind, not to mention money. But on this occasion, evidently, my people are seriously getting ready to return. Papa is being promised a flat, but nothing has come of this promise nor will it come. One has to bear them in mind in planning one's own prospects.

3

In the summer of 1936, as soon as the boys had finished their classes, Zinaida Nikolayevna transported the necessary furniture and effects to Peredelkino and travelled there herself. After a while Pasternak moved there too.

That very first summer in Peredelkino was marked by the composition of a large poetic cycle. Its biographical basis was the 1931 journey to Georgia, under the fresh impressions of which "Waves" and the Caucasian verses from *Second Birth* had been composed. The cycle gave deeper expression to aspects of Georgian national life, its manners and customs and its poetry, understanding of the origins of which had grown in the course of work on translations, in correspondence and friendships with its poets.

Back in July 1932, Pasternak wrote to Paolo Yashvili: "Whatever I may have intended, there is now no way I can ignore Georgia in my next work." The outcome of this undertaking was the cycle "From My Summer Notebooks". It was dedicated to "Friends in Tiflis". Its chief heroes were the two poets, Tabidze and Yashvili.

The last three in the selection of winter poems published in *Znamya* reflected impressions of the journey in November 1933 and Pasternak's acquaintanceship with the family of G. Leonidze. In the summer ones, Pasternak sketched out, from the examples of Tabidze and Yashvili, his understanding of a people's poet, expanding on the ethical-spiritual category of the artist's close relationship with the people. In the spring, the clouds gathered over Tabidze's head: there were mounting attacks on him as well as repercussions from the dialogue on formalism. Pasternak wrote to him in support and encouragement: "Plunge the drill in deeper, without fear or pity, but into yourself, into yourself. And if you fail to find there the people, the earth and the sky, abandon the attempt, the search is pointless."

The unhewn block of Titsian Tabidze's hidden talent, "the sense of inexhaustible lyrical potential" and "the predominance of the unsaid and of what he has yet to say over what has been said" was the subject of Pasternak's verses about him:

> He inhabited a block of stone
> so he could step free of his shroud,
> born more clearly, fraction by fraction,
> as a thousand fragments fall away.
>
> Even when his measureless gift
> is barely warmer than a candle,
> he is the kick in banquet wine
> downed in the ashen dawn.

Remembering the time he first fell in love with Paolo Yashvili who had invited him to Georgia and taken them around to visit a variety of sights and people, Pasternak calls in his poem for their differences of the past months to be forgotten:

One doesn't carry wilfulness
across the threshold of the past.
Let's embrace, Paolo,
in the very first lines.

I never offended intimate friends
by applying a set of absolute rules.
In those days, you were everything
I loved and all the company I saw.

Taking issue with the widespread opinion of Georgia, in particular that of Mayakovsky, as a land of carefree bliss, Pasternak valued above all the creative character of its people, its links with historical tradition. In *An Essay in Autobiography* Pasternak wrote about "the symbolism of folk traditions, full of mysticism and messianism, which gives imagination its cue, and makes a poet out of everyone, as in Catholic Poland";* he also wrote about it in a 1936 poem:

The fresh free breezes
would not strike me as paradise.
That rich country has endeared itself
for quite a different reason.

You can live by the shore
of a lake and be blind and deaf.
But here the visionary element
is palpable beside the other four.

The fifth elemental force, as Pasternak explained in his commentary on the notion of "quintessence", is man as an integral element of the universe. In "Waves" Pasternak enumerated the other "basic elemental forces" of this land:

And we will understand the exact amounts
of success, striving, service, air,
in combination with the earth and sky,
that go to give us such a race of men.

Twelve poems "From Summer Notebooks", with certain editorial cuts, did appear in the October issue of the journal *Novy Mir*.

The notion of popular quality as an inner, inherent quality of a poet, which has nothing in common with a veneer of general accessibility and stylization was misinterpreted by the Secretary

* *An Essay in Autobiography*, p. 56.

of the Union of Writers, Vladimir Stavsky. In his report to the All-Moscow meeting on 16 December 1936, he said:

> The poet, who has been all but proclaimed the highest peak of Soviet poetry, writes and publishes, with the blessing of the editorial board of the journal *Novy Mir*, verses in which he slanders the Soviet people:
>
> > As if it were his hobby,
> > he takes a chisel
> > to your hopes and dreams.
>
> One cannot read these lines and speak of them without indignation!

In his letter to *Literaturnaya Gazeta* (No. 1, 1937) Pasternak clarified the sense of the passage: the third stanza, which gave rise to the rebukes, speaks of

> the fact that individuality without the people is transparent and that in any emanation of it, the authorship and the merit of the primal driving force goes back to it – the people. The people is the master craftsman (carpenter or lathe operator) and you the artist are the material. Such is my genuine thought and whatever subsequently happens, I cannot perceive in it anything incompatible with the idea of the people. I explain to myself the misunderstanding that has occurred solely in terms of the inadequacy and infelicity of the passage in question and, equally, of these verses of mine in general.

Moreover, this poem was cut down in publication by three stanzas.

4

Pasternak spent the winter of 1936–37 in the dacha at Peredelkino, visiting Moscow on business about twice a month. Zinaida Nikolayevna and the boys were living in Moscow.

At the end of September he again resumed work on his prose. In a letter written on 1 October 1936 to Olga Freidenberg, he acknowledged that the crisis of the previous year had been caused, in part, by the impossibility of continuing with the work of developing the questions raised in *Safe Conduct* about the origins of art:

> It has been just now, the last two or three days or so, that I have

devoted myself in fits and starts to thematic linkage, a task which since 1932 has barred all way ahead for me until I manage to get the better of it – however, it is not only lack of strength that acts as a brake but the sideways glance at objective conditions which holds this whole project to be an aspiration of impermissible naïveté. And yet I have no choice. I shall write this novel.

Work alternated with spells of reading.

Ah, history is a great thing. Here I am reading Michelet's 20-volume work, *Histoire de la France*. I am now on Volume VI, dealing with the fearful period of Charles VI and VII and with Joan of Arc and her condemnation and burning at the stake. Michelet has page after page drawn from original source material . . . Splendid, the contemporary of that age who recorded what he went through, even if it meant him seeing his days out in the Tour de Nesle prison and therefore made him appear a dullard to the cynics!

Back at the end of 1928, when analysing Konstantin Fedin's novel, *Brothers*, Pasternak had written of "the subconscious concern for the restoration of the broken chain of moral continuity" springing up in recent art, which, in his opinion, simultaneously represented "concern for both posterity and for contemporary man." Fedin's novel was close to his heart because of its unformulated striving "to propitiate memory". "There was a time," he wrote, "when people like us were not duty bound to be historians or to nurture that vocation in ourselves. Very few have recognized the necessity for it in our days." Now, in the middle of the 1930s, Pasternak had fully determined his duty as a historian, witness and chronicler.

His parents congratulated their son on his birthday. He replied two days later, on 12 February 1937:

Thank you for your congratulations. I always remember the 29th because it is the date of Pushkin's death. And this year, in addition, it is the 100th anniversary of his death. We here are having very great celebrations in this connection – very noisy ones. It is shameful that I am not taking part in them, but of late I have been the subject of several misunderstandings – that is they do not always understand me in the way I speak and think. I physically cannot stand public places and I am capable of giving voice to my own words only in times of quiet. If it were not a question of Pushkin, the possibility of being misinterpreted would not deter me. Against the background of his name any awkwardness or slip of the tongue would seem to me an intolerable vulgarity and act of indecorum to his memory.

This was written ten days before the opening of the Fourth Plenum of the Board of the Union of Writers which concluded the Pushkin celebrations and which took place in the same Hall of Columns at Trade Union House where the 1934 Writers Congress had been held. The Plenum demonstrated the startling change in public atmosphere that had taken place over this period; and which influenced in turn the overall attitude to literature and, in particular, the assessment given to Pasternak's works.

The speakers were nonplussed by the juxtaposition of contemporary poetry with that of Pushkin, and the desire to measure the achievements of the former against the incomparable marker of the latter's eminence. Tikhonov's report was subjected to reproach for its unduly gentle criticism of Pasternak – "a poet who does not have the slightest claim to be a representative of the Pushkin tradition". The most explicit attempt at pitting the Plenum against the atmosphere of the Writers' Congress found expression in the speech by Aleksey Surkov, who recalled "the canonization of that part of our Soviet poetry which is characterized by its notorious subtlety" that had taken place "here in this hall two and a half years ago." This primarily implied Pasternak and Selvinsky. Dzhek Altauzen, Dmitry Petrovsky and Aleksandr Bezymensky openly accused Pasternak of deliberately pursuing alien and hostile ideas under the guise of subtlety and complex imagery. The line from *My Sister, Life* about the ventilation pane,* with the addition of the stanza from "Summer Notebooks" quoted by Stavsky, was adduced as proof.

The psychological climate of the time, pervaded by fear and the practice of denunciation, which had become a norm of human conduct, is strikingly illustrated by Anatoly Tarasenkov's account of a speech by one of Pasternak's old friends, Dmitry Petrovsky. Two years previously in the same hall Petrovsky had sworn loyalty and devotion to Pasternak; now he was openly testifying:

---

* i.e. the one in which the poet calls through the pane to the children in the yard to ask them "what millenium is it out there, my friends?"

I do not want anyone to tell me that Pasternak's poems are a jumble. They are a coded message addressed to someone with a quite unequivocal label. This is duplicity. Pasternak's publications of late have also been rich in duplicity. There is no degree of talent that can justify his anti-civic actions (I hesitate to put it more strongly). What is in question is not the complexity of his style but the fact that Pasternak has decided to use this complexity to serve aims that are alien and hostile to us.

Tikhonov attributed the absence of Pasternak, Selvinsky, Aseyev and other poets from the Plenum, and their refusal to make speeches, to their failure to understand the significance of the historic moment which the country was undergoing. Pasternak had to go in to attend the final session and make a speech following Fadeyev, who had somewhat toned down the Plenum's inquisitorial character. After recalling his previous, misunderstood speeches and the misconceptions that had resulted from them, Pasternak merely said that he had never thought of setting himself up against society and the people and that he did not understand the accusations brought against him.

In a letter to his parents on 1 October 1937 he explained how difficult at times it became for him to write.

The times are alarming not only because of family occurrences; and the tension creates such suspiciousness around one that the most innocent correspondence with relatives abroad sometimes leads to misunderstanding and forces me to abstain from it . . .

Recalling the most critical period of his illness, the loss of his own self, Pasternak acknowledged that he had recovered ". . . Now it is over and that is such a joy. I took such a deep breath, stretched out to my full height and so it was when I again recognized myself . . . – and fell back among the hunted!"

What most contributed to this feeling was his winter time isolation in Peredelkino. He was then living in the dacha which faced on to the highway in the wooded part of the settlement, with Bespalov and Pilnyak as his neighbours.

"One good thing," he wrote to his parents on 12 February 1937:

is winter in nature's setting. What a source of health and peace! I have again returned to prose, again I want to write the novel and I am gradually doing so. But, in my poems I am always master of the situation and know roughly what will come out of it and when. But in this case I cannot see ahead and I never believe in prose having a happy outcome. It is my affliction and it always attracts me, the more strongly for that. But what I like best of all is chopping down fir branches for the stove and collecting twigs. And then if only one could give up smoking for good, although now I smoke no more than six cigarettes a day. Maybe, when I write the novel, it will release my hands. Maybe, when practical will power awakes in me, plans and lady luck will come with it. But for the while I am like someone bewitched, as if I had cast a spell over myself. I have ruined the life of my family on Tverskoy Boulevard. With that feeling and my awareness of having done so, what am I to say of my own life? And in matters public not everything is as clear to me as previously – in other words I am more inactive because I am less sure of myself. Well, see for yourself, but there's only one healthy element in me or around me – nature and work. The one and the other absorb me entirely; and can this devotion to them be such a sin and crime that for this some sort of misfortune is lying in wait for me, and I am fated not to see you or the changes in Zhenya's life, nothing, nothing of what worries me and keeps urging me on? However, there is no choice and I live in faith and grief, faith and fear, faith and work. Is this not what is called hope?

At the beginning of April, the work made progress and Pasternak had hopes of finishing the first part of the novel by the autumn. On 12 May 1937 he wrote to his parents:

If owing to my physical separation from young Zhenichka and you, and to Zhenya's* cantankerousness, I am never to be and cannot be happy, I do now hold in my grasp the core, the dazzling core of what may be called happiness. It is the manuscript, thickening out stupendously slowly, which after a break of many years gives me possession of something substantial, expanding symmetrically, growing vigorously as if the same involuntary nervous system, the disruption of which afflicted me two years ago were gazing at me from its pages and from these is now returning back to me. Do you remember that little thing of mine called A Tale? By comparison with this work, that was a decadent fragment, while this one is growing into one large whole, using far more modest but by the same token more durable elements.

* i.e. his first wife, Evgeniya Vladimirovna.

I called it to mind because if it did have any merit, it was solely of an inner kind. The same conviction is at work in this case but at full stretch and, as I said, in a straightforward, transparent form, I keep on thinking of Chekhov but the few people to whom I have shown some of it, again bring up the name of Tolstoy. But I do not know when I shall go into print with it and I do not think about that (when shall I write more?).

At the end of the year an extract, "From the new novel, about 1905", was passed to *Literaturnaya Gazeta*, with an explanatory note enclosed with it:

I shall be writing the first part of the novel this year. The novel will be in three parts. I do not know yet what it will be called. The first part will be about children.

The question set down in the hand of the editor of the literary section is: "Boris Leonidovich, may one publish it in the general conspectus 'What works Soviet writers will be writing in 1938'? E. Nelson. If possible, add details."

Pasternak crossed through the original text of his note and added:

No, it is not possible. Please, there's no need for anything. It is not a matter of State and I do not understand the newspaper's persistence. Publish the extract, but I generally dislike talk about what we have on offer to brighten up the world; please spare me this chore. Greetings. Yours, B. Pasternak.

The extract from the chapter "A December Night"* was published on 31 December 1937.

5

In the summer of 1937 Pasternak refused to put his signature to the demand for the execution of Tukhachevsky and Yakir. Zinaida Nikolayevna, who was at that time expecting a baby, recalls how she flung herself at his feet, begging him to bow to circumstances; and how she got no sleep that night, awaiting the worst. On 15

---

* Dealing with the rising of December 1905, this chapter did not finally appear in *Doctor Zhivago*, though it is indirectly related to the chapters on the 1905 revolution contained in the novel.

June *Literaturnaya Gazeta* came out, with Pasternak's signature figuring among those appended to a letter from the writers' community, headed "We will not permit the existence of the enemies of the Soviet Union". He immediately went to see Stavsky to demand a printed disclaimer. "No one gave me the right to decide questions of life and death," he said.

"When, five years ago," Pasternak recalled in a letter to Korney Chukovsky on 12 March 1942:

> I refused Stavsky my signature to that infamous letter and was ready to die for it – and he threatened me with just that, but then inserted it nevertheless, fraudulently and spuriously – he yelled: "When will this Tolstoyan playing of the holy fool stop?"

In August came the news, a month late, of the suicide of Paolo Yashvili. Pasternak vented his first attack of grief in a letter despatched on 28 August 1937 to Yashvili's widow:

> Tamara Georgievna, my sweet, my poor dear, what is happening! I have been living for about a month as if there was nothing the matter; and I knew nothing. For some ten days I have known and I have been spending the whole time writing to you and destroying the result. My existence is rendered valueless and I myself need reassurance; and I do not know what to say to you that would not seem idealistic drivel and unctuous hypocrisy. When they first told me, I did not believe it. On the 17th I received confirmation in town. There was now no place for nuances or semitones. The news grabbed me by the throat, I submitted to its orders and I am still possessed by it.

Pasternak was given an account by the poet, Simon Chikovani, of his last meeting in the autumn of 1937 with Paolo Yashvili, who had been publicly slandered and had become mentally troubled as he awaited his impending arrest.

"Why were these two people sent to me?" wrote Pasternak in *An Essay in Autobiography*.

> How can one describe our relations? They both became an integral part of my private world. I did not prefer one to the other, they were so inseparable, they so complemented one another. The fate of both of them, together with the fate of Tsvetayeva, was to become my greatest cause for grief.*

* *An Essay in Autobiography*, p. 58.

Two years later, on 1 November 1939, Pasternak told Anatoly Tarasenkov:

In those horrendous, blood-stained years anyone might have been arrested. We were shuffled like a pack of cards. I have no wish to give thanks, in a philistine way, for remaining alive while others did not. There is a need for someone to show grief, to go proudly into mourning, to react tragically – for someone to be tragedy's standard bearer.

In the fearful years we lived through, I wanted to see no one – even Tikhonov, whom I love, used to stay with Leonov when he came to Moscow; he refrained from phoning me and if we met, averted his eyes. Even Ivanov, the most honest of writers, committed all sorts of odious acts at that time – God knows what he got up to, putting his name to all sorts of vile fabrications so as to keep his own last refuge – the temple of art – inviolate. He was trundled out like a bear on a lead with a ring through his lip; he was obliged, like all of us, to repeat parrot-fashion all the fairy tales about the plots. He would do so and then retire to his refuge, his art. I forgive him. But there were those who liked being bears: they had the ring removed from their mouth and still they kept on happily lumbering down the boulevard, dancing to amuse the public.

The experience of those years taught Pasternak once and for all "to be true to himself" and "not to renounce his dignity" whatever the situation. His fidelity to life's undistorted prompting allowed him to preserve his sense of inner freedom and his moral integrity in the very worst times.

6

On 1 October 1937 Pasternak wrote to his parents:

I might be earning more, I might try harder to want my vast, empty house in Peredelkino to resemble as cosy and agreeable a human habitation as does Zhenya's* miniscule two-bedroom flat, elegant, proper and asking to be put on canvas as an "intérieur". I might spend less time in the wilderness, absent myself less from

* Pasternak's first wife, Evgeniya Vladimirovna.

town, devote less time to the woods and the river, to reading multi-volume histories. Instead of the novel which I am writing slowly and to the best of my capability, I might be dashing off more profitable trivia, etc., etc. But evidently there is nothing predestined about all of this. So, at the present time the choice made has been mine, and if Zina's* lot is a bitter and unenviable one in terms of the difficulty she has to bear . . . the responsibility does not scare me; for those with me the going has to be difficult and cannot be easy. And if I spent less time getting in firewood for the winter, devoted less time to the air and nature (its October, there's ground frost in the mornings, but I'm still going for a bathe) and read less of Michelet and Macaulay, maybe I would not be able to work.

In the autumn of 1937 Zinaida Nikolayevna's twelve-year-old son, Adrian Neigaus, started to feel extremely ill. He was taken for a while out of school and brought to Peredelkino.

It was at this time that Pasternak, on his own and over a ten-day period, assembled and packed up the things for the move to Lavrushinsky Lane. He wrote to his parents describing how this occupation had resurrected in his memory the circumstances of similar preparations in 1911, how, sorting through old sets of *The Artist*† containing his father's sketches, hampers and trunks full of his papers, drawings and portfolios, he had relived afresh the family's entire life and his own, rejoicing in the fullness and fruitfulness of the former, despairing at the meagreness and state of incompletion of the latter.

In the large writers' house in Lavrushinsky Lane they received a small apartment in the tower under the roof which had first been intended as a bachelor pad for the theatrical compère Garkavi. It consisted of two small rooms located one above the other, on the seventh and eighth floors, connected by an inner staircase. When Garkavi renounced it in favour of something better, it was passed on to Pasternak. In order to increase the size of the flat, Zinaida Nikolayevna gave instructions for the removal of the inner staircase, thus obtaining an extra room, six metres square, on each floor.

The rooms on Volkhonka Street were more spacious, but they had to be surrendered: the wing of the building which housed the Pasternak's flat was to be pulled down a little while later. In the

* Pasternak's second wife, Zinaida Nikolayevna.
† Pre-Revolutionary fine art magazine.

move most of the furniture was left to the neighbours or distributed among friends.

On New Year's Eve 1938 his younger son, Leonid, was born.* A week later Pasternak wrote to his parents:

> The baby boy is sweet, healthy and, it seems, jolly. He contrived to make his appearance on New Year's Eve with the last, twelfth stroke of the clock and thus, according to the statistics of the maternity ward, immediately made his way into print as the "first boy of 1938, born at 00.00 hours on 1 January". I have named him Leonid after you.

A child's cot was squeezed, with difficulty, into the minute little room, in which Zinaida Nikolayevna slept.

With their move into town and the birth of the child, work on the novel had to be set aside "in favour of more petty and more lucrative work". "I do not regret it," wrote Pasternak on 14 April 1938 to Raisa Lomonosova:

> because sometimes it is useful to forget about self and get lost in some form of dogged, rapidly alternating and almost artisanal activity. I am still doing a lot of translating work, of whoever and whatever comes to hand. This may cover one or other Georgian poet or someone from the German revolutionaries, and Verlaine and the French Symbolists and Hans Sachs from the sixteenth century and anyone else. Among others I shall be dealing with an Englishman too for one anthology; I do not know who, probably Keats or Byron, maybe Blake, maybe even Spenser.

The contract for the collection of translations of poetry had been signed back in June 1936. At that time *Literaturnaya Gazeta* had itself announced the forthcoming issue by Goslitizdat of *Translations From Kleist* and of a collection of poems by Rainer Maria Rilke then under preparation. But in the light of political events these editions of German poets were adjourned and remained unrealized.

The inner reasons for Pasternak turning to translations at this time were his anxiety about the fate of Europe and European culture and his bitter sense of severance from his family. As early as 25 April 1936 he had written to his sister, Lydia, in England:†

* Pasternak's only son by Zinaida Nikolayevna.
† Lydia left Russia for Germany in 1921, and moved to England with her sister and parents in 1939.

How is their appearance [i.e. the translations] to be explained; is there a place for what is out of place; can one make the meaningless meaningful? One can. Their sole meaning for me is that they correspond to my yearning for Europe, my constant intellectual absorption in it. The meaning of these translations is that we too live in just the same way as do these translations; that you are abroad and, moreover, in a number of countries; that life has transformed our flat on the Volkhonka. Finally the meaning of these shamefully meretricious translations is that there will just have to be the likes of Bovary and Dombey because they are all that is left to write about – there is nothing more to be done: because there has been a revolution and as soon as man receives the freedom to distance himself from it just a little in order to recall it in its entirety and to think about it – what then can emerge other than great realistic art. And if I shall be alive. I shall then live to see it happen.

Now, in the spring of 1938, Pasternak alternated translations from Simon Chikovani with poems by Rafael Alberti whom he had recently got to know. On 30 July 1938 *Literaturnaya Gazeta* published a poem by Johannes Becher, "Luther", in Pasternak's translation; and *Novy Mir* (No. 8, 1938), Verlaine and a Shakespeare sonnet. *Krasnaya Nov* (No. 8, 1938) came out with Byron's "Stanzas to Augusta", two short poems by Shakespeare – "Music" and "Winter" – and four by Verlaine, among them the famous "L'Art Poetique". The following number included Hans Sachs' Shrovetide play, *Eulenspiegel and the Blind Men*, in a reworked version of the 1918 translation.

On New Year's Eve, 31 December 1938, two poems by John Keats were printed in *Literaturnaya Gazeta* and in April 1939 two others in *Ogonek*. Pasternak recalled his enthusiasm for English poetry in the letter to Lydia in Oxford quoted above: England, "the object of my dreams in 1913 when as a self-taught student I got to know Keats and Coleridge, Swinburne and Poe, and others in the original."

The choice of poets was far from being random, they were all lifelong objects of love and veneration; from his youth onwards the world of their poetry was close to Pasternak's heart and the translations of their poems a duty imposed by the apprenticeship and devotion, and the desire to give the Russian reader some idea of them. This feature of Pasternak's work on translation was picked up and appreciated by the critics. A. Evgenyev wrote in *Literaturnoe Obozrenie*:

Pasternak's translations merit the highest respect if only because ... they enter into the creative world of the poet like milestones, defining to some degree his own creative path, and because Pasternak, in his love for the poets he is translating, has managed to convey this splendid artistic enthusiasm to the reader as well.

In the autumn Pasternak, who had stayed on in Peredelkino after Zinaida Nikolayevna and the boys had moved back to town, translated Shevchenko's great poem "Maria".* He read it in public on 25 December 1938 at a ten-day creative session of the poetry section and published it in *Krasnaya Nov* (1939, No. 2). Pasternak was very fond of this poem written in a popular vein, dealing with the subject of the Gospel and of the life of the Mother of God in the naïve style of a primitive painting. In 1947 he ventured to set down his own version of this theme in the poem "Christmas Star".

7

"I continue to live here," wrote Pasternak on 30 October 1938 to his sister Lydia,

alone in a large two-storied, badly-built house (built only three years ago but already rotting and collapsing), in a damp wood where it starts growing dark at 5 o'clock and it is far from cheerful at night, only because the household routine imposed by all this (meaning the heating, the cleaning, the washing and so on) reminds me of '19 and '20, the last years in time sequence that I spent with you and our parents; and to live with this evocative simulacrum, even if it is not a real tryst, has become such a vital need, to the exclusion of all else, that I am willing to go to any lengths for its sake, and in fighting to protect that delight, I grow wilder and am capable of forgetting myself. Because, apart from everything else, it is indeed a joy ... I am an incorrigible and convinced frequenter of bunks and attics (the student who "rents a cubbyhole") and my very best recollections are of the difficult

* Shevchenko, Taras Grigoryevich (1814–61): Ukrainian poet whose "Maria" is regarded as the Ukrainian national poem.

and modest periods of my existence: in them there is always more earth, more colour, more Rembrandt content. What I need is that life should make it hard for me . . . It is just as pleasurable as bathing in the river. It is 1 November and I have not given up the custom . . .

The winter solitude in Peredelkino was connected with work on the prose. He read fragments to his friends and gave a public reading on 25 December at the ten-day meeting of the poetry section; extracts from the first chapter "District Behind the Lines" were published in *Literaturnaya Gazeta* (15 December 1938) and the chapter "A Beggar Who Is Proud" in *Ogonek** (1939, No. 1).

I have seven or eight such recopied chapters, 3–4 in rough draft which need processing, and several in head; the whole subject is thought out and although I cannot even put my finger on the main difficulties, it is shameful that there is no novel (only talk) despite everything . . .

wrote Pasternak on 12 January 1939. Five chapters of the first section were earmarked for *Krasnaya Nov*. Among the provisional headings proposed for them were: "When the boys grew up", "Patrick's notebooks", and "Zhivult's notebooks".

While preparing to move to Moscow, on 5 November 1938, Pasternak wrote to Lydia Chukovskaya:

My choice of a place to stay is dictated by the type of work ahead of me. If it were possible and it made sense (not for my friends and wellwishers, but it's not at all clear for whom) to carry on with this prose (which I have got used to considering part of a certain novel), then I would hibernate in Peredelkino because the amplitude of the decision would correspond to that of securing the most favourable possible working conditions.

But this initiative, just like my other attempts at getting on with the novel . . . is limping lamely along: it is a matter of no interest to me whether the lameness in my prose comes about from an excess or a deficiency – it is so evident in its trial runs in the outer world where a book with literary pretensions is not supposed to suffer from lameness.

---

* *Little Flame* – a weekly social – political and artistic, illustrated magazine, published in Moscow since 1923, with a circulation of over two million.

Ten years later when Pasternak was completing work on the first part of *Doctor Zhivago*, an acquaintance of his, N. Muravina* – a student at Moscow University, noted down in her diary what it was that Pasternak had said to her over the telephone, indicating what aspect of his 1930s prose he saw as giving rise to this "lameness":

> I asked him about "A Beggar Who Is Proud" which I had come across in an old literary journal.
>
> "It is part of the same project as the novel," Boris Leonidovich explained. "But it consists only of scenes from everyday life. The artist is within his rights to sit back and deal with everyday life when literature is living through normal times and there is a general harmony of understanding. Then everything falls naturally into place."
>
> "But it gives such a rich portrayal of Moscow!" I said on behalf of the book, of which he had just been so unduly dismissive.
>
> He retorted: "Yes, many people, like yourself, will talk of life's rich canvas, but when the writer finds himself at odds with the general view, he has to offer an explanation of himself and his conceptions. If the writer cannot be understood when held up against the background of generally held impressions, it is not enough to offer scenic descriptions of daily life."

Pasternak was evidently unable before the outbreak of war to complete the writing of a novel already so clearly delineated in its subject matter. He lacked "the distant echo" of actual human reality; he lacked the feeling of a climate of freedom, of any universality of social life based on a unity of perceived values – without such attributes any attempt by the artist to write broadly-based, narrative prose is predestined to failure.

8

At the beginning of 1939, at Meyerhold's request, Pasternak started work on the translation of *Hamlet*, which the former was proposing

---

* Muravina's memoirs seem not to have been published in full. A small part of them appeared in the American-based emigré newspaper, *Novoye Russkoye Slovo* under the pen name Nina Skorbina. She herself emigrated to Paris.

to stage in Leningrad at the former Aleksandrinsky Theatre. By early April he had translated the first two and a half acts. He wrote to his parents on 29 April 1939:

> . . . There is no need of new translations, especially of *Hamlet*. But if they keep on at me with a proposal to that effect, whether from snobbery or some other reason, why should I not profit from such a theatrical whim – even without any hope of measuring up to my predecessors. For this gives me justification for an escapade into Shakespeare-land and for plunging myself into him. And a sojourn there, even in the form of reading him at a snail's pace, is in itself an incomparable treasure.

Pasternak goes on to explain that this year's move to the dacha has been put off because they had decided to exchange their large six-room cottage for a smaller one that had become vacant but

> . . . it is being repaired, the floors relaid and the painting done, hence the obstacles to the move. For in fact it was the other, enormous one on which I had reckoned for your arrival, and then, forgetting about the root cause, I got all amazed as to the reason for such a vast, unmanageable stable. Now, it will be half the size, and not in the wood but beside the fields, in the sun, better for the vegetable plot."

Zinaida Nikolayevna and her sons moved into the newly-refurbished dacha but Pasternak stayed behind to finish off rapidly the translation of some poems by the Hungarian romantic writer Aleksandr Petöfi:

> At first I had no feeling for him but then I discovered something sympathetic about him and I warmed to him. At one time I used to be enthusiastic about Lenau and came under his influence, and this Hungarian has something about him that recalls Lenau, Franz Liszt and others: common fundamentals, a single basic approach and so forth, so that I do not regret having taken him up. I have put together the best of my translations of recent years and I will issue them.

The booklet *Selected Translations* came out in the autumn of 1940 in the Sovetsky Pisatel Publishing House and included Kleist's drama *Prince Friederich of Homburg*, a Shrovetide play by Hans Sachs, and translations of poems by Shakespeare, Walter Raleigh, Byron, Keats, Petöfi, Verlaine and Becher.

After the Petöfi translations and the publication of five of his poems in *Literaturnaya Gazeta* (26 July 1939), Pasternak again returned to work on *Hamlet*. An extract from the second scene of the third act, "The Performance in the Court", was published in *Ogonek* (No. 18, 1939).

In the first few days of July Pasternak went to visit his family at Peredelkino in the new dacha which stood right on the edge of a large field. From the house there was a view of the little river beyond the field, the Setun, and of the church on its high bank. "The move was completed without me," he wrote to his father:

Zina spent a month and a half settling into the house, bringing it back into shape and looking after the vegetable garden – such a large one that we can hardly manage it – by dint of her own hands and efforts. It's magical here. I have been wanting to write to you since day one. It hurts that you cannot see this . . . But seriously, without exaggerating or overdoing it is just what one might dream of one's whole life. As regards views, abundance, commodities, tranquillity and husbandry, it is precisely what, even from a distance, observing other such, used to put one in a poetic frame of mind. Such slopes spun out by the course of a river right across the horizon (in the forest of silver birch), studded with gardens and little wooden houses with attics in a would-be Tyrolean cottage style – a glimpse of them at sunset from a train compartment window, in the course of one's journey, would make one lean out as far as the waist, and stay there lost in contemplation of some wayside settlement irradiated with an unearthly and covetable perfection. And suddenly life turned about and on its slope I myself plunged into this soft, evocative array of colour, seen from afar.

In Pasternak's letters of this period the feeling of "there being a limit to the years and the strength left to me" and of his "unbearable shame and grief" in the face of what was being perpetrated on all sides, filters through. Work on the translation of *Hamlet* was an antidote to this torture. Pasternak subordinated his whole order of life to its demands, sparing no effort, and set himself scarcely practicable daily targets, working for 10–12 hours a day. He forced himself to give up smoking, alternating periods sitting at his desk with physical work in the kitchen garden.

At the very climax of his work came the terrifying news of the arrest of Meyerhold on 20 June 1939 and of the murder of his wife

Zinaida Raikh twenty-five days later. At the end of August, a week before the start of the Second World War, Pasternak learnt of his mother's sudden death. Without replying to the letters of condolence, he stunned himself into silence by intensified work, fearing that a chance event might prevent him from completing the translation.

He gave readings of the acts he had managed to complete to a circle of his Peredelkino neighbours. Vsevolod Ivanov passed on news of the new translation to the Moscow Arts Theatre, where Nemirovich Danchenko was preparing to stage the tragedy.

At the beginning of 1939 Pasternak gave a reading of the first two acts in the Arts Theatre. And thus he struck up a friendship, which was to last many years, with the theatre and, primarily, with Boris Livanov, who was picked for the role of Hamlet.

After the reading Nemirovich Danchenko tore up the contract with Anna Radlova, whose translation had been specially commissioned by the Arts Theatre. In substantiation of his rejection, he wrote to Anna Radlova on 6 November 1939:

I received your letter the day after I looked at B. L. Pasternak's translation. His translation is exceptional in its poetic quality and is, undoubtedly, an event in literature. Nor could the Arts Theatre, which has been responsible for its own productions for many years past, afford to pass over such an outstanding rendering of *Hamlet* . . . I continue to consider your translation a good one, but with such an exceptional translation becoming available the Arts Theatre had to accept the latter.

Pasternak read the last three acts in the Arts Theatre on 18 November 1939. Vitaly Vilenkin, head of the literary section, recorded his impressions:

He reads, as usual, rhythmically, with powerful gushes. There is something of Hamlet about him; he captivates you by the rhythmical quality of his delivery which seems to come from within. Leonidov happened to hear extracts when visiting Trenev and then came to see me the following day with the words: "You have prevailed, O Man of Galilee . . . And you know what – he himself is Hamlet, he should play the role, and I will produce it."

That same summer, on 18 June, two days before Meyerhold's arrest, Marina Tsvetayeva arrived in Moscow. Her daughter and husband, who had returned from Paris two years previously, were living in a large dacha in Bolshevo which belonged to the Ministry of Foreign Affairs. Ariadna was working as a translator and spent most of her time in Moscow. Marina Ivanovna and her son took up residence in Bolshevo. Pasternak expected nothing good from their arrival and had been opposed to this decision back in 1935 – the tragedy of the family immeasurably exceeded his apprehensions, as he subsequently wrote in *An Essay in Autobiography*.

Pasternak used to tell Tarasenkov that Tsvetayeva had been instructed to live under the strictest incognito and that she, when in Moscow, looked in on Pasternak and left with him her notebook containing written entries with her last poems written in defence of the Czechs. On 28 August her daughter was arrested; on 10 October her husband. In the first few days of November, Pasternak went to see her in Bolshevo. Soon after, she moved out of the dacha and for a while lived with the sisters of Sergey Efron in Moscow. Pasternak took her to see Goslit, introduced her to the Director, Petr Chagin, and the editor in charge of the USSR People's Literature Section, Aleksandra Ryabinina; and translations began to come her way.

In November 1939 Akhmatova paid a brief visit to Moscow. Lydia Chukovskaya has recorded Pasternak's words, uttered after Akhmatova read out to him some of her new poems: "I now fear death no longer . . ." These were probably, as Chukovskaya infers, verses from Akhmatova's *Requiem*.*

On 27 November the Arts Theatre signed a contract with Pasternak and work started on the text of *Hamlet*, with the aim of achieving greater fluidity and intelligibility.

Vilenkin became the intermediary between Pasternak and the theatre – in the person of Nemirovich Danchenko and the actors, who were demanding further work on the text.

Pasternak readily, even too easily, as it seemed to me, agreed with them and from the very start was patently ready to put in additional work,

Vilenkin recalled.

* A long poem by Anna Akhmatova (1889–1966), occasioned by the imprisonment of her third husband, Nikolay Punin, and her son, Lev Gumilev, which was also a lament for the country as a whole. It has only recently (1987) been published in full in the Soviet Union.

. . . Of course, I checked everything against the original and tried to eliminate from the critical comments the casual, the superficial and the trivial, but I nevertheless agonized over having to pass on to Pasternak even the sort of objections with which I could not myself agree. But he took it all, however unusual, in good part. Perhaps in one or other instance of the most utter and complete nonsense he might suddenly groan: "Lord, what fools! . . ." or make some ironic comment. Just occasionally he did flare up, not at me, of course – he understood my position perfectly well – but at "the absence of an ear among theatre people in general." He readily inserted the majority of corrections – not immediately, not there and then, but used to bring them to me the next time he came. There were occasions when Boris Leonidovich used to say, gently but firmly: "In that case it was not me you should have invited . . ."

After handing over the reworked text of *Hamlet*, Pasternak wrote to his father on 14 February 1940:

This work was for me total salvation from many things, especially from Mama's death – the rest you do not know and it would take a long time to tell – without it I should have gone out of my mind. I achieved the aim I set myself: I rendered the thoughts, concepts, pages and scenes of the original and not individual words and lines. The translation is utterly simple, fluid, intelligible at first hearing and natural. In a period of bogus rhetorical pomp the need for a straightforward, independent word is very great and I involuntarily succumbed to it.

The same day he wrote to Olga Freidenberg:

The supreme indulgence, one quite beyond compare, is to read *Hamlet* out aloud, without cuts – even if only half of it; for three hours you feel yourself a human being in the highest sense of the word – endowed with the divine gift of words, a person in your own right, full of fire; for three hours you find yourself in spheres familiar to you from birth and from the first half of your life – and then, limp from spent energy, you fall back into the unknown, you "return to reality".

Pasternak very much wanted to see *Hamlet* on the stage. "My only solace is the Arts Theatre," he wrote on 24 November, thinking that revision of the text was now at an end. But further revision continued into the following winter too, when he travelled to and fro from Peredelkino in the mornings for twice-weekly meetings with Vilenkin and spent up to half a day in the theatre. These morning journeys formed the basis for the poem "On early trains":

> My winter quarters are outside Moscow.
> But whenever it was wanted,
> I took myself to town on business,
> be it blizzard, storm, or ten below.

Work on the play proceeded at a slow, typically Arts Theatre pace. It was interrupted by the outbreak of war. It was resumed in 1943, continued by Vasily Sakhnovsky after Nemirovich Danchenko's death, but the play was not in fact staged.

The original text of the translation had been intended for Meyerhold's theatre which, in Pasternak's opinion, represented a Russian offshoot of the Shakespearian tradition. It was printed in *Molodaya Gvardiya* and introduced by a note "From the translator". "The work needs to be judged," Pasternak wrote, "as a Russian original dramatic production because apart from accuracy, symmetry of line with the original and so forth, there is more in it of the deliberate liberty without which there is no way of approaching great things."

The second version of the translation, a polished one in a literary form, from which at the request of Nemirovich Danchenko and the actors the "folksiness", the "popular speech" and the "Griboedov intonations" had been removed, and which had been gone over additionally by the author, was submitted to Goslitizdat* in June 1940 and came out in book form on the eve of the war. Pasternak's aim in the foreword to this edition was to clarify the rationale of the translation's first version:

> The translator had been preparing a work on Shakespeare, Apollon Grigoryev, Ostrovsky and Blok, which he had in mind to use as a preface to the translation. But his intentions did not fit in with the time schedule. In issuing *Hamlet* in a somewhat different form from that in which it was printed in Nos. 5–6 of *Molodaya Gvardiya* for 1940, he is acting under the pressure of necessity. He refers readers with taste and understanding, who are able to distinguish between truth and its appearance, to the original version in the journal.

* State Literary Publishing House.

On 19 April 1940 Pasternak gave a reading of his translation in the Writers' Club. For that evening he invited Marina Tsvetayeva. Anna Grishina recalls that Marina Ivanovna arrived after the reading had already begun. Seeing her in the doorway, Pasternak halted, went over to her, kissed her hand and led her to the seat which awaited her in the front row.

The reading of *Hamlet* in the University club was a great success.

The text came across immediately, in a flash; and the reaction of the rapturous and responsive audience communicated itself to the author and confirmed his awareness of his artistic success. He made preparations to give a reading in May in Leningrad, followed by another in Tiflis. But a sudden acute attack of rheumatism put him in hospital for a month.

The critics differed in their assessment of the new *Hamlet*. Mikhail Morozov and Nikolay Vilyam-Vilmont congratulated Pasternak on the success of the translation which "springs organically from the bowels of the Russian language" and reproduces "the living tissue of Shakespeare's text" by its widespread use of folklore – a feature on which Shakespeare, too, had relied in his time. Mikhail Alekseyev and L. Reztsov saw the colloquial language as "pollution" and vulgarism. Such a *Hamlet* had no business in the realistic Arts Theatre; he was more akin to the Vaktangovites, wrote B. Solovyev.

As previously, Pasternak continued to take a direct part in all Tsvetayeva's tribulations and failures. She had spent the winter in Golitsyno, close to the writers' House of Retreat. For the summer, it proved possible to fix her up with the Gabrichevskys, who had gone away to Koktebel until the beginning of September. Pasternak introduced her to his friends, Vilyam-Vilmont, Neigaus, Asmus, Aseyev, Akhmatova, the Tager sisters, and Aleksey Kruchenykh. On one occasion he took her to see Elena Tager on Tverskoy Boulevard. Pasternak told Zoya Maslennikova the story of how Marina had complained to him that she was only producing twenty lines of translation a day and then had to spend another four days revising them. "I said to her," he recalled, "to justify doing it, one needed to get through 100 lines a day, and at that time I could produce 150 a day."

Aleksandra Ryabinina used to pay Tsvetayeva, sometimes without waiting for the work to be handed over. Pasternak helped out on a regular basis. But he had absolutely no success in finding her a room in Moscow and so, in the hope of help from the Union of

Writers, he decided to introduce her to Aleksandr Fadeyev. At one point when Tsvetayeva was on a visit to Peredelkino, he had wanted to take her to see Fadeyev who lived nearby, but the latter refused to receive an émigré. Some time later Fadeyev looked in on Pasternak, as if by chance, and Tsvetayeva had the opportunity of putting her requests to Fadeyev. In the same way she came to meet Petr Pavlenko, to whom she addressed a letter on 27 August 1940, with a note from Pasternak in support.

In July Pasternak had staying with him Nina Tabidze, who had made the journey to intercede on behalf of her husband.* He, too, personally took part in the attempt to intercede; and in the Museum of the History of the Peoples in Tiflis there is a letter from Pasternak to Beriya. But nothing could be learnt of Titsian.

9

"Ah, how often I need you," wrote Pasternak to Olga Freidenberg on 15 November 1940.

Life slips away or maybe has already departed for good, but, as you wrote last year, we live in fragmented bursts of some kind of "seventh youth" (your expression). I had many such this year. After a long period of solid translation I started to get down something of my own. However that was not the main thing. What is amazing is that the abundance of this wonderful, vital summer has played no less a role in our lives than in the life of any collective farmer. I and Zina (the initiative is hers) have established the most enormous vegetable plot so that this autumn I was afraid of our not having the strength to get it all in and store it. I and Lenichka† are spending the winter in the cottage, while Zina is tearing herself to bits between us and the boys who are studying in town. What incommunicable beauty there is, living in the woods in winter, in the frost, when there's firewood to be had. The eyes dazzle, one is completely blinded. The magical quality is not only in the contemplation but in the minutest detail of the laborious, anxious daily round. Let things go for an hour and the house will get so cold that however you

* Titsian Tabidze was arrested (and executed) in 1937.
† Leonid, Pasternak's son by Zinaida Neigaus.

stoke the fire you will not get it warm again. Be caught napping and the potatoes will start to freeze in the cellar or the cucumbers go mouldy. And it all breathes and has its own smell, it is all mortal and can die a death. We have half a cellarful of our own potatoes, two barrels of shredded cabbage and two barrels of cucumbers. And then there are journeys into town, waking up before six in the morning and a two mile walk through the dark, still nocturnal fields and woods, and the line of the permanent way in wintertime, ideal and severe like death, and the flame of the morning train for which you have arrived late and which overtakes you at the point where you emerge from the edge of the wood and the crossing confronts you. Ah, how delicious it still is to be alive, especially at times when things are difficult and there is no money (a situation which has, for some reason, affected us these last months). How premature to give up, how one wants to live!

In passing, Pasternak mentioned that he had "started to get down something of my own" – the first poems of the Peredelkino cycle, "Summer's Day" and "The City". They were published in *Molodaya Gvardiya* (No.1, 1941) in their original versions which differed markedly from the definitive ones. The first is devoted to the lush abundant summer of 1940 and his work at the vegetable plot which washed his soul clean of its moribund accretions and, as had once happened in 1918 in Ochakovo, a few kilometres from Peredelkino, restored to Pasternak his purity of perception and joy in creativity. In the winter of 1914 he had written to his parents that it was necessary to put a pitcher of water "under the freshly-picked words" of his new book – now the author himself was akin to the pitcher of water with the flowers in it.

> As a vase is filled with flowers
> and water, night will pour in
> through the casement and fill me flush,
> when I walk up into the mezzanine.
>
> Night will remove the shawl
> of warmth from the walls.
> And when the walls have cooled
> will wrap it round a local girl.

The poem "The City" represents a new variant of the theme traditional to Pasternak of today's metropolis as a living embodiment of history.

It has fathered a thousand miracles
and need not fear the permafrost.
The million souls who live here
make it a city all soul.

From its commanding heights,
arms akimbo in the snow,
it seems a timeless grove of firs,
where all the cones are centuries.

And isn't it eternal when it hurls –
from running start to furthest point,
through intersecting multitudes –
its main arterial road into the west?

This form of address to the earth and the sky – since, for Pasternak,
the city as an embodiment of history was a substitute for the sky
(and not merely in childish dreams) – became for him the starting
point of a new awareness and a new approach to poetry.

But these two poems were not worth a mention in Pasternak's
eyes. Speaking of "getting down something of my own" he had in
mind his return to prose. This becomes clear from his letter to
Evgeniya Pasternak:

After a break of many years during which I was busy on all sorts
of rubbish, the sole exception being *Hamlet* (although that too is
a translation), I had a try at turning my hand to something of my
own. I was astonished at first to find how far I had lost the art
of writing but then things tightened up and now I quiver with
my old excitement at each hour given up to work. This is again
still the same novel: either – if things go well – I shall finish it or
I shall cause it to move somewhere ahead or to one side . . .

wrote Pasternak on 3 July 1940.

The creative surge which had welled up in the summer also left
its mark on a lyrical cycle of nine poems written in 1941.

"After an interval of 15 years or more I again feel as I did once
before," he wrote on 8 May 1941 to Olga Freidenberg.

I find my daily work bubbling up spontaneously inside as before,
and not because of some imperative requirement – and this is the
only way in which it can come naturally without the feeling of
being under guidance towards focussing on "the entire country"

and so on and so on. I am already getting something down and I shall be doing more still.

He told her what a big role his intensive correspondence with her was playing in his spring upsurge of lyric writing. And in fact his letter of 15 November 1940 quoted above can be regarded as the outline for the poems "Summer's Day" and "On early trains".

> At the level crossing, wild pussy willows
> whitely awaited my arrival.
> Overhead, the high stars
> lay in January's cold pit.
>
> As a rule, in the woods,
> the night mail or the No.40
> would try to overtake me,
> but I was after the 6.25.
>
> Sly hints of light about me
> would suddenly tighten their grip,
> the searchlight fling its flood
> the length of deafened viaduct.

Akhmatova recalled her meeting with Pasternak at this time: "In June 1941 when I arrived in Moscow he said to me over the telephone: 'I have written nine poems. I am coming over straight away to read them.'" Akhmatova remembered his earlier mood during "the long and painful interval when he really was incapable of writing a single line." "I can still see it," she noted, "I can just hear the perplexity in his voice: 'What is the matter with me?'" She paid a visit to Peredelkino in August 1940, spent several days with Pasternak at his dacha and adjudged that it was indeed life in Peredelkino when "he, in effect, completely abandons the city," his "encounter with nature", which had helped Pasternak to surmount the difficulties of that period.

> His whole life long Nature was his sole and omnipotent Muse, his secret collocutor, his Betrothed and his Beloved, his Wife and his Widow – she was to him what Russia was to Blok. He remained faithful to her to the end and she rewarded him right royally. The asphyxia was over.

But for Pasternak nature was not an object for countryside sketches; it was another name for life, an example of spiritual well-being, spontaneity and beauty which had to be translated into art and made part of man's spiritual world. In *An Essay in Autobiography*, he called her "imagination's successful design" which "serves the poet as a better model than anything he can find in the studio." His verses about nature in Peredelkino speak of the memories of childhood and the sea, the expectation of the end and the fundamentals of artistry; they evoke hope and gratitude and kindle the feeling of admiration for simple people who readily and manfully bear with the deprivations that are their lot.

The critics who had accused Pasternak's poetry in the Twenties of "hermeticism" now rewarded him with the persistent tag of "summer cottager". But if twentieth-century art is pre-eminently city art, it is quite natural for contemporary man to encounter nature in his country cottage; and for his reflections to derive from his impressions of genteel suburban rusticity. "The lands where the wild birds fly" remain in the realm of the exotic, and the heart of the city dweller, as before, quickens more to "the sandy slope with the two rowans in front of the garden gate."

The cycle of poems, entitled "Peredelkino" in the book, written in the spring of 1941, was the justification for the restructuring of which Pasternak had spoken at the 1936 Minsk plenum. If the notions of spontaneity and simplicity in art were formulated in the *Second Birth* poems, in this cycle they were given practical expression.

Noting his movement towards "unparalleled simplicity" in his most recent works of translation, the critics expressed the hope that "the same simplicity would characterize Pasternak's new original poems."

Such was indeed the case. Pasternak's new poetry showed the influence of the "Shakespeare bath" which Romain Rolland had advised as far back as 1930. In the period when he was establishing a creative style for himself, Pasternak had learnt from his translations of Swinburne and Kleist the art of conveying the terms of thought of another poet in a succinct and lively manner; and this newly-acquired talent had helped with the writing of *Over the Barriers* and *My Sister, Life*. His experience of Shakespeare and Verlaine now enabled him to rise to new heights of mastery. He now gives precedence to the rational desiderata of relevance and a sense of proportion over the subjective irrational aspects of perception and the wish to project life in a rapidly changing sequence of impressions. The sensibility and excitability which characterized his lyric poetry in the Twenties is not lost; it is purified and made lucid by a calm understanding of life's fundamentals and their basic permanency. Pasternak consciously restricts the metaphoric loading of detail while reducing to a minimum the figurative structure of the verse, and he increases the overall metaphoric impact of the poem as a whole.

At one point in a letter to Sergey Spassky of 30 April 1933 he depicted the maximum degree of perfection attainable – "in principle only" – by his striving after a "circumspect style", which presupposed giving the meaning of each word its full weight.

> Only when it has reached a certain height can poetry allow itself the final and broadest metaphor of casting itself in the role of ordinary man who uses language as a natural means of communication. Only at this final peak can it succeed with the image (already a dramatic one) diffused to the ethereal extreme, which it provides uncircumscribed by detailed metaphor because the image, if it is not to fall apart, must be maintained in existence by the metaphoric force of the energy which sustained it. Only then are all the words meaningful and does the very sub-fusc quality of their precise sense become music.

The poetic cycle of the spring of 1941 became a definite step in this direction, one which was governed by Pasternak's entire previous development of poetic mastery with its emphasis on clarity and sobriety of thought. In his letter to Simon Chikovani of 6 October 1957 Pasternak wrote of the relationship between image and thought in poetry, "about the insubstantiality of the differences in poetry between direct and limpid speech, shorn of symbols, and those occasions when it uses metaphors."

> Direct formulation and metaphor are not opposites but different stages of thought, distinct in time: an early stage, one of instant inception, unelucidated by metaphor; and a mature one which determines its own meaning and is merely perfecting its own projection in non-metaphoric assertion.

In *An Essay in Autobiography*, Pasternak acknowledged: "I do not like my own style before 1940 . . . The disintegration of forms, impoverishment of thought and the littered and uneven style, then general, are alien to me."* The results achieved in the winter of

* *An Essay in Autobiography*, p. 39.

1940–41 and those attained later on enabled him to come to such a categorical verdict.

The Peredelkino poems were first published only in October 1943 in a small booklet under the title *On Early Trains*. With a copy to Olga Freidenberg in blockaded Leningrad, Pasternak wrote on 5 November 1943:

> I am sending you a slim volume, too meagre a volume, very late in appearing, and much too insignificant for it to be worth talking about. It does contain just a few worthwhile properly-written pages. They belong to the early 1941 cycle "Peredelkino" (to be found at the end of the book). It is a sample of how in general I would now be writing if I were able to do free original work. It was done just before the war.

10

> The war wrested me away from the first pages of *Romeo and Juliet*. I had given up working on the translation and, what with seeing off my son who was going to do defence work, and other commotions, I forgot about Shakespeare. In the weeks that followed, every mortal thing became involved willy-nilly in the war. I was doing fire duty on the roof of a twelve-storey house during the night time bombardments – the witness of two incendiary bombs hitting the building during one of my spells of duty; I also helped dig air-raid shelters here on the city outskirts and attended military training courses, which disclosed that I was a born sniper. My family was sent out to the depths of a remote country district. I kept trying to join them. At the end of October I went off to join my wife and children; and the winter in a provincial town, remote from the railway, on a frozen river – which itself represented the sole means of communication – cut me off from the outside world and for three months incarcerated me with my interrupted *Romeo* . . .

was how Pasternak began his note published in the journal *Ogonek* (No. 47, 1947) under the title, "My New Translations".

The first to be evacuated were small children, and three-year-old

Lenechka* Pasternak had his name put down for the writers' children's school contingent due for evacuation to Bersut on the Kama on 9 July.

That same day Pasternak wrote to Olga Freidenberg:

> My Dearest, Precious Olyushka! How about this for a piece of news? I am writing to you, in floods of tears, but – just imagine it – with the first happy news, news of the first fright (the first in an impending series) to have passed us by safely: Zina has been taken on as a helper with the train contingent with which Lenichka* is to be evacuated, and thus, with the Lord's help, he will not be alone and will know who he is and what he is. They are being sent away shortly and I am parting with all for which I have latterly lived and laboured. Zhenichka† is in the army, somewhere in the heat of the fighting, out in your direction.

Circumstances were complicated by the fact that since the spring Zinaida Nikolayevna's eldest son had been gravely ill in a tuberculosis hospital and a few days before war being declared had had an operation to remove the affected area of bone. Zinaida Nikolayevna took thirteen-year-old Stasik with her, leaving the sick Adik to the attention of Boris Leonidovich.

Zhenya Pasternak, who had only just finished tenth class, had been immediately despatched, together with pupils from the senior classes, to dig trenches around Smolensk. After enduring German bomber attacks, they returned in mid-July.

> Sad in our garden.
> Every day, more beautiful.
> Even this year, life here
> the cup that runneth over.
>
> But the householder can't find
> the love he felt for the house.
> He's sent his family away
> and the enemy isn't far. [. . .]
>
> Yet he keeps on, keeps on
> going into the garden,
> a home guard at his post
> seeing the sunset towards Smolensk.

* Alternative, double diminutive forms for Leonid, Pasternak's son by Zinaida Neigaus.
† Double diminutive form for Evgeny. Likewise Zhenechka for Evgeniya.

Every four or five days Pasternak wrote to his wife with detailed news of Adik and of his Moscow life.

On 20 July 1941:

. . . Yesterday morning I was with Adik and said goodbye to him. They are moving out to the town of Ples on the Volga. I found him in better shape than used to be the case . . . As I have written more than once to tell you, I could not leave the flat, the dacha and the kitchen garden in the state to which they had been reduced at the time of our parting. I have gradually got it all back into shape with my own hands . . . I now find the most agreeable and congenial occupation to be physical labour: it confers oblivion from my tiredness. I kiss you and Stasya and Lenya.

On 24 July 1941:

Dearest Dusya! They have been bombing Moscow for the third night running. The first night I was in Peredelkino and also the last one, the 23 to 24, but yesterday the 22 to 23 I was in Moscow on the roof . . . of our house, together with Vsevolod Ivanov, Khalturin and others in the fire-watching operation . . . How often during the course of last night, with high-explosive bombs coming down and bursting on every second or third house, and incendiaries setting entire street blocks almost instantaneously alight – as if at the wave of a magic wand – did I mentally say goodbye to you both, Mama dear and my Dusya. Thank you for all that you have given me and brought me; you have been the best part of my life, and you and I have been insufficiently conscious of this, of how profoundly you are my wife and what a lot that means.

With only a few hours to get ready and without time to say their goodbyes, Evgeniya Vladimirovna and Zhenya left for Tashkent on 6 August. The next day but one, Pasternak saw off Marina Tsvetayeva, who was being evacuated.

From the first days of the war, especially after the seven bombing raids around 20 June when her son, Mur, spent the nights on roof duty, Tsvetayeva was possessed by a frenzied urge to get out of Moscow. Pasternak sought to dissuade her, since Moscow was a source of work contracts and earnings, and he could not afford a break with the city.

At Pasternak's request, Viktor Bokov went with him to the South Moscow river port. Bokov recalled how Mur did not want to leave and went off somewhere; how they bought open sandwiches for the journey in the nearest food store because Tsvetayeva had not brought any food along with her, relying on there being a buffet; and how she stood on the deck and waved her hand to them as the steamer moved off.

". . . I have again begun to earn something, just recently," Pasternak wrote to his wife on 20 August:

They accepted the article for VOKS and I am writing them another (even at a fee of only 200 roubles a time). I have written several new poems for *Krasnaya Nov* in substitution for the other, pre-war ones. I want to write a play and yesterday I submitted an application to this effect to the Arts Committee. I am irritated by the still prevailing cult of the routine in literature, and on the publishing side, etc. After people have tasted the smell of powder and death, and looked danger in the eye, and walked on the edge of the abyss and so forth – after all that it is not possible to sustain them with the same joyless trivialities, so dear to the heart of the people who churn them out – people in their majority devoid of talent and devoid of willpower, with minimal appetites, who do not even suspect that there is such a thing as the taste of immortality, happy on a diet of ham sandwiches, saloon cars or limousines, and scones . . . with gongs. You remember the mood I was in before the war and how I used to want to do everything at once and to pour it all out, right down to my innermost thoughts. This is now so ten-fold.

On 1 September 1941:

I do not complain of my existence – I love my arduous fate and I cannot stand inactivity – I do not complain, as I say, but I am being literally torn in pieces between two empty flats and the dacha, my worries about you, my fire-watching duties, my literary earnings, my military training . . . In the spring, after *Hamlet* I wrote the best I had ever written. This upsurge is still continuing. I do everything that other people do and I turn nothing down: I have joined the fire brigade, I am taking part in drill instruction and shooting practice. You saw what I wrote for the newspaper at the beginning of the war – it was so simple, so sane and so robust and all the rest . . .

Of Pasternak's four wartime and nine pre-war poems, *Krasnaya Nov* (Nos. 9–10) published only two: "On Early Trains" and "The

Villein", two others were given to *Ogonek* (No.39) and one was published in *Literaturnaya Gazeta* (24 September 1941). The articles written for VOKS were not accepted, nor was the one written at the beginning of the war. The translations from Simon Chikovani and the Latvian poet, Yan Sudrabkaln, were published much more easily. Pasternak considered his poem "To Russian Genius" the most important of them all. In it he sought to give a definition of the moral origins of a nation's genius. It was an outline in verse form of the thoughts which were later set out in fuller form in his essay *A Visit to the Front*: "Genius is primary and unobtrusive. The same features of novelty and originality formed our revolution." *Literaturnaya Gazeta* demanded it be revised: the second stanza was thrown out, the first rewritten, and the title changed. Pasternak had his appeal to Russia and Russian patriotism struck out more than once by the editorial boards of the wartime newspapers. The articles he wrote at the beginning of the war were not accepted. Lydia Chukovskaya read one of them. It contained the words: "Because for us Russia is not only the name of our country but the name of our sisters, mothers and wives."

"I have seen and gone through a very great deal," he wrote to Olga Freidenberg on 18 July 1942.

It all offered unrivalled opportunities for reflection, observation and proving my worth in both word and deed. I kept trying to express myself in different ways but each time with that measure of truth and effectuality (perhaps imagined or mistaken) which I consider incumbent on me, and scarcely one of these efforts bore fruit.

Pasternak's proposal for writing a play, mentioned in his letter to Zinaida Nikolayevna, has been preserved in the personal papers of N. N. Chushkina, who was then working in the Arts Committee. His work on *Hamlet* and then on *Romeo and Juliet,* the Arts Theatre rehearsals and his contacts with the actors had all made Pasternak want to write a drama. In his application, he wrote of his preference for the Arts Theatre to which he would like to offer his work for staging:

The experience, both in the present and in the immediate future, of the organization of the defence of Moscow is to serve as the basic material for a four-act play "In a Soviet City". This will depict a large Soviet town in winter – on the analogy of Moscow or Leningrad, with the front approaching ever nearer, and then under conditions of frequent bombardment, counter-raids, and hostile provocation; amid privations, dangers, and the need – becoming an ever more customary feature of life – to keep up their spirits. *The author set as his task** the attainment of the gentle, natural, pervasive dramatic atmosphere *of Chekhov and Ibsen. In depicting* the general psychological bases of existence in the enhancing focus which the presence of danger imparts to life . . . the play will be an attempt to study and outline the initial features of a historically new type; and pay tribute to *themes scarcely touched upon or left totally ignored by Soviet literature.* Thus the author will attempt, for example, to show that the two words "Russian" and "Socialist" stand for similar things and that this is the main and most substantive fact of world history in the first half of the twentieth century. He will seek a formulation for the concept of "Soviet-ness" as such, as being the most elementary and evident of spiritual truths, residing identically in innocent and guilty alike, in both adherents and opponents and indeed in everyone without distinction, be they only the progeny and the product of the past quarter of a century.

At the end of his application, Pasternak cautioned that "the play will be written in a new, free way".

While living on his own in Peredelkino, he had come more and more acutely to feel an identity with Russian history and nature, an understanding of the inimitable features of the national character, forged and shaped in adversity. Pasternak made new friends among the workers and caretakers of the writers' settlement, of the most varied composition and origins, who had made their way in life through long years of hardship and deprivation. "People of an artistic cast," wrote Pasternak to his parents as early as 6 June 1938, "will always be drawn to the poor, to people of a working and modest background; things are warmer and more cosy with them, and have more spirituality and colour than anywhere else:

> All the upheavals of the past,
> years of war and privation,
> and I have come to recognize
> Russia's face without a word.

* See footnote on p. 65.

Checking my adoration,
I observed and adored.
Squatters, old women,
students, locksmiths,

and need created
nothing servile.
They suffered change,
discomfort, like gentlefolk.

The start of the war sustained and prolonged this quest. It became
the basic content and motivation of his new artistic upsurge. "The
tragic, painful period of the war was a period of vitality and in this
sense an untramelled, joyous restoration of the sense of community
with everyone," wrote Pasternak in a note of 1956. Just as he had set
out in a letter to Obradovich of the summer of 1927 to explain that he
"had grown accustomed to see in October the chemical composition
of the air we breathe," so now he wanted to depict in his play the
commingling in the face of adversity of the Russian and the Soviet
elements in the soul of all who had been formed in the post-
revolutionary period – "the progeny of the quarter of a century".

11

On 10 September 1941 he writes:

Last night Fedin told me that it seemed that Marina [Tsvetayeva]
has taken her own life. I do not want to believe it. She is
somewhere near you, in Chistopol or Elabuga. Please find out
and write me (telegrams take longer than letters). If it is true,
what a horror! If so, see what you can do for the boy, find out
where he is and how he is . . .

It will never be forgiven me. This last year I stopped bothering
about her. She was very highly thought of by intellectual society
and, among those who knew, was coming into fashion; she had
been taken up by my personal friends, Garrik, Asmus, Kolya
Vilyam, and, finally, Aseyev. Since it had become very pres-
tigious to call oneself her best friend, for this and other reasons,
I stayed away from her and kept my distance: but this last
year virtually completely forgot about her. And now this! How
dreadful it is.

The grief and horror evoked by the news alternate in the letter with tortured pangs of conscience. Perhaps, had Pasternak been closer to her, and had not allowed her to leave – and he had been so very much against her leaving! – perhaps then this would not have occurred. His desire to reverse events and reshuffle them bred excessive self-reproach. He had not "forgotten about" her in her last year, but had helped her materially on a regular basis. According to Ariadna Sergeyevna, from sometime in the early summer of 1941, Marina Tsvetayeva came to Peredelkino and Zinaida Nikolayevna did the rounds of all the neighbours and assembled the sum necessary to pay for the room on Pokrovsky Boulevard. After rescuing her from her spiritual gloom and despair of the autumn of 1939, putting friends at her disposal and doing something towards regularizing her outward life, Pasternak anguished over having relinquished her; he had given way, as always, to her own insistent wish. But Tsvetayeva was the architect of her own life, brooking no one's interference in her own decisions; she made and unmade her own friendships. Later he was to outline her character in *An Essay in Autobiography*:

> Tsvetayeva was a woman with an actively male soul, decisive, militant and indomitable. In her life and works she rushed headlong, hungrily and almost rapaciously, into the search for finality and definition, in the pursuit of which she had ventured far afield and outstripped everyone else.*

> If there is anything I can do,
> let me know. Somehow or other.
> I could sense a complaint
> in the silent way you went.

> The enigma of all loss –
> at which I worry away,
> seeking an answer. Useless.
> Death has no definition.

In the first few days of October Pasternak had a meeting with Mur, Tsvetayeva's son, who had returned to Moscow. After their talk he noted down in Aleksandr Kruchenykh's scrapbook: "How does that strike you, Alesha! We always felt it coming. Who can go on living after this? Borya, 12 October 1941."

---

* *An Essay in Autobiography*, p. 55.

At this time Akhmatova arrived by plane from blockaded Leningrad. Pasternak was proposing to install her for the winter in Evgeniya Vladimirovna's flat under the eye of the wise and energetic E. P. Kuzmina. But Fadeyev had included Akhmatova, along with Pasternak, Fedin, Leonov and their families, in the contingent due for immediate evacuation from Moscow on 14 October to Chistopol on the Kama. The train departed at 8 a.m. The Vakhtangov and Maly theatres were travelling on further, into Siberia: the writers descended at Kazan. They continued their journey to Chistopol in a steamer, and arrived there late in the evening on 18 October. These were the terrifying days of the German advance on Moscow.

Zinaida Nikolayevna rented a room for Pasternak. She herself lived as a warden in a boarding house where the boys, too, were. An account of the life in Chistopol, the suppers in the Litfond Canteen and the Wednesday literary get-togethers in the Teachers Club has been given by Aleksandr Gladkov, then a young playwright, in his memoir *Meetings with Pasternak*. He records one of their walks together through the town on 20 February 1942:

A fine, spring-like day and a long interesting conversation of which I am writing down only a small part. It begins with B.L. speaking of the barges which have frozen solid in the ice of the Kama which, when he looks at them, always remind him of Marina Tsvetayeva.

"I loved her very much and now I regret not having sought opportunities to tell her so as often as she, perhaps, may have needed to hear it . . .

"One day I will write about her, I have already started . . . Yes, both in verse and in prose. I have long wanted to do so. But I am holding myself back so as to accumulate strength worthy of the theme, that is of her, of Marina. One needs to write about her with tautly-stretched expressive power . . ."

This warm February day in Chistopol, with icicles and the snow thawing out, is captured in the poem "In Memory of Marina Tsvetayeva" which was conceived and started at that time and then completed in Moscow in December 1943.

> The grey day prolonging its gloom.
> Inconsolable streams across the porch
> to the door of the hall,
> and in at the open windows . . . [. . .]

It was time long ago to take
your scattered remains from Elabuga
and lay them to rest in a requiem.
Ah Marina, the obstacles were small.

Last year I saw it celebrated
all along the snowy reaches of the river,
where the long ships lay up
in pack ice for the winter.

Pasternak took two contracts for translations with him to Chistopol: that for *Romeo and Juliet*, on which he had already begun work in the spring, and one for a collection by the Polish romantic writer, Juliusz Slowacki. On arrival he got down to Shakespeare immediately. He marked his completion of the work by giving a public reading of the tragedy in the Teachers Club.

This took place on the evening of 26 February 1942 and the collection went as a donation to the front. "B.L. in a black suit and a bright woollen tie," noted Gladkov, "with white felt boots on his feet. He takes a long time unwrapping an untidy bundle done up in old, crumpled newspapers from which he extracts his manuscript text . . . He is absolutely no actor and when he sort of starts to act out the speeches of the character parts, such as the nurse, it produces an effect of naïveté. He does best with reading the speeches of Romeo and Lorenzo. The scene of Mercutio's death came over dramatically. The translation itself is very good, almost better than *Hamlet*."

Pasternak's letters to his wife, Evgeniya, are full of details of daily life of the winter of 1941–42.

12 March 1942. Dearest Zhenya, I received all your letters and telegrams, including the last one with the news about young Zhenya starting at the Military Academy. I am very happy to hear this and congratulate you both from my heart. I have not written to anyone for two months – a conscious sacrifice I made towards the work on *Romeo and Juliet* which was finished during that period. It has caused me a lot more effort than *Hamlet* because of the comparative thinness and affectation of some aspects and parts of this tragedy, one of Shakespeare's first, they say . . . I have been preparing myself the whole while for failure and disaster with this thing and if I have escaped disgrace, as it seems, it is precisely thanks to putting more effort into it than into *Hamlet* and making a few changes . . .

I have got through this winter happily and with a sense of happiness amid privations and in the very heart of the most impenetrable backwardness, thanks to the concord established between myself, Fedin, Aseyev, and also Leonov and Trenev. Here we feel ourselves freer than in Moscow despite the nostalgia for her, affecting each of us equally.

At the moment I am busy with translating the Polish classic Slowacki. This also is a commission for which I am paid; that is, it is work for one's daily bread. Later I shall put in some time on something of my own, for myself . . . I want to write a play and a story, a long poem in verse and some minor poems too. This mood of mine – perhaps in anticipation of death – is the one I had last year and the last pre-war months, and it has flared up still more vividly in the war . . .

The translation of Slowacki's selected works was sent to Chagin in Goslitizdat on 30 May 1941. Its publication did not come about and Pasternak's work was lost. Its text was not found till 1972, in Rovno, in the collection of a Chistopol friend of Pasternak's, Valery Avdeyev, a Professor of Botany. Before leaving for Moscow in the summer of 1943, Pasternak had deposited with Avdeyev all his papers, the manuscripts of the works completed in Chistopol and the letters he had received.

12

The Novosibirsk "Krasny Fakel" Dramatic Theatre put on *Hamlet* in Pasternak's translation and with Serafim Ilovaisky in the title role. On 20 February 1942 a contract was signed with the same theatre for a play "on a theme and subject topical at the present day . . . Completion date July 1942." His conversations with Gladkov reflect Pasternak's starting work on the play. The first scene was to take place in a potato field. "And after that an old estate. The theme – the continuity of culture . . . I dream of reviving in this play the forgotten traditions of Ibsen and Chekhov. It is not realism but symbolism, is that it?"

His work on the play created the need for him to refamiliarize himself with Apollon Grigoryev's articles on the theatre, and on 22 March 1942 Pasternak requested Aleksey Kruchenykh to send him the one-volume work edited by Strakhov.

Summer 1942 was devoted to work on the play: ". . . I am writing it freely like writing verse, and entirely to please myself – a contemporary realistic play in prose," Pasternak wrote to Chagin on 14 June.

At the same time the proofs of *Hamlet* for Detgiz* were inspected and gone through once again. Replying to M. M. Morozov's criticisms of the translation, Pasternak wrote on 15 July 1942: "I have begun a large play in prose form, a realistic one, contemporary with the war – Shakespeare will help me here a lot; it is an all-Russian Faust in the sense in which Faust should comprise Gorbunov and Chekhov."

In a letter to Olga Freidenberg of 18 July, sent to blockaded Leningrad, the sketches of daily life in Chistopol intermingle with thoughts of and ideas for the play developed, in part, from the self-same background material of a provincial town in wartime.

18 July 1942. Sunday, seven o'clock in the morning, a rest day. This means that Zina has been here overnight and Lenechka will be arriving at 10 a.m. The rest of the week they will both be in the children's home where Zina works as a warden . . . I got up at six in the morning because there's often something wrong with the connection of our local stand-pipe where I go to get water and, besides, it's only available twice a day at fixed hours. One has to catch the right moment . . . One of my windows gives on to the road, beyond which there's a large green expanse calling itself "Park of Culture and Rest", and the other on to the daisy-infested courtyard of the local people's court to which they escort contingents of emaciated prisoners evacuated to the jail here from other towns, and where people start keening at the top of their voices the moment sentence is passed on one of the local lads.

The road is covered with a thick layer of black mud that oozes up between the cobblestones. Here one has a soil with magical properties, rich black earth of such a quality that it seems as if it is mixed with coal dust, and if such soil were to be had by a hard-working, disciplined population who knew its own capacity, what it wanted and what was within its rights to demand, no economic or social task would be too hard for it to accomplish; and in this New Burgundy art would blossom forth on the lines of Rabelais or Hoffman's *Nutcracker*.

* Children's Publishing House (literary and popular scientific).

The final passage of Pasternak's letter above was dictated by his acute need for a self-sufficient existence; he had found it painful to put up with its atrophy ever since the First World War. For Pasternak there was a metaphorical connection between the notion of a fruitful existence and the cultivation of the soil, just as cultivation has its etymological origin in the word "culture". In one of the two surviving scenes from the 1942 play, the heroes find themselves in an unknown estate on the edge of the town which has been abandoned by the Soviet troops and not yet taken over by the Germans. The plot development was probably on lines analogous to the stay of Zhivago's family in Varykino during the Civil War.

Pasternak ended his letter to Olga Freidenberg by listing what he had managed to achieve that winter – the winter's productivity had engendered in him a feeling of freedom:

> An official government order is required for me to be able to return to Moscow. They are reluctant to issue them. I asked friends a month ago to try and get me one. It will be, probably, another month before I do get one. When I do, I will make the journey to Moscow out of a whole variety of natural feelings, curiosity among them. For the time being I am free and writing fast; I am rewriting and destroying a contemporary play in prose, which I write solely for myself from pure love of art.

In Chistopol, Fedin and Leonov and Gladkov were each writing plays. Pasternak read and praised Gladkov's *Long, Long Ago*, was enthusiastic about Leonov's *Invasion*, though the artificial – "conference style", as he called it – ending of the play grieved him, and took pleasure in the success of Fedin, who gave a reading of his *Test of Feelings* on 5 July. At the same time Pasternak explicitly recognized that the notions of freedom and self-sufficiency which he championed in his own play, in other words "the concept of Soviet-ness as such, as being the most elementary and evident of truths, residing identically in innocent and guilty alike", would be misinterpreted.

He wrote to Tairov that the play was "cast in so independent a form that unless serious changes intervene in our literary and theatrical productions, it will scarcely be fit for staging and publication."

He received a Moscow travel order at the end of September and on 2 October was excitedly walking along its empty streets. He stayed with his brother on Gogolevsky Boulevard. The flat in

Lavrushinsky Lane had been taken over by anti-aircraft gunners. The previous winter in Chistopol he had learnt of the loss of his personal papers and now, on his arrival in Moscow, he came upon a scene of total devastation.

"I went away amid the panic and chaos of the October evacuation," he wrote on 5 November 1943 to Olga Freidenberg,

> I and Shura* went to the Tretyakov Gallery to request them to accept my father's portfolios for storing. Nowhere was anyone accepting anything except at the Tolstoy Museum, and that was a long way off and there were no hand-carts and no cars. The anti-aircraft gunners have taken over our town flat (on the eighth and ninth floors). They have turned the upper floor, which they have not occupied, into a passageway with the doors left wide open. You can imagine the state I found everything in during the mere 5–10 minutes I spent there. Our soldiers are quartered in Peredelkino. Our things were transferred to Vsevolod Ivanov's house, among them a large chest with quantities of papa's oil sketches; and soon after the Ivanov's dacha burned down to the ground. This, my major wound, was so painful for me that I waved goodbye to all remaining traces of my own sojourn there, now that the main thing that used to link me to my memories had gone.

His desire to spend the winter in the woods of Peredelkino turned out to be a total impossibility and he spent his three months in Moscow alternating between his brother Shura and Asmus. At some point soon after his arrival he read his new play to them and a few other friends. The degree of freedom and independence postulated in it alarmed his listeners. A few days later, on 22 October, meeting Gladkov in the Writers Club, he said, in answer to a question about it, that not only had he not finished his drama but "rather, in fact, he had not started on it" and was preparing to return to the idea. The second and third scenes of the first act of this play have been preserved: one of them is in a potato field, the other in a bomb shelter. The frightening story of the wayside railway hut, written in Platonov's prose style, was used by Pasternak in an epilogue to the novel *Doctor Zhivago* as the story of Tanya the laundry girl.

The Sovetsky Pisatel† publishing house was offered a book of

* His younger brother Aleksandr.
† Soviet Writer Publishing House.

poems *On Early Trains*, consisting of four cycles: "War Months" (end of 1941), "The Artist" (winter 1936), "Travel Notes" (summer 1936) and "Year in Peredelkino" (beginning of 1941).

Pasternak gave a reading of poems from this book on 15 December 1942 in the Moscow Writers Club. Gladkov recalls how:

> B.L. came out on to the low little stage in the large hall of the club (now its dining room). There were a lot of people . . . B.L. read his poems in a state of high excitement. The discussion spilled over into a torrent of acclaim and gratitude.

The newspaper *Literatura i Iskusstvo** carried an announcement about the evening on 19 December 1942.

Pasternak was invited to give a reading of his translation of *Romeo and Juliet* to the All-Russia Theatrical Society and he then gave another to the Maly Theatre troupe at its administration's request. On 26 December 1942 *Literatura i Iskusstvo* announced that Pasternak's translation had been accepted for staging by the Maly Theatre.

A contract was signed with the Arts Committee for the translation of *Antony and Cleopatra*; the Arts Theatre was interested in this work.

On 2 November 1942 Pasternak wrote an article "On Shakespeare" for the Sovinformbyuro.† It was a persuasive answer to those who have taxed Pasternak with occupying himself with subjects remote from reality at so tense a time.

> Shakespeare will always be the favourite of generations which are historically mature and have been through a lot. Repeated exposure to experience teaches people to appreciate the voice of fact, genuine perception and the grave art of realism.

In November Pasternak asked Fadeyev to arrange for him to visit the front. The visit kept being put off from one day to another, leaving him uncertain about returning to Chistopol. Negotiations dragged on for two months and came to nothing.

The poem commissioned from him for the twenty-fifth anniversary of October was not accepted by *Komsomolskaya Pravda*. Before leaving for Chistopol, Pasternak wrote the text of it down in Kruchenykh's scrapbook.

---

* *Literature and Art* – bi-monthly journal.
† (Wartime) Soviet Information Bureau.

I promised to write down for you the poem which I had written in honour of 7 November for *Komsomolskaya Pravda*. A great stroke of luck that they did not publish it. It is very feeble rubbish, and in the given instance particularly foolish for its misplaced intimacy. The only valuable thing about this page is that I am jotting it down in a fearful haste when I have other things on my mind. Yours, B.P.

The poem expressed Pasternak's recent shock over the devastation of the flat and the loss of his father's and his own works, among them the manuscript pages of 1929–40 of his novel in varying stages of preparedness.

> You celebrate the anniversary
> of your triumph 25 years ago.
> Unforgettable dawn! As then,
> because of you, I regret nothing,
>
> not even works that came to nothing.
> My readiness for new hardships
> this October morning tells me
> once more what I feel for you.

The day after writing this entry in the Kruchenykh's house, on 26 December 1942, Pasternak left. He made his way from Kazan to Chistopol by a Po2 plane. It was the first flight he had ever made. Fedin recalls Pasternak's impression: "You find yourself flying as if at telegraph-pole height." At the New Year his son Lenechka had his fourth birthday.

13

Pasternak repeatedly wrote how near and dear to him was Chistopol, with its magnificent snows, its houses with fretworked windows and gates, the panorama of the town and anonymous meetings with unknown passers-by.

> Houses in the stern north
> are roofed with sky like slates.
> Remote lairs, you bear the legend:
> "With this, you will conquer."

His declaration of love for Chistopol started with his letter of 19 January 1943 to Aseyev. The previous winter had brought the two old friends together again. In his letter of 12 March 1942 to Vsevolod Ivanov and Evgeniya Vladimirovna, Pasternak had written of the unanimity between himself and Aseyev and of the freedom and boldness of the latter's work. Again in Moscow, during the three months Pasternak spent there, they had had congenial and happy meetings with one another, as in the far off days of their youth. Aseyev was rapturous over the book *On Early Trains* and spoke accordingly at a meeting in the Writers Club. Pasternak wrote:

My great, quiet pleasure of late has been my friendship with you, just as I dreamed of some long while ago when, because of our youthfulness, we both had to work to keep it alive; and this is always exhausting with the one desisting, the other persisting, and I always kept suspecting that I was not being sufficiently responsive; but now we are both being brought together not only by our feelings, but by the facts which surround us; and – which is the main thing – by the best and most interesting of them . . .

Pasternak added that, at Nemirovich Danchenko's request, he was getting on with *Antony*

It occurred to me to write to you because between translations I hope to write two chapters for the continuation of *Safe Conduct* and a few poems for "no one particular" which I shall doubtless send to you.

In all probability, the poems in question are those "In Memory of Marina Tsvetayeva", which he had yet to complete.

In a letter of 26 March 1943, Pasternak again wrote to Aseyev about his upsurge of energy and the happy feeling of being spiritually close to one another:

It seems to me that I am full of strength and inventiveness as before (maybe this is self-deception); that I have only now understood what I need; and that I am capable of doing what I want to do. As before, I am glad of you and of your being near to me, irrespective of what use we put this to.

14

On 25 June 1943 the remnants of the Chistopol writers' colony were loaded on board the steamship *Mikhail Sholokhov*. Pasternak brought his family to Moscow. Their flat was still occupied by anti-aircraft personnel. Their eviction, the subsequent repairs and getting things in order took them up to late autumn. Pasternak alternated between his brother and Asmus, and Zinaida Nikolayevna between the Pogodins and the Trenevs.

In the first few days after his arrival Pasternak gave readings in the Theatrical Society and in the Writers Club of his completed translation of *Antony and Cleopatra*. He prefaced them with a few remarks on the tragedy which put one in mind of *Anna Karenina* and *Madame Bovary*.

> Cleopatra herself is Nastasya Filippovna of times long past. All the tragic elements have merged and only death disentangles them and neatly snips off the protruding ends.

Later, these judgements were formulated and recorded in 1946 in his "Notes on Shakespearian tragedies".

A fortnight before his arrival in Moscow, Pasternak's book *On Early Trains* appeared on sale. In accordance with the contract he had already signed, before the war, with the Chief Administration of Artistic Literature, Pasternak started to put together a volume of *Collected Works* in which, according to Gladkov, he was preparing to include whatever of his was "the most descriptive".

Gladkov invited Pasternak to attend a performance of his own play *Long Long Ago* at the Red Army Theatre. On 31 July 1943, on their way back from the theatre, Pasternak shared his doubts and hopes. Pasternak had written a review of a collection of Akhmatova's poems which had appeared in Tashkent. This brief but significant – in terms of its contents – work was due to appear at any moment in *Literatura i Iskusstvo*. He himself was being invited to work for *Pravda*.

His article on Akhmatova was not printed. On 21 August 1943 an article by Pasternak, "A Slav Poet" – on Ondra Lysohorsky, together with five of his verses translated from the Lachian* appeared in the monthly *Literatura i Iskusstvo*.

Pasternak's letters of this period evince an acute longing for the mass reader without whom, he considered, there can be no great literature, and he is afflicted by the "shame and pitifulness" of his isolated position. He is full of creative plans and wants to "establish a natural relationship of his own with fate, reality and the war." His requests for an official trip to the front were insistently renewed.

Pasternak joined a contingent of writers who set off to visit the area of the recent battle for the liberation of Orel. The group had received an invitation from the Military Council of the 3rd Army to take part in the preparation of a book *In the Battle for Orel*. Those who left Moscow for this purpose on 27 August 1943 were Serafimovich, Simonov, Serova, Azarkh; and arrangements were made to pick up in Peredelkino Fedin, Vsevolod Ivanov and Pasternak. Serafimovich, who had recently celebrated his 80th birthday, was seated next to the driver, the rest were put in the back of the lorry, a Dodge. Tregub has given a detailed description of this journey in his sketch "The field mission of the Union of Writers". Pasternak's daily entries about it in his diary, which he subsequently used in his notes from the front, have survived:

> Very many people have written about this devastation, about the horror of Russians rendered homeless, about German bestialities etc., laying it on thick. The real picture is more horrific and stronger. One must clearly not use tidily isolated feelings wrapped up in neat packages to describe it: one must conjure up all the associative thoughts and emotions it evokes.

Pasternak took part in a Young Komsomol meeting on 4 March and read poems from *On Early Trains* to the wounded in a field hospital. Tregub recorded what he said about poetry, about Mayakovsky, and about what made a man great:

> We discussed a lot of things . . . He was good at listening and established this with his endlessly repeated "Yes, yes, yes . . ." throughout the conversation. This, however, by no means meant that he fully agreed with you. At some point in a peaceful chat, he would unexpectedly explode and utter a sustained, trenchant "n..nn..no!" and everything would go to smithereens. We used

---

* A transitional Czech-Polish Slav dialect. An English language edition of his works was published by Jonathan Cape, London, 1971.

to argue. But mostly we tried to understand one another. It was interesting talking with him. I would even say – it was easy.

"My visit to the front," wrote Pasternak to Avdeyev on 21 October 1943,

was of exceptional importance to me for it not so much showed me what I could not have expected or anticipated as gave me inner release. Suddenly everything turned out very sympathetic, natural and familiar, more in line with my normal thoughts than with the standard stereotype. I am not afraid of seeming boastful – and I can say that of the entire, fairly large group who went on the journey, which included Konst. Al.,* Vsev, Ivanov and K. Simonov, I was the one most at home among the senior military, and it was with me that the generals who received us during our month there came to be on the closest terms.

The references to the straightforwardness and ease of Pasternak's relations with senior commanders are born out by the fact that it was to him they turned with a request to write an "Address to the Men of the Third Army", to which he responded with pleasure.

Men of the Third Army! For the past two weeks we, a number of writers, have been visiting your Divisions and taking part in your route marches. We have gone past places covered in the unfading glory of your prowess. We have marched in the tracks of a cruel and pitiless enemy. We have been met by an inhuman spectacle of devastation, by unending rows of villages, blown up and burnt to the ground. The population had been deported into slavery or, having taken to the woods, was waiting for the monstrosities of the retreating enemy to peter out, before returning in sparse clusters of homeless unclad waifs and strays to the incinerated ashes of their own homes. The heart contracted at the sight of this spectacle. It prompted the question: what wonder-working forces will get these districts back on their feet and restore them to life? Comrades, Men of the Third Army, these forces are yours. They are in the valour of your hearts and the accuracy of your weapons, in your well-merited good fortune and in your loyalty to your duty . . .

* Konstantin Aleksandrovich Fedin.

146

This Address is quoted in *Visit to the Front*, written immediately on his return. It contains loving and detailed sketches of people they met: Zhavoronkov, the hero and organizer of the defence of Tula, and A. A. Kukushkina, Secretary of the Chern district committee, and her woman assistants, women active in the Komsomol and the urban organizations whose intelligence and ease of manner reminded Pasternak of the best university youth of the past. As always, he was very attentive to language; and enchanted and delighted by the beauty and naturalness which came out in the words and manner of his interlocutors:

> We are at the fountainhead of our greatest national treasures. It was in these provinces that our literary language, on which Turgenev pronounced his famous words,* was formed. Nowhere but here has the spirit of Russian inimitability – the highest thing in our possession – found such comprehensive and free expression. The womenfolk we have got to know are born and bred in these heartlands. They bear the imprint of Russian talent. They are flesh and bone descendants of Liza Kalitina and Natasha Rostova.†

Pasternak gives a vivid portrayal of the figures and characters of the members of the Military Council, with particular emphasis on the affable General Gorbatov.

> His intelligence and cordiality rescue him from the slightest suspicion of putting on airs. He speaks in a quiet voice, slowly and straightforwardly. His air of authority derives not from the tone of his words but from their soundness. This is the best but most difficult form of the practice of command.

Gorbatov also recalled his getting to know Pasternak:

> In 1943 we in the Third Army had a visit from the writers, among them Boris Leonidovich Pasternak. His openness and his lively and sympathetic attitude towards people made a good impression on us. I was then totally unacquainted with his poems. I know little of them now and those I know I do not find sympathetic, though I believe them to be talented. It was clear to us that

* This appears to be a reference to Turgenev's prose poem, "The Russian Language".
† Heroines of, respectively, Turgenev's *A Nest of Gentlefolk* and Tolstoy's *War and Peace*.

Pasternak was someone of a completely different origin, from a different sort of life and of different literary views from Tvardovsky. However, for all that, he spoke so sincerely of his admiration for *Vasily Terkin* and was so interesting on the meaning of this book that we took him to our heart for that too.

Pasternak noted particularly that Gorbatov was "a close friend and comrade-in-arms of the late Gurtyev." The figure of Gurtyev could not have failed to claim his special attention. "The modest and glorious grave of General Gurtyev, Commander of the 308 Rifle Division, hero of Stalingrad and Orel", was located in the park and Pasternak noted it in his description of the monstrous spectacle of a city razed to the ground. The writers' group spent three days casting around in search of the 308 Division – travelling out to Zhizdra, Shchigry and Bryn. But the Division proved elusive and they did not succeed in catching up with it. Pasternak met and produced a vivid description of the elegant and sardonic Commander of the 380 Division, Colonel Kustov, whose units together with Gurtyev's 308 Division began their attack on 12 July.

Shortly before Pasternak's journey, Vasily Grossman's book *Stalingrad* had come out in the Sovetsky Pisatel publishing house. The author, who had met Pasternak in the spring of 1942 in Chistopol, presented him with an inscribed copy. The central section of the book, "The Main Line of Advance", is dedicated to Colonel Gurtyev and the prowess of his Siberian regiments, which, after sustaining 80 hours of constant bombardment, stood up to the superhuman pressure of many hours direct assault by three German divisions.

Gorbatov, who together with Gurtyev, had been caught in the bombardment of 3 August 1943 during the fight for the liberation of Orel, was present during Gurtyev's last moments. The scene of Gurtyev's death has been described in Gorbatov's book *Years and Wars*.

Pasternak's poem, "Fresco Come Alive", which was originally entitled "Resurrection", is devoted to Gurtyev's end. The rough draft has, in the upper margin of the last page, where Gurtyev's death is described, his last words: "I am dying, it seems." In early versions of the poem, Gurtyev, feeling death approaching, returns in his mind to Stalingrad where beside the Barrikady Factory he had maintained the defences with his regiments and personally taken part in a counter-attack.

Obedient to a kind of deadly logic,
his wounds have brought him back
to where the factory in Stalingrad
still stands at the maelstrom's edge.

The rough draft is dated the afternoon of 26 March 1944, when as the author noted, "our troops reached the former frontiers of Roumania."

15

His immediate impressions of the journey to the front were reflected in Pasternak's war sketches, "A Liberated Town" and *Visit to the Front*, the second of which was published in shortened form in the newspaper *Trud* on 20 November 1943. At the same time the idea for a poem on the subject which dated back to the previous year came to fruition. It was due to bring together all he had seen in the army and create a generalized image of a Russian soldier or, more precisely, a non-commissioned officer. Pasternak's admiration for *Vasily Terkin,** which he considered the supreme piece of literature about the war, came through in the intonation he imparted to his army tale and the character of the hero who combines instinctual bravery with a humorous attitude to his own actions. The poem was intended for publication in *Pravda* and a "Preface to the Poem" appeared in that newspaper on 15 October 1943. A week later the first chapter was submitted but not accepted by Yury Lukin and this put an end to work on the poem.

Later drafts became individual poems: "A Sapper's Death", "Pursuit" and "On Reconnaissance". These were written in the same metre and the narration is by a direct participant in the events, the NCO in charge of a group of sappers. The hero's account – which has survived in draft form – of his deeds on the Zusha, a tributary of the Oka, near the village of Vyazhi-Zavershye enables one to identify him as the sergeant who narrates the death of the sapper. The individual poems which form part of the whole show a good knowledge of the Orel operation and are indeed based on material taken from the War Diary of the Staff Headquarters of the Front which remained among Pasternak's papers.

* A long poem (written 1941–45) by Tvardovsky about Soviet experiences in the Second World War viewed through the eyes of a Soviet private, Vasily Terkin.

These poems were printed with editorial changes in *Krasnaya Zvezda* on 10 December 1943 and 9 February 1944. On the subject of "A Sapper's Death", Pasternak wrote to Daniel Granin on 3 January 1944:

> I had really serious intentions when I wrote "Sapper". The poem has been slightly mutilated (even he, too) like everything we write. All the rhymes in it were full and exact. . . . The alterations, made in my absence, have in fact been to the rhyme. In addition they have dropped one line – It is obnoxious.

The "serious intentions" which Pasternak had in relation to "A Sapper's Death" also related to its expansion in the poem "Nightglow". "I started it with other hopes," he writes further on, "but the general atmosphere for literature and the reception accorded to the individual, odd literary work, actually embodying a thought of some kind, discourages me."

The reference is to Fadeyev's report, presented to the Union of Writers on 30 December 1943, in which Fedin, Zoshchenko, Selvinsky, Aseyev and Pasternak were sharply criticized for "ideological distortion".

It was during these days in December 1943 that Pasternak finished off the verses dedicated to the memory of Marina Tsvetayeva. Pasternak attributed their completion to the insistence of Aleksey Kruchenykh.

> Here is a multitude of broken words,
> shades of meaning, slips of the tongue,
> self deception and only one signpost:
> faith in the resurrection.

In a note appended to his signature in the copy he presented to Kruchenykh, Pasternak linked "the idea behind these poems . . . with the projected article on Blok and the young Mayakovsky."

The "circle of ideas" sketched out at the beginning of 1944 was somewhat expanded in an article devoted to the hundredth anniversary of the birth of Verlaine. It was placed in *Literatura i Iskusstvo* for 1 April 1944. The article asserted the realistic essence of the work of Verlaine, who had left behind him "a vivid account of things experienced and things seen"; and it traced his kinship with the later works of Blok, Rilke, Ibsen and Chekhov. It paid particular tribute to:

Evgeniya Vladimirovna and Boris Pasternak, with their
son, Evgeny Borisovich, 1926. (*Pasternak Trust*)

Boris Pasternak, Viktor Shklovsky, Neznamov, Osip Brik,
Sergey Tretyakov, Vladimir Mayakovsky, 1927. (*Pasternak Trust*)

Mayakovsky at the exhibition *Twenty Years' Work*, Moscow, 1930. (*Museum of Modern Art, Oxford*)

Evgeniya Vladimirovna with Evgeny Borisovich, Berlin, 1931. (*Pasternak Trust*)

Zinaida Nikolayevna Neigaus, 1932. (*Pasternak Trust*)

Marshal Tukhachevsky.
(*David King Collection*)

Marina Tsvetayeva, 1940.
(*Olga Ivinskaya*)

M. Asmus, M. Vilyam-Vilmont, Irina Vilyam-Vilmont,
Leonid Borisovich Pasternak, Zinaida Nikolayevna, Boris
Pasternak, Valentin Asmus, Irina Asmus, Peredelkino, 1945.
(*Pasternak Trust*)

Anna Akhmatova and Boris Pasternak, 1946. (*Pasternak Trust*)

Photograph of a portrait of Andrey Zhdanov by Vasily Efanov. (*Society for Cultural Relations with the USSR*)

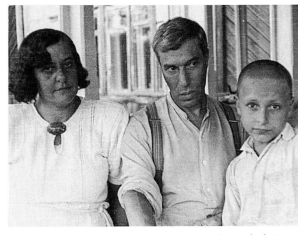

Zinaida Nikolayevna and Boris Pasternak, with their son Leonid Borisovich, Peredelkino, 1947. (*Pasternak Trust*)

The approach to Pasternak's dacha in Peredelkino, 1958.
The bay-windowed room on the first floor was his study. (*L. N. Shapiro*)

Boris Pasternak with Zinaida Nikolayevna at the
Sanatorium at Uzkoye, 1957. (*Pasternak Trust*)

Boris Pasternak and Olga Ivinskaya
in the late 1950s. (*Pasternak Trust*)

Konstantin Fedin. (*Society for Cultural Relations with the USSR*)

Aleksandr Fadeyev. (*Society for Cultural Relations with the USSR*)

Aleksey Surkov. (*Novosti Press Agency*)

Giangiacomo and Inge Feltrinelli. (*Olga Ivinskaya*)

Boris Pasternak toasting the Nobel Prize, with Nina Tabidze (left) and Zinaida Nikolayevna (right), Peredelkino, 23 November 1958. (*Pasternak Trust*)

Korney Chukovsky, with Boris Pasternak and Zinaida Nikolayevna, Peredelkino, 1958. (*L. N. Shapiro*)

Pasternak's funeral, 2 June 1960. (*Pasternak Trust*)

the sense of the pertinence of earthly life, inseparable from genius, and his boundless facility for communicating Parisian colloquial speech in all its artlessness and its enchanting pithiness.

By comparison with the naturalism of de Musset, Verlaine arrives at his naturalism without seeking to charm and without stirring from the spot; he is colloquially, super-naturally natural – that is, he is simple not so as to make people believe him but so as not to hinder the voice of reason which is bursting to emerge from him.

Pasternak was again obliged to turn to translation. Contracts were signed for *King Lear* and *Othello* and translations of Shelley done for an anthology of English poetry. Publication of four of his poems in the journal *Znamya* (No. 2, 1944) was accompanied by a short prefatory article on his attitude to translation as "a means of communication between cultures and peoples over the centuries". The second part of his "A Translator's Notes" was devoted to the role of Shakespeare in English poetry, his presence "and influence in a whole number of the most effective and typical English devices and ways of speech."

Nikolay Zhdanov wrote much later in the journal *Druzhba Naro-dov** (No. 11, 1979) about Pasternak's collaboration in the newspaper *Krasny Flot*. The first of the contracts was for a poem on the institution on 3 March 1944 of the Orders of Nakhimov and Ushakov†. Pasternak immediately responded with the poem "The Boundless Perspective . . ." It was published on 8 March 1944. The next one, "In the Lower Reaches", was published on 26 March. It dealt with Pasternak's recollections of his Odessa childhood and his overall frustrated longing for fruitful employment.

> Drifting grains of amber on the flats,
> the glint of jet-black earth.
> Local people busy with rigging,
> tackle, ferries, boats.
> Rapture in the estuary of night.
> Bright dawns.
> Black Sea foam
> sighing on sand banks. [. . .]

* *Friendship of the Peoples.*
† Both Russian Admirals. Nakhimov (1802–55) was in charge of the defence of Sebastopol in the Crimean War. Ushakov (1744–1817) created the Black Sea Fleet.

Did this ever exist? New style or old style?
Where are those years?
Is it possible to recreate this life,
this truth, this freedom?

When Odessa was liberated on 10 April by the troops of the Third Ukranian Front, Pasternak was again commissioned to write a poem. But Zhdanov was bothered by what he termed its "involved imagery" and its "excessive naturalism". At his demand the title of the poem was changed, it was cut by three stanzas and the remaining ones were re-edited by the author in response to comments.

In January the blockade of Leningrad, which Olga Freidenberg and her paralysed mother had lived through, was broken. Pasternak dedicated his poem "The Victor", written in the rhythm of Blok's poem "Prowess, Feats and Glory", to the liberation of Leningrad:

And now the story reaches a crescendo.
He has torn away the seige's torques.
The wider world, ecstatic it should end so,
crowd in to see the way a hero walks.

The poem was published in the newspaper *Trud* on 28 January 1944. Pasternak sent his poem "Spring", written for the 1 May to the same newspaper. It was simultaneously demanded by *Pravda*, where it appeared only on 17 May with emendations to two of the lines. Pasternak explained to Kruchenykh on 21 May the story of its publication:

In *Pravda* there was speculation about the possibility of having the plural in the passage "the flowering for these centuries" for it to sound more extensive – although one staunch century counts for more than several rhetorical ones. Then instead of the word "He" they asked for "I", the author, to be inserted. You remember, Alesha, I told you about the scandal in *Pravda* and *Trud* when both set the poem up in type for 1 May. B.P.

The daydreamer, the late-night strategist
feels more at home in Moscow
because it is the source and seedbed
of all the flowering for this century.

In July 1944 the manuscript of a book with the title "A Free Sweep of the Horizon", which included ten poems from the spring of 1941 and thirteen from wartime was submitted to Sovetsky Pisatel. Just as Pasternak failed to get the, for him, very essential poem "To Russian Genius" included in the book, so too the texts of the wartime poems were subjected to editorial revision along lines corresponding to the more hostile climate of the time. After Fadeyev's winter speech, in which he had accused Pasternak's recent poem "Winter Approaches" of "Great Power chauvinism", the lines:

> Heavy transports manoeuvre and turn,
> leaving cyrillic letters on the fields.
> Russia opens up right down the centre
> like a magic book.

were replaced by a new version without any mention of "Russia", and this destroyed the poem's syntax and the sense. The poems "On Reconnaissance" and "Pursuit" lost the stanzas realistically depicting the cruel circumstances of the war, as traducing the image of the Soviet fighting man:

> Businesslike, they burst on the village
> like pedlars or a gang of thieves.

or:

> We used, as was usual,
> filthy language with refinement.

Another poem, "Odessa", was left out: Pasternak wrote to Tarasen-kov that he had simply overlooked it. The whole book came out in January 1945 under the title *The Vastness of Earth*.

At the same time Pasternak's wartime poems were included in the same, unchanged versions in a smaller volume of his *Selected Works* being put out by Goslitizdat. In June 1944 Pasternak corrected the proofs.

He spent the summer with Stasik Neigaus, then a sixteen-year-old student at the Conservatoire. Zinaida Nikolayevna and Lenechka moved into the ruined dacha in Peredelkino and set about cultivating the kitchen garden. She came to Moscow twice weekly to visit her eldest son in hospital.

Akhmatova returned from Tashkent and on 13 May she was in Moscow. At Nadezhda Mandelstam's request, she handed over to Pasternak the letter written by Mandelstam on 2 January 1937 but not sent off at the time, in which he expressed gratitude for the great range and unrivalled scope of Pasternak's life work. How prophetically the wishes of the dead poet coincided with Pasternak's present strivings and tribulations: "I want," wrote Mandelstam, "your poetry, of which we are all the spoiled, undeserving recipients, to explode further afield into the world, among the people, among the children . . ."

Against his will, Pasternak was then translating *Othello* which, as he acknowledged, he had "never taken to. I am now working on Shakespeare semi-subconsciously," he wrote to Olga Freidenberg on 16 June 1944. "He now seems to me like a member of a former family of mine, from my Myasnitsky Street period, and I am simplifying him terribly."

At that same time he did several translations of Chikovani, Avetik Isaakyan, Samed Vurgun, Gaprindashvili, and Maksim Rylsky, and two poems by Shevchenko.

The third scene from the fourth act of *Othello* in which Desdemona sings the Green Willow song, was published in *Literaturnaya Gazeta* on 9 December 1944. Pasternak prefaced it with a note in which he wrote:

> In our works we have followed in the steps of the old translators, but we are striving to go further still in pursuit of the lifelike, of naturalism and of what is called realism. We are far from cherishing the illusion that every particular of our work successfully replaces previous examples. We are not challenging anyone in terms of individual lines; we are contending in terms of building entire constructions; and in assembling them together with our fidelity to the great original, we are guided by ever greater reliance on our own system of speech and a thousand other secrets, half of which we are not able to comprehend and which with the years are becoming ever more numerous and demanding.

Morozov gave Pasternak credit, in accordance with what he had said, for having "decisively broken with literalism, and striving for an inward, not an outward likeness; for a likeness, not for a copy." In

Pasternak's translation, Shakespeare's personages, to use Morozov's words, acquired "their own movement, their own animation, their own voice."

His work on endless translations caused Pasternak to keep putting off his own projects and left him exhausted. He wrote of this to Olga Freidenberg on 30 July 1944:

> My trouble is not in life's superficial difficulties but in the fact that I am a man of letters, that I have something to say and thoughts of my own – yet we have no literature and in the present circumstances there will be none nor can there be any. This last winter I signed a contract with two theatres to write at a point in the future (which, according to my calculations, I was visualizing as being in this coming autumn) an original tragedy on a contemporary, wartime theme. I thought that by that time circumstances would change and things would become a little freer. However the situation is not changing and all one can dream of is that the staging of one or another of these translations will secure one a degree of material independence enabling one to write what one wants to, freely, and put aside for an indefinite time any thought of getting things published.

17

In January 1945 a new contract was signed for the translation of both parts of Shakespeare's *Henry IV*. Pasternak wrote the rough draft of the translation with his left hand because he had overstrained the right and this had led to acute inflammation of the nerve in his shoulder. As a pianist, he had trained himself to write left-handed.

> It is the result of over-exhausting myself scribbling – not over-exhausting myself writing, [as he wrote to Nina Tabidze] for my earnings are proportionate to the amount of ink I use but not to the purpose or quality of the product. I am proud, after all, like you, Ninochka! But there's no virtue in complaining, Nina dear! The whole time there is something alive and present in my soul which even in my grief is a source of joy and constantly captivates and possesses me and enables me to bear the blows. And therefore

– praise heaven – one should in fact marvel at that instead of getting depressed.

The newspaper *Sovetskoye Iskusstvo** commissioned at short notice an article from Pasternak on Chopin for the 135th anniversary of the composer's birthday. He completed it within two days. Developing the ideas set out in his articles on Verlaine and Shelley, Pasternak wrote of Chopin as a realist in music and provided a definition of terms that was absolutely fundamental to his own artistic philosophy:

> When we speak of realism in music, we do not at all have in mind the illustrative bases of music, whether operatic or programme music. We are talking of something entirely different. Whatever the branch of art, realism stands in fact not for a separate trend but forms a special degree of art, the highest grade of authorial precision. Realism is, in all probability, that crucial measure of the admixture of artistic detail which neither the general rules of aesthetics nor the listeners or viewers of his time stipulate from the artist. Romantic art comes to a halt at precisely this point and is happy to do so. How little is required for it to prosper! At its command it has stilted pathos, pseudo-profundity and simulated sensitivity – all forms of artificiality are at its disposal.

For some months the newspaper's editorial board remained "delighted" with this article, as Pasternak wrote, but still did not get around to printing it. It was published in the journal *Leningrad* (Nos. 15–16, 1945) in a truncated form.

The collection *The Vastness of Earth* came out in February 1945. Tarasenkov's review published in *Znamya* (No. 4, 1945) contrasts Pasternak's landscape poems, in which "there is something of the paintings of Serov and Levitan", with the rhetoric and aridity of his poems about war, shorn of the "artistry" with which he previously used to write and is now writing about nature and love and art.

This spurious, aesthetically subjective opinion determined the unjust attitude of his contemporaries towards Pasternak's wartime poems, the "discreet style" of which corresponded to his austere and serious attitude to events, his desire to show the war in all its unvarnished nakedness, with no concession to the romantic

---

* *Soviet Art.*

exaltation of which he had written with such irritation in his article about Chopin.

In the journal *Zvezda* (Nos. 5–6, 1945) P. P. Gromov wrote:

Hitherto Pasternak's poetry might at times have been considered one unbroken cascade of associations, one long hyperbolic metaphor. The wonderfully well-observed detail, as it proliferated and expanded, tended to fill all the space in the poem so densely that getting through to the poetic emotion and meaning was like going through a thorn bush. Pasternak's charm lay in this wealth of fantasy, but it was also a source of weakness. The poet's new book is on more prudent and more simple lines.

Adrian Neigaus, the elder son of Zinaida Nikolayevna, died in the spring, on 29 April 1945, and within a month came news from Oxford of Leonid Osipovich Pasternak's death.

"Dearest Olya!" wrote Pasternak to Olga Freidenberg, "on 31 May, Papa died. A month before that they had removed the cataract from his eye and he had started to recover in hospital. He moved back to his home, but there his heart gave way and he died on Thursday, three weeks ago."

Sovetskoye Iskusstvo for 13 July 1945 carried an article by Igor Grabar "In Memory of Leonid Pasternak":

The death recently occurred in Oxford of the outstanding Russian painter, L. O. Pasternak. In his time, in the nineteenth and at the beginning of the twentieth century, he played a most notable role in Russian art as a prominent artist and a wonderful teacher, bringing up several generations of artists, of whom many subsequently became major painters.

His father's death served Pasternak as a painful reminder of the unfinished state of his novel: he had justified his inability to take time off to travel abroad and see his parents by his urgent need to work at his book. The new climate around him and the immediate post-war omens of freedom contributed towards sustaining and reinforcing his desire to discharge his duty. He was further persuaded in that direction by renewal of contact with his extensive reading public and the lively and grateful response he received from that quarter.

The evenings in the University, the Polytechnic Museum and the Scientists' Club organized at the initiative of P. I. Lavut, were of great importance in this respect. At first Pasternak considered appearing in public risky and, as he wrote to Durylin:

> expected nothing from it but failure and public disaster . . . [yet] imagine it, it gave me nothing but pleasure. From my modest example I learnt just how many, many people are even now disposed in favour of what is worthwhile and serious. The existence of this unknown reservoir right here among us was a revelation to me.

Pasternak learnt that his work was being translated and published in the West by Professor Maurice Bowra of Oxford University and a young group of "personalists" headed by the poet and critic, Herbert Read. This, in turn, exposed him to attacks from the leadership of the Union of Writers.

In the autumn of 1945 Pasternak, in a letter to Nadezhda Mandelstam, defined his position in the following terms:

> All of a sudden, my life has (as I shall put it for brevity's sake) . . . taken an active turn. My links with certain people at the front, in auditoria, in various remote corners and in particular in the West have turned out to be more numerous, more direct, and more straightforward than I could ever have supposed in my wildest dreams. This has wonderfully and miraculously simplified and facilitated my inner life, my way of thinking, my activity and the tasks I set myself: it has also severely complicated my outward life. Things are especially difficult because not a trace has remained of my former equability and public sociability. Not only do the Tikhonovs and the majority of the Union members not exist for me – and I repudiate them – but I let no moment slip to proclaim this publicly and openly. And they are of course right to give me as good as they get. The line up of forces is, of course, uneven, but my fate is settled and I have no choice.

Such a turn of events necessitated a serious and significant response, and this entailed risk-taking and self-sacrifice. "I sensed," wrote Pasternak to Durylin:

> that I was no longer in a mood just to put up with being classified in the administrative rubric as an undesirable; and over and above doing submission (albeit on a ridiculously small scale), one must do something costly and of one's own, and try, in a more hazardous form than has been the case, to get through to the public.

III

DR ZHIVAGO
(1946–55)

I

A historic premonition of victory was felt by everyone, beginning with the successful battle of the Kursk bulge and the subsequent advance in Byelorussia. Pasternak opened his sketch *Visit to the Army* with the words:

> Of late we have been gripped increasingly by the progress and logic of our wonderful victory. With each day its all-embracing beauty and strength become ever clearer . . . It is the population as a whole which has triumphed – every sector of it – with its joys and its griefs, its dreams and its thoughts. Variety is victorious.
>
> Everyone has triumphed, and they are inagurating a new, supreme era of our historic existence here and now, before our very eyes.
>
> Universality and breadth of vision are beginning to pervade everyone's activity. This atmosphere is affecting even our modest labours.

Victory was the result of a heroic feat by all; it was purchased by vast losses and deprivation. Everyone was painfully conscious of their irredeemable debt to the dead:

> We will punish the evil ones.
> But for the widows and the families
> honour charges us to find
> some new word to wipe away their tears.
>
> Inspired by all the heroes
> and all the martyrs of the victory,
> we swear on all our Russian genius
> to raise an everlasting monument.

The atmosphere of those years was one of the festive anticipation for the end of universal enmity and the start of a free, productive existence. Pasternak designed his novel *Doctor Zhivago*, begun in the winter of 1945–46, to be the artistic embodiment of those years. The need for such a work was borne out by many contemporary events.

The Shakespeare translations were an undoubted success. They had also attracted attention in England. Pasternak was preparing a broadcast on Shakespeare to be put out by Moscow Radio in English. He was very pleased by an article by Christopher Wren in the *British Ally* newspaper which was published in Moscow.

2

The draft version of *Henry IV* was completed at the beginning of August 1945 and after revising it Pasternak turned to the translation of the great Georgian lyrical writer, Nikolay Baratashvili. "I looked to see what had been done earlier in this respect," he wrote to Chikovani on 9 September,

> . . . An attempt has already been made to make a rhyming conversion from the original words of an interlinear crib, and it is not worth repeating. One must turn it into Russian verse as I did with Shakespeare, Shevchenko, Verlaine and others – that is how I see my task. I have already been at it for the last half week and am content with my progress: not only did I not have to switch from the way in which I have been writing these last years, but, on the contrary. Baratashvili has provided a helpful opportunity for taking a few steps further in the same direction. I shall get it done quickly.

And, indeed, by the end of September he had translated everything that had been written by the poet and had discerned in him an originality, similar to Baratynsky's and noted by Pushkin as embodying "a constant thought process". "His poems," Pasternak wrote in a comment published in the Tiflis newspaper *Zarya Vostoka*, "are very dramatic, even the most contemplative of them, and bear the personal imprint which makes one suspect that behind each thought there lies some real occurrence that provoked it."

In October there were great celebrations in Tiflis to mark the centenary of Baratashvili's death. Pasternak was invited to take part and gave a public reading of his translations on 19 October in the Rustaveli Theatre. Nina Tabidze recalled that Pasternak made her presence in the auditorium a condition of his participation. This was her first appearance in public for eight years. As he read, he made a point of turning in her direction. His two weeks in Tiflis were full of enormous and tragic joy. He returned to Moscow with the resolve to repay this pleasure in the near future with his new work. At their parting, Nina Tabidze presented him with a large stock of high quality, watermarked writing paper. Pasternak was conscious of the demands made upon him by such a gift.

3

On his return to Moscow, he set about putting his plans in concrete form. He now saw the prose he had written before the war in a new light. He recommenced work on it. Isaiah Berlin, who met him in the autumn of 1945, recalls that even then Pasternak had told him of his project for a new novel and that, at Pasternak's request, he carried a letter to the Pasternak sisters in Oxford.

Many years later Pasternak told Vyacheslav Ivanov what this important step in his life meant to him:

> For a long time previously, since during the war I had been irked by the complacent continuity governing the basic axioms on which my poetry has been constructed, my literary activity conducted and my name built up. It seemed to me like one long accumulation of failures and blunders, to which I wanted to put a drastic, tangible and absolutely final end; a sequence liable to involve retributive satisfaction – along lines outside one's normal bounds of comprehension such as other people's suicides and political trials. It was not imperative that the response to it be a tragedy or a catastrophe, but it was imperative that the outcome represent a radical and major break with all past habits and the start of something new, something tremendously and irreversibly transforming: the irruption of the human will on to the scene of tragic destiny and the intervention of the spiritual self into matters in which it supposedly took no part, nor had any part to play.

Pasternak's correspondence indicates the utter intensity of his work on the novel during the 1945–46 winter months. Some of his

January 1946 letters do already hint at his project acquiring an overall outline, albeit of the most general kind.

> I now have the chance to put in three months work or so at something completely of my own, without having to think about earning my daily bread. I want to write a prose work about the whole of our life from Blok to the present war, of maybe 10–12 chapters, not more. You can imagine in what a hurry I work and how afraid I am of something happening before I finish!

he wrote in his letter of 26 January to Nadezhda Mandelstam.

> I am furiously writing a large prose narrative taking in the years of our life, from Musaget* to the last war – once again the world of *Safe Conduct*, but without the theorizing, in the form of a novel on wider and more intimate lines; with topical events and dramas, closer to reality, to the world of Blok and the ideas expressed in my letter to Marina. My rush to get it done is quite natural – I can hear the days and the weeks whistling past my ears . . .

he wrote to Sergey Durylin on 27 August.

By February 1946 the initial design of the novel had sufficiently taken shape in Pasternak's mind for him to envisage getting it down on paper within the next few months.

"Wish me strength," he wrote to Olga Freidenberg on 1 February

> that will keep me from drooping under the load of fatigue and tedium. I have begun a long prose piece in which I want to incorporate the main thing which caused my life to "spark" and I am in a hurry to finish it in time for your summer visit so that I can read it to you then.

The first public reading of Pasternak's translation of *Hamlet* took place in February in the club of Moscow University. Pasternak was present. The first version of his poem "Hamlet", with which Yury Zhivago's notebook opens, is also dated February 1946:

> Every bit of me is here on stage.
> At the door, I pause and try
> to work out from a distant echo
> what will happen in my time.

* Moscow Publishing House of ("junior") Symbolists; ("seniors" belonged to the rival "Scorpion"), 1910–17. Both Pasternak and Durylin were connected with it.

The echo of an action some way off.
For as long as it lasts, I play my part.
Alone. Everywhere, the letter killeth.
Life's ways are not the way across a field.

"There shall be no more death" – are the words inscribed by
Pasternak in a bold, sweeping hand on the cover of the manuscript
draft of the novel's first chapters: they comprised one of the early
titles proposed for it – a title which made its appearance that same
year, 1946. Below them is an epigraph indicating the source from
which the words were taken:

> And God shall wipe away all tears from their eyes; and there
> shall be no more death, neither sorrow, nor crying, neither shall
> there be any more pain for the former things are passed away.
> (Book of Revelation (of St John the Divine) XXI.4).

"Your words about immortality were dead on target!" wrote
Pasternak on 24 February 1946 in answer to a (non-extant) letter
from Olga Freidenberg.

> This is the theme, or rather the primary mood, of the prose I
> am now writing. I am writing it very much at random, not the
> way writers do, almost as if I were not writing at all. If only I
> have enough money to finish it, since it has put a temporary
> stop to my regular earnings and has upset my calculations. But
> I feel as I did more than thirty years ago – it's almost embar-
> rassing.

4

Akhmatova came to Moscow for a short while in the spring. A
joint writers' evening for her and Pasternak was organized in the
Writers Club on 2 April. The following day they read their works
at a meeting of Leningrad and Moscow poets in the Hall of Columns
of Trade Union House. Pasternak was late and turned up in the hall
while Surkov was giving his reading. The latter had to break off in
mid-sentence because the hall greeted Pasternak with applause as
he tried to slip unnoticed into his seat on the platform. Akhmatova
rounded off the first part of the meeting. Pasternak opened the
second. With a slight change in the roll of speakers the evening

was repeated the following day in the University's Communist auditorium. The audience would not let Pasternak leave the stage, making him read twice as much as any one participant was allowed. This was the first time, at the audience's request, that Pasternak read his "In Memory of Marina Tsvetayeva".

A particularly memorable impression was created by the Pasternak evening held in the large auditorium of the Polytechnic Museum on 27 May 1946. His one-volume 1936 collection and his *Selected Works* of 1945, annotated in Pasternak's hand for the public reading that evening, have been preserved. The substitution of lines and titles, the sequence and even the musical intonation of individual passages was carefully thought out. The audience sensed this. One of them, B. N. Dvinyaninov, recalls:

> There was not a trace of what we call "expressiveness" in B.L.'s reading. There was no hint of the six (or thirty-six!) tonal leverages which public recitation experts have at their command . . . And what was the result? There was symmetry! I have never forgotten and shall never forget the feeling: in front of us was the poet-architect of his own Poetopolis:
>
> Each syllable adds centre and suburbs
> to this town or that of the opening lines.

But this was not the erection of walls on the "brick-on-brick" principle but on the principle "How one image fits into another". Pasternak's Poetopolis rose before the eyes of the delirious auditorium not because of its superabundance of precious materials but because of its inner loading, the growth of one image with the support of another.

5

Pasternak was delayed in his move to the dacha. He was in a hurry to write his foreword to the collection of his Shakespearian translations for a two-volume edition in *Iskusstvo*.

"I did not believe that I would get on top of it," he wrote on 5 October to Olga Freidenberg.

To my surprise, I succeeded. I have managed to say in thirty pages what I want about poetry in general, about Shakespeare's style, about each of the five plays I translated; and, in relation to some questions connected with Shakespeare, about the state of education at that time, and the authenticity of Shakespearian biography.

In the belief that what he had written was of intrinsic merit, he sent a copy to V. Sayanov in the monthly journal *Zvezda*.

Pasternak's treatment of Hamlet in this work took on a distinctly autobiographical aspect, the key to which was to be found in a quotation from the New Testament setting out the Christian understanding of sacrifice:

> Hamlet renounces himself in order to *do the will of him that sent me*. *Hamlet* is not a drama of weakness of character but a drama of duty and abnegation. When it emerges that appearances and reality do not coincide but are divided from one another by an abyss, it is not of the essence that the reminder of the world's falsity comes in a supernatural form and that the ghost demands vengeance of Hamlet. It is much more important that by force of destiny Hamlet is made judge of his time and the servant of a higher force. *Hamlet* is a drama of high destiny, forbidden exploits and accomplishment of a mission.

Similarly, Pasternak's poem "Hamlet", in its final version dated December 1946, takes on the meaning of the voluntary acceptance of the inevitability of the route of the Cross, as the guarantee of immortality, in harmony with Christ's prayer in the Garden of Gethsemane.*

On arrival in Peredelkino, Pasternak again turned to his prose work:

> . . . since July I have been starting to write a prose novel, "Boys and Girls", which in ten chapters should cover the forty year period 1902–1946. I have written a quarter or a fifth of the book, with intense absorption. This is a very serious undertaking. I am already old. I may die soon and one cannot put off indefinitely the free expression of one's real thoughts. My activities this year are the first steps along this path, and they are unfamiliar ones.

---

* Abba, Father, all things are possible unto thee; take away this cup from me; nevertheless not what I will, but what thou wilt (Mark xiv.36).

One cannot at thirty and forty and fifty, endlessly live off what one lived by as an eight-year-old child; on passive indications of your abilities and the goodwill of those surrounding one. Yet my whole life has been spent under this compulsorily restricted regime.

On 3 August 1946, he read the first chapter of the novel at home – to Zinaida Nikolayevna and the Asmuses; and Fedin was also invited. On 14 August the Decree on the Journals *Zvezda* and *Leningrad** appeared in the press. Although the decree did not concern Pasternak directly, Fadeyev made use of it to accuse him of losing touch with the people. In his speech to the presidium of the board of the Union of Soviet Writers on 4 September 1946 he warned against "currying favour" with a poet who did not recognize "our ideology". Fadeyev saw Pasternak's refusal to take part in the last war with his creative work, and his "seeking refuge from topical poetry in translations during the war days", as a "definite stance" and recalled that he had uttered a warning in 1943. A few days later he repeated this at a general meeting of Moscow writers in the Scientists' Club.

The draft of a letter in reply – which may, or may not have been despatched – has survived among Pasternak's papers.

According to the information of the Union of Writers certain literary circles in the West are attaching undue importance to my activity, incommensurate with its slightness and unproductiveness . . . There is no point in setting me up as an opposite to reality which is in all respects stronger and higher than I. Like all normal people with vivid, natural feelings, I am bound by an identity of mind and spirit to my century and my homeland and I would be an undiscerning nonentity if behind certain transient and inevitable rigours of the time I failed to see the spiritual beauty and greatness which have marked the strides of present-day Russia and which were predicted for her by our great predecessors.

The cause of the disquiet was that Pasternak had, for the first time, been put forward for the Nobel Prize, and this had become known.

---

* The Party decree (widely known as the Zhdanov decree) denouncing the two Leningrad journals for having published work by Zoshchenko and Akhmatova which blighted the artistic atmosphere for nearly forty years.

Recollections have it that friends approached him advising him to come out in print with a criticism of Akhmatova. He replied that this was absolutely impossible because he loved her very much and she seemingly took a positive attitude towards him.

His all-consuming work on the novel enabled him to avoid getting worked up over the development of events, and he gave a humorous account of this in a letter to Lado Gudiashvili, whom he had met on his last visit to Tiflis:

The ground was shaking under me and I was reproached . . . for not noticing anything, for continuing to walk along without checking in my stride, for not tumbling over. They then persuaded me to move into town, to avoid giving cause for irritation – at such(!) a time – by my sojourn in nature's bosom – like a scene from Manet or Renoir.

Seeking to reassure Nina Tabidze, Pasternak wrote on 4 December 1946:

Nina, my dear, all that twaddle this last autumn did not in the least distress me. Can there conceivably be anyone among us so dull and vain as to start sitting down and thinking whether he is or is not on the side of the people? Only word-mongers and show-offs such as those have the nerve to keep using that terrifying, majestic word . . .

I have been fine this last winter, spring and summer. I not only knew (as I know now) what was mine and what Divine providence required of me – it seemed to me that it could all be achieved in communion with others, in one's daily activity, at public meetings. I put a great deal of enthusiasm into writing an introduction to my Shakespearian translations . . . And even more into the two months spent writing the novel. I approached it anew, with a sense of doing so for the first time, a feeling which I have not previously had since the very outset of my venture. The events of this autumn slowed things down outwardly and put a temporary halt on my work (all the time I find myself having to solicit money as if it were alms), but I have now resumed it. Ah, Nina, if only people were set free, what a miracle it would be, what happiness! I cannot escape the feeling that reality is like a fairy-tale trampled under foot.

The mood of that autumn was captured in the poem "Indian Summer" written at the time:

Here the road drops into a depression
and sorrow sweeps over you
for the ancient, arthritic twigs,
for autumn itself, the rag-and-bone man

who has swept everything here.
You mourn that everything is simpler
than the wiseacres suppose.
The copse is downcast. Everything ends.

Pointless to pretend not to know
when the world is ablaze
and white wisps of autumn soot
trail like gossamer past your window.

By the end of 1947 ten poems from Yury Zhivago's exercise book
had been written. The inter-relationship between the poems and the
novel's hero allowed a further step to be taken towards attaining
greater transparency of style and imparting greater clarity to a conscious, determinate concept. In attributing the authorship of the poems to his hero, an amateur poet, Pasternak consciously renounced
the specifics of his own artistic manner of writing which bore the
imprint of his professional biography; renounced the emphatic sub-
jectivity of perception and personalized association. The removal of
the autobiographical element from the lyric poetry unexpectedly enabled him to develop the poems' themes. This particularly applied to
those on biblical themes, and is in no way at variance with the verses
also relating to the facts of his own life. These two trends found
particularly harmonious unity in the poem "Hamlet", the final version of which conveys the fervour and pain of Christ's prayer in the
Garden of Gethsemane, his last before Golgotha.

6

Pasternak derived help and support for his new lyrical upsurge in
consciously turning to the experience and achievements of Blok's
poetry. The 25th anniversary of the death of Blok was due to have
been held in August 1946. It had been frustrated by the Zhdanov
decree and the ensuing political campaign. When preparing, back
in the winter of 1943–44, to carry out his planned intention of

writing an article about Blok, Pasternak had pencilled annotations in the margins of the first volume of the Alkonost edition of Blok and had jotted down some notes for his "Towards a Character Sketch of Blok". In this respect, Pasternak's presentation of Hamlet as a hero personifying duty and self-sacrifice, abjuring self "in order to do the will of him who sent me", acquires additional depth from its indebtedness to Blok's "Hamletian" affinities.

In a letter of New Year 1948 to Vera Zvyagintseva, containing his poem "Nightglow", Pasternak called it "bad Blok". The similarity of theme allows it to be related to Blok's "Second Baptism".

> Entering into the new world, I know
> there are people and tasks to perform,
> that probably there is a path to paradise
> open to all who walk in evil ways.

For Pasternak, the "second baptism" was the conscious turning to the sources of love, goodness and beauty which had nurtured the poetical generation of the 1910s.

> I want to rush out to the people,
> into the crowd and the mania of morning.
> I could smash it all to smithereens,
> bring the world to its knees.

> So I clatter downstairs and out,
> as if for the very first time,
> into streets silent with snow
> and the empty main road.

At that time, characterizing the generation to which both he himself and the heroes of his book, *Doctor Zhivago* (the first title of which was "Boys and Girls"), belonged, Pasternak wrote:

All these boys and girls had stuffed themselves on Dostoevsky, Soloryev, socialism, Tolstoy's teachings, Nietzsche's doctrines and the latest poetry. They had jumbled it all up into a heap which was left lying alongside them. But they are completely right. It all comes down to approximately the same thing and constitutes our present-day thinking, the main peculiarity of which is that it is a new, unusually fresh phase of Christianity,

Our age has understood anew that part of the Gospel which from time long past has been best felt and expressed by artists. It was prominent with the Apostles but then dropped out of sight with the church fathers, in the church, in morals and in politics. Francis of Assisi bore vivid and passionate witness to it and the Age of Chivalry reproduced in part certain of its features. And its breath has been very strongly felt in the nineteenth century. It is the Gospel spirit, in the name of which Christ spoke in parables drawn from daily life, explaining the truth in terms of everyday reality. It is the concept that communication between mortals is immortal and that life is symbolic because it is meaningful.

When pointing out the volumes of Chekhov's Collected Works which he had borrowed from Korney Chukovsky, who lived in a neighbouring dacha, Pasternak let slip to E. A. Krashennikova, who often used to visit him, that he had read all his theology in Chekhov.

7

By the end of 1946 the first two chapters of the book, "The Five O'Clock Express" and "A Girl from a Different World", were written. Pasternak started to give readings of them in friends' houses.

One such reading took place on 27 December in M. K. Baranovich's flat. Those invited were K. N. Bugaeva, Maria Petrovykh and A. S. Kochetkov. As a memento of the evening Pasternak presented Baranovich with a copy of a recently-issued collection of his *Georgian Poets*, on the title page and endpapers of which he had inscribed the poems: "Improvisation at the Piano" (a reworked version of the 1915 poem), "Hamlet", "Indian Summer", and "Winter's Night" with the date 1946.

A contract was signed with *Novy Mir* in the person of A. Yu. Krivitsky for a novel under the title of "Innokenty Dudorov" or "Boys and Girls", 80,000 words long, due for completion in August 1947. At the same time the journal was offered three of Pasternak's latest poems, "March", "Winter's Night", and "Indian Summer". Krivitsky spoke out strongly against their publication and Simonov was forced to agree with him. Lydia Chukovskaya remembers how offended the latter was by Pasternak's tactlessness in expressing surprise that anyone could stop the chief editor of a leading journal from printing what he liked and considered desirable.

Among the *Novy Mir* editorial staff, Pasternak got to know Olga Vsevolodovna Ivinskaya,* in charge of the poetry section. He invited her and Lydia Chukovskaya to his next reading of the novel, on 6 February 1947 at the house of the pianist Maria Yudina. That day he read his recently written "Christmas Star".

The following day Yudina wrote straight back to him with her impressions:

> . . . It became suddenly quite clear who you are and what you are. Some fruit take longer to ripen and do so less perceptibly. It is as if your spiritual power suddenly shed all lesser values, smiled gently at dispirited amazement and said to it "How come you recognized me so late in the day? I have always been here . . ." It would take too long to say what one thinks of your book but in terms of one's feelings and impressions, my brief response is that it gives an uninterrupted majestic view of perfection and undeniable integrity of *style*, proportion and detail – the *classic* combination of feeling sealed in deeply behind external clarity of form (as with my beloved classicism in all forms of art – Mozart, Gluck, or the architecture of Petersburg: I deliberately omit any literary parallels) with the grandeur of the overall design; it conveys a rare feeling of the immutability, the rightness of every word, expression, turn of speech, and length of sentence. At first, especially . . . I was inexpressibly struck by the brevity of your lapidary sentences – and this impression was fortified by the brilliant expressiveness imparted to the book by your reading – by the radiance of the metaphor and the ethical content which knits it all together . . . It is impossible to speak of the poems. If you wrote nothing in your life other than "Christmas",† that by itself would be enough to ensure your immortality here on earth and in heaven.

Two months later, when he had finished the next chapter, "A Christmas Party at the Sventitskys'", Pasternak gave a reading of all three chapters on 5 April, at Olga Ivinskaya's request, in the house of her friends, the Kuzkos. Lydia Chukovskaya was invited and she succeeded in taking a shorthand note of some of the remarks with which Pasternak prefaced his reading:

* See *A Captive of Time* by Olga Ivinskaya, Collins Harvill, London, 1978.
† i.e. "Christmas Star".

I think when theatre is fully extended in literary form it produces not drama but prose.* In the field of the printed word, I love prose most but I have found myself writing poetry. Poetry stands in the same relation to prose as a sketch to a painting. I visualize poetry as being a large literary portfolio.

Like Mayakovsky and Esenin, I started my profession at a time of the disintegration of forms, a disintegration which has continued since Blok's time. For the purpose of our talk it will be sufficient to say that prose has split into different segments. In prose there now remains the descriptive approach, on the one hand, and the conceptual – that is, in terms of concept per se – on the other. The very best prose now is, I dare say, descriptive. Fedin's descriptive prose comes high up, but any sort of creative benchmark is now absent from prose. I have long wanted – and now I am beginning to have some success – to realize some sort of boost to my life, to find a way out of this situation. I have not the least idea of what my novel represents objectively but for me, within the framework of my life, it is a strong onward stimulus to my ideas. On the stylistic side, there is the desire to create a novel which would not be solely descriptive but would render feelings, dialogue and people in a dramatic embodiment. This is the prose of my time, of our time, and very much my own.

In the summer I had been asked to write something for Blok's anniversary. I very much wanted to write an article on Blok and I thought to myself what am I doing writing this novel in place of an article on Blok. (Blok had fleeting moments of supreme prose – extracts, passages.)

I surrendered to the force of these strivings, these elements which derive from thence – from Blok – and drive me on further. My idea was to create a realistic – in my understanding of the word – prose work, to portray Moscow life – its intellectual life in the Symbolist period – but to embody it in the form not of sketches but of a drama or tragedy.

Emma Gershtein, who was present at the reading, sent Pasternak a rapturous letter in which she called the novel "a book about immortality . . . the most contemporary of all the ones we know. I sensed Russia," she wrote, "with my eyes, my ears and my nose.

* See *Hope Abandoned*, Chapter 31, "Major Forms" (particularly 1: Tragedy), by Nadezhda Mandelstam, Collins Harvill, London, 1974, republished 1989, pp. 337–443.

I sensed the epoch . . . To how many people will this novel serve as a companion on their journey, how many thoughts and feelings will it inspire, for how many years will it continue to have its followers and imitators . . ."

N. I. Zamoshkin discerned in the novel the new opportunities opening up for Pasternak, the prose writer, when he wrote on 21 April 1947:

Who of your enemies might have thought of you as a realist; thought that your "word is made flesh", that it sparkles, that it is flexible and well-lubricated, that it is simple and exact – after the manner of Pushkin. Who might have thought that life's mouse-like scurry was no less within your reach but maybe even more so than the life of the spirit, the imagination and the philosophical dream.

He saw in the style of the novel an echo of "Tolstoy and Dostoyevsky, and even Rousseau."

N. M. Lyubimov noted the presence in the book of "the world of goodness, beauty and truth". He wrote to Pasternak on 30 April: "Your novel provides brilliant confirmation of the Apollon Grigoryev-Dostoyevsky idea of the universality of Russian genius."

The reading arranged for 11 May in the house of the painter Petr Konchalovsky evoked quite different responses. Lydia Chukovskaya recorded her conversation with Pasternak on this subject:

Boris Leonidovich phoned me this evening. He had phoned yesterday too but was in a highly emotional state, tired, and confused. He said he had been giving a reading at the Konchalovskys', where all the names were due to turn up: the Ivanovs, the Livanovs and many others besides. And nobody turned up, apart from Ivanov and Koma (Vsevolod Ivanov's son). Moreover Ivanov found fault with the novel.

It is evidently this evening that is referred to in the memoirs of Tamara Ivanova (Ivanov's widow) where she says:

On one occasion Vsevolod took Boris Leonidovich to task for allowing himself to write in such a slovenly style after such stylistically impeccable work as *The Childhood of Luvers, Safe Conduct* and others. Boris Leonidovich retorted that he was "writing almost like Charskaya on purpose", that in the given case his interest was not in the search for style but in its "accessibility" and that he wanted his novel to be fit for anyone to read . . . at a single gulp.

Such objections vexed Pasternak, who knew that minor blemishes cease to be visible when a thing has captured the reader by its strength and profundity. He wrote in this sense to M. M. Morozov a propos of the latter's quibbles over his translation of *Hamlet*.

> One constantly forgets that one is not at all obliged to be right or wrong in order to merit gratitude, just as vivid expression wresting itself free from the very heart of matter does not depend for its strength on its rightness or wrongness. Since you choose to object and argue the point that means that the triumph of the protoplasm is not total, that its possession has been prematurely terminated, that the sirens are giving a poor performance. But what sort of rightness reigns at the topmost peaks towards which we are both clambering?

Pasternak arranged for his next reading to take place in the Serovs' flat, in memory of Olga Valentinovna, the daughter of the painter and a contemporary of his, who had recently died. To pre-empt at the outset any reproaches about stylistic oversights, he cautioned his listeners that he had written the novel after consciously abandoning his usual style – "in fact without any sort of fixed style, just as I used to write when I first started."

Among those invited were Olga Berggolts, Neigaus and Dmitry Zhuravlev. Turning to those present, Pasternak said that what he had written was not the "product of a colossal memory" but a product of fantasy.

> I fantasized. No such philosophies, no such conversations occurred in actual fact. It is something embodying a universal concept. I have a cardboard Tolstoy in it, who is credited with judgements he never made.

He requested Sofia Tolstaya, who was present in the room, to judge how far it was all in the spirit of Lev Nikolayevich.

> The novel is not yet completed, I thought up the surnames out of my head, although some of them turned out to be familiar; and I came across the main hero's surname in Andrey Bely.*

---

* The attribution may well derive from the presence in *Dramatic Symphony* (1902), one of Bely's early works, of a minor character, an elderly religious lady of apocalyptic views, named Mertvago (meaning "dead") which could be regarded as an antonym for Zhivago (meaning "alive"). In fact, both Mertvago and Zhivago, though not commonly met with, are old Russian names.

The evening has been recorded by N. A. Muravina. A year previously she had graduated from university and had written an article on Pasternak. He had wanted her to get to know the chapters he had completed of the novel.

The house in which his hosts, the Serovs, lived is situated on the corner of Serebryany Lane and Molchanovka. It was here that Zhivago had the most astonishing experiences and meetings. It was here that he first read the special government announcement about the establishment of Soviet power in Russia.

He found that he was standing once again at the bewitched crossroads of Serebryany Lane and Molchanovka at the entry to a tall five-storey building with a glass-fronted door and a spacious, well-lit hall.

8

During Akhmatova's visit to Moscow, Pasternak gave a reading at the Ardovs' flat on the Ordynka, where she was staying. Akhmatova was acutely unhappy with the novel, exasperated first of all by its heroine, who seemed to her banal and pedestrian. The tragic love of the author for "this girl from a different world" who had become a woman too early, was incomprehensible to her.

This genuinely distressed Pasternak. The heroine's image was very precious to him as representing the development of a theme on which he had been working throughout his life and as the historical expression of the fate of women in Russia. In revising the novel Pasternak cut down on the physiological detail of the relationship between Larisa Gishar and Komarovsky. These scenes had exasperated Zinaida Nikolayevna too, Pasternak having stripped her first love of its halo by representing her cousin, Nikolay, as a scoundrel and cad. But, in cutting out detail, Pasternak was unable and did not wish to change anything in his treatment of the main characters. He had conceived them back in his boyhood and their characterization was shot through with the bitterness and pain of 1917, the personification of which he saw in the fate of Zinaida Nikolayevna, who had become the heroine of his earlier, never-published novel of the 1930s about Patrick Zhivult.

The external portrayal of Larisa, and of the lyrical warmth which pervades the chapters devoted to her, may be considered to bear the imprint of Pasternak's relations with Ivinskaya, which were then happy and radiant. Pasternak always considered that the evocation in him of a "sharp and vibrant personal response" gave him strength to cope with the difficulties arising out of his work on the novel. The consciousness of the sinfulness and the avowedly foredoomed nature of their relations lent them a special glitter at that time. Pangs of conscience, on the one side, and thoughtless egoism, on the other, frequently faced them with the need to part, but compassion and the longing for emotional warmth again attracted him to her.

> Take your hand off my breast.
> We're conductors crackling with current.
> Willy-nilly, without knowing what's what,
> we'll soon be stuck together again.
>
> The years will pass. You'll marry.
> You'll forget this mess. It's something,
> something great, something heroic,
> to be a woman, to drive men mad. [. . .]
>
> But no matter how much night
> drags on me with its dreary fetter,
> the ebb away is the strongest pull
> and passion tempts me to break-up.

9

From the beginning of 1947 intensive preparation of a small collection of Pasternak's poems, to be issued in a series devoted to the 30th anniversary of the October Revolution, had been under way. An autobiographical note was written and individual passages from the poems *Nineteen Five* and *Lieutenant Schmidt* were recast with the aim of "simplification" at the request of the book's editor, F. M. Levin. The collection included several poems from the novel.

The translation of *Hamlet* was edited and shortened for Detgiz. Unfavourable reports from the well-known Shakespearian scholar, A. A. Smirnov, hindered publication of the two-volume translation of Shakespeare and this deprived Pasternak of the possibility of working on the novel.

In a long article "On B. Pasternak's Poetry", printed in *Kultura i Zhizn** on 21 March 1947, Aleksey Surkov bore sharply down upon "the meagre spiritual resources" of the poet which were incapable of "giving birth to major poetry". Misread lines from twenty to thirty years before were quoted by way of proof. He cited: "The universe's tears inside the seedpods", from the 1917 poem "Definition of Poetry" as an example of the remoteness of Pasternak's verse from "public human emotions".

Pasternak wrote to Olga Freidenberg that such reprimands did not bother him and did not affect his work:

> . . . I feel fine and in a cheerful mood despite the attacks having grown more frequent (for example the article in *Kultura i Zhizn*).* Apropos of "Tears inside seedpods" – "pods"† was sometimes used in place of "hulls". In the greengrocers' shops, when we were children, they used to sell peas in their pods, that was the only way they said it. And now everyone thinks they are bones in ones back.
>
> It stands to reason that I am ready for everything. Why should it happen to Sashka‡ and everyone else and yet not to me? I write nothing to anyone. I never answer. There is no point in it. I do not justify myself. I do not enter into explanations. Probably, things will become more difficult as far as money's concerned. I am writing to tell you this so that you do not take it to heart and start worrying. Maybe it will all pass over. I did have a lot of stupid confusion to my credit in the past. But then my present clarity is even less acceptable . . .

By the summer of 1947 the novel's narrative had reached the beginning of the First World War and a start had been made with the chapter "The Advent of the Inevitable". Pasternak described to Lydia Chukovskaya the feelings of depression and melancholy that came over him when he read books about this period. His financial resources were petering out and he again had to switch to translation work.

"I have long ago grown out of translating," he explained on 20 May 1947 to Olga Freidenberg,

* *Culture and Life.*
† Russian word "lopatka" means both "shoulder blade" and (now rare) pods, as in pea pods.
‡ Olga Freidenberg's brother.

but since circumstances have latterly taken an unfavourable turn I had, with disgust, to go back to putting up some proposals of that sort. Even those were not at first accepted, so I kept switching them around until suddenly they were all accepted. The result is that by the end of the summer I have to produce translations of *Faust*, *King Lear* and a poem by Petöfi, "The Knight Janos". But I shall spend the twenty-fifth hour of every day writing my novel.

Two-and-a-half thousand lines of rhyming verse from Petöfi's lyric poetry were translated in one month and a week. Agnessa Kun has given an account of the difficulties of this work in her memoirs. Pasternak completed the translation of *King Lear* in a month and a half. On 8 September he wrote to Olga Freidenberg to express his satisfaction:

> This summer (as regards work) I am taking my first steps along the new path I have set myself (it is very difficult and it is the first thing in my life of which I might be proud): to live and work on two planes – part of the year (working in a great hurry) for covering the whole of the year, and the other part doing proper work – for myself.

Pasternak was very forthright in disposing of his earnings: he sent money to the most varied addresses and, while continuing to help his first wife, also gave regular support to Nina Tabidze; to Marina Tsvetayeva's daughter, Ariadna Efron, and Marina's sister, Anastasia Tsvetayeva, living in exile; to Andrey Bely's widow, Klavdia Bugayeva; and to many others. Among Pasternak's surviving papers are vast numbers of receipts for money orders despatched to a variety of addresses, including camps. With Olga Ivinskaya giving up her work, Pasternak took on the responsibility for her and her family. Zinaida Nikolayevna always complained that Boris Leonidovich deliberately created money problems at home.

10

Pasternak's *Selected Works* was due out from the Sovetsky Pisatel Publishing House in the spring of 1948. But the 10 February 1948 decree on Muradeli's opera *The Great Friendship* marked the start of a new period of ideological pressure. At the writers' meeting on

1 March devoted to this decree, Surkov "also dwelt on the individualistic work of B. Pasternak, praised to the skies by foreign aes-
thetes". The April issue of *Oktyabr** contained an article by N.
Maslina, "Mayakovsky and the Present Day". This accused Pasternak of sacrificing "content – of any kind, including reason and
conscience" for the sake of form and of turning art into a catalogue
of "subjective feelings". It concluded that Pasternak's work "caused
severe damage to Soviet poetry".

The arguments advanced in this article were repeated by B.
Yakovlev in *Novy Mir*. The print run of Pasternak's *Selected Works*
was not put on sale and was destroyed.

The Peredelkino dacha was, under the pretext of having repairs
done to it, taken over as a hostel for Litfond workers. Zinaida and
Lenya† were issued passes entitling them to a stay in the local
writers' Rest House. Pasternak remained in Moscow, where he
was, as he wrote to Olga Freidenberg:

> finishing writing the first book of the prose novel and at the same
> time trying to recut and re-recut my translations of seven of the
> Shakespearian dramas, which have reached me from a variety of
> publishing houses, in line with the contradictory requests of
> innumerable editors ensconced therein . . .

The two-volume edition of his works which for three years had
lain motionless in the Iskusstvo Publishing House was now issued,
but Pasternak's article "Notes on Translations from Shakespeare's
Dramas" was not included in it.

Anna Akhmatova came to Moscow on a visit at this time and
Pasternak did all he could to protect and look after her. She proudly
declined all his attempts to help her with money so that his basic
task became to obtain a Litfond grant for her. In his letters to his
wife, despatched from Moscow to Peredelkino by casual hand,
Pasternak wrote of his efforts on Akhmatova's behalf:

16 June 1948
Spent the whole day trying (and succeeding) to get Anna Andreyevna 3000 roubles, but in order to receive them she has to submit
a written application and she does not want to. I approached
Muzfond about Scriabina.

* *October* – Soviet political and cultural monthly journal, organ of the RSFSR
Union of Writers, founded in 1924.
† Pasternak's son, Leonid, by Zinaida Nikolayevna.

22 June

I managed to arrange for Anna Andreyevna to be given work in all the publishing houses.

23 June

I got Anna Andreyevna a Litfond grant of 3000 roubles. She needed to fill in an application, but she is refusing. The Central Committee and the Union have issued permission for the publishing houses to give her translation work. I phoned Golovenchenko. A bored, haughty voice: "Ah, Akhmatova . . . ? Yes, they told me. We shall have to see whether she is capable of doing translation." I told him to go to blazes, and threw the phone down.

It is her birthday today. If possible, let Galya* have some berries and I will give them to her as a present, if I have time to look in on her this evening.

The first chapters of the novel were being retyped at this time and amendments and additions made to them. Pasternak went to Peredelkino to read through the typescript, leaving one copy behind in Moscow for Anna Andreyevna with the request that she take it with her to Leningrad and hand it over to Sergey Spassky for him to read. Aware of the singularity of his work, due to his desire to make it as well-devised and intelligible as possible, Pasternak wrote to him on 12 June 1948:

> Find out if Akhmatova has arrived back and brought the thing with her, go and get it and read it. Send me a line about your impression, if you think it necessary. Give me your opinion straight. Is it trying to bite off too much? My break with custom, with my previous experience and with whatever may still remain of what has to be considered art, is so evident and such a major one that the whole endeavour is dogged by a degree of arrant effrontery and there is no reason to spare the author, and maybe it is nowhere near as good as it seemed to me when reading it – in my half-histrionic style. Perhaps my eyes need opening and I need teaching a lesson.

In sending Spassky the unread typescript, Pasternak wrote that he was not worried by:

---

* Galina Sergeyevna Neigaus, the wife of Stanislav Neigaus, Pasternak's younger stepson.

minor oversights, in some cases exasperating ones . . . They will not be a real bother to you and they are of so little significance that I have been quite right to send you an unchecked and at certain points immature manuscript. So many years of one's life have gone by selecting and polishing, exercising prudence and patience, that all there now remains for me is to stop wasting time and get a move on. There are few people in this world who are as well able as you to understand what this is about and what it is for, so, unless it is too awful, it should give you pleasure.

Spassky sent back an excited and rapturous reply, expressing his delight in the beauty and boldness of the images resurrected in their full array in the new novel:

Dearest Borya! Quite a time has passed since I read your manuscript. I started by going through it slowly but it sucked me in immediately and I kept returning to it every spare moment I had until I reached the end . . . First of all, it is a great success for you . . . the result is a genuine narrative and a genuine book. The external objectivity so vital in prose is not impeded by our having here alternating sequences, with the changes rung on the widest possible range of information on a whole number of individual human fates and circumstances. All those particles are charged with the same source of energy: they are, as it were, distributed over a magnetic field, so that, responding to the effect of this force, they line up with one another and combine to form a harmonious pattern. I did not find this quality in those of your earlier prose experiments which I used to come across earlier on, for you did read a number of your things to me at various times. One did occasionally come across superb passages – I remember, for example, one description of a river, of its current; or how you described the grown-up Zhenya Luvers. But one had no sense of the direction of flow of all this material. Now, however, it's quite different. A spring of pristine, creative energy has gushed forth from inside you and now you know for certain what is the one most important thing of all about which you now have to speak. With it the question of the relative validity of one or other set of stylistic approaches has dropped away and it is now simply a question of putting your entire poetic arsenal into use.

"Dearest Serezha!" Pasternak replied on 14 August:

Do not be offended by my letting you know on what is but a mere postcard the delight your long and important letter gave me. What a lot of astonishing understanding and what goodness and generosity you showed by giving me so unsparingly of your time. I am compelled to do things in a hurry: you must forgive me. Just so as to be able to continue work on the lines in your letter I have, at one fell swoop, to get the better of *Faust*, and that is what I am about at the moment.

II

The first part of *Faust*, 4700 lines of rhyming verse, was translated over a six-month period from August to February. Pasternak's own spiritual and artistic experience had prepared him for this labour. His excellent knowledge of German philosophy and literature, and his sympathy with Goethe's views on art were prerequisites for performing it successfully. But in the foreground stood the task of making the translation a feature of Russian literature, of creating a Russian Faust.

This too was achieved.

"It is working out, fancy that," he wrote to Olga Freidenberg on 6 November 1948:

and that is natural because the ground has been laid by all that has gone before: much of what is most powerful in Lermontov, Tyutchev, and Blok has come from Goethe. I am surprised at this continuity having escaped Bryusov and Fet (in their translations of *Faust*). The Russian-language *Faust* has to be captured by lack of design – impulsively.

Goethe's lyric poetry captivated and bewitched the translator as he endeavoured, in the course of his labours, to understand its peculiarities, its magic:

Faust is the magician who conjures up men's fates, the elements and the spirits of the past and the present with the force of lyric poetry. The lyric contents of collections of poetry are inconsequential lyrics, the lyrics of emotional titillation of the reader. The lyric poetry of *Faust* is all related to evident, readily perceptible consequences. The dramatic contents of *Faust* are the spectacle of these achievements and results.

Pasternak identified the basis of Goethe's design for his composition while doing the translation. He made a note for himself "for a possible future foreword, explanatory notes, and so forth":

Goethe's attempts in the second half of his life and before his end to hang his new afterthoughts, ideas and views onto the connecting rod of his strongest and most vital work are natural and correct. A strong, vital artistic production that is full of warmth is just as capable as an organism of sustaining a graft with growth potential etc.

This observation is equally applicable to Pasternak's own work on the novel where he was "capable of inserting as trip wires the most startling aspects of what he had managed to discern or rethink."

At one stage he thought of calling his novel "Attempt at a Russian Faust."

It was not only the completion date in the contract and his own desire to get on as soon as possible with the writing of his prose novel that required the earliest possible completion of his translation; there was also the string of demands from *Novy Mir* for the return of the advance made for the novel "Innokenty Dudorov". In February 1949, precisely at the time when the manuscript of *Faust* lay on the publishing house's table, the matter was taken to court.

It was not only pointless but even dangerous to offer the chapters to a journal. Pasternak understood that his freedom of manner, style and treatment of events ran contrary to the generally accepted norms which in those years became even more rigorous.

Pasternak wrote on 1 October 1948 to Olga Freidenberg:

I am translating the first part of Goethe's *Faust* with frenzied haste so as to earn by my intensive stint the opportunity and the right to continue and, maybe, complete my novel in the winter – a completely disinterested and non-profitable undertaking because the novel is not earmarked for current publication. Moreover, I am not writing it in any way like a work of art, even though it is closer to belles lettres than my past efforts. But I do not know whether there is any art left in the world or what art still means.

Pasternak was very concerned about the fate of Olga Freidenberg, then in charge of the classical philology faculty in Leningrad University. The political clouds which went under the name of the struggle against cosmopolitanism erupted into open persecution of science, art and literature.

The slim collection of Pasternak's work which had been run off in print and then destroyed continued to be discussed in the press as a malicious breach on the ideological front. F. M. Levin, the book's editor was charged with having extolled the work of the "aesthetically-minded formalist" Pasternak in 1937; and in 1947 of "complacently" helping to edit his book. A. Tarasenkov did public penance at a session of the Poetry Section for having "given support to Pasternak". There were insistent rumours of Pasternak's arrest. Anna Akhmatova and Olga Berggolts were so alarmed they phoned to enquire from Leningrad.

12

The sense of danger speeded up his work on the novel. He needed to finish writing it in time. When sending Maria Yudina a number of Goethe poems which he had translated for the same edition in which Faust was due to appear, Pasternak wrote on 27 March 1949:

> It was important to me to get Faust moving as a whole; in its own fluid, mobile world, in its dramatic integrality, and I have, it seems, achieved this, but my thoughts are now directed elsewhere – to the completion of the novel, and it will be a while before I tackle that . . . There are many reasons why I must not delay my own work, everything is in such a state of uncertainty.

The danger was enhanced by the growing interest in Pasternak in the West. He had been put forward as a candidate for the Nobel Prize each year since 1946. Pasternak had again to justify himself to Fadeyev.

> Dearest Sasha! *Iskusstvo* has put out my translations in a very nice edition (though a very modest print run). You helped in their publication. Thank you . . . You know I have been on the point of writing to you about a lot of other things because I find nothing easier than to talk with you (I almost said – and only with you) with sincerity, love and respect, but over the passing years it has become an ever more pointless and absurd occupation. Instead I will just say the following to you.
> Of late the number of people outside Russia to have studied Russian has increased a hundredfold over what there was at the

beginning of the century. Russian has displaced German and French in international importance and shares first place with English. This has, of course, been brought about by our revolution in its most general, its primary significance: it has been brought about by the victory of Russian weaponry, but it has been brought about by Russian literature too . . . and in some measure, somewhere between Blok and Esenin and you and certain others besides, among those who helped towards this, however unimaginable, stupendous and undeservedly improbable it may seem to me myself, was I. That is the source of my patriotic feelings.

On 7 August 1949, Pasternak wrote to Olga Freidenberg, enumerating the English anthologies of Russian poetry which included his poems and also the book by the Oxford professor, Maurice Bowra, on Apollinaire, Mayakovsky, Pasternak, Eliot and Lorca:*

Five years or so ago when facts such as these were not liable to be made to look discrediting (even subjectively, to oneself) by the use of a distorting mirror, information of this sort might have seemed a cause for satisfaction. Now their effect (again, speaking for myself) is quite the reverse. They underline for me the shame of my present downfall (both on the official plane and, evidently, vis-à-vis the public itself). What am I in fact worth, in the final count, if the barrier of blood and origin has remained unsurmounted (all that there remained to surmount) – and may mean something, albeit in intimation; and what a pretentious nonentity I must really be if I end up the focus of a narrow, private popularity cult among the most oppressed and unhappy members of the Jewish intelligentsia. Oh, if it be so, then I ask for nothing; and who am I or what point is there in bothering about me when the heavens turn aside from me so readily and so fully.

13

The four chapters retyped in the summer of 1948 made up what was originally to have been the first part of the novel. Pasternak sent

* *The Creative Experiment*, Maurice Bowra, Macmillan, London, 1949.

off copies to various people for them to read and make comments.

They elicited an impassioned, fervent response from Olga Freidenberg. As someone close to Pasternak, she immediately appreciated the spiritual message of what Pasternak had written:

> Your book is beyond judgement. One can apply to it what you say about history being a second universe . . . It is a special version of the Book of Genesis. I became numb with cold when I got to its philosophical passages. I was simply frightened that any moment now the final mystery would be unveiled, the one you carry inside you, which you want to express your whole life long; you wait for its revelation in art or science – but you are in mortal dread at the prospect since the mystery is due to stay a riddle for ever . . . I have the impression that you are afraid of death, that this explains it all – your passionate preoccupation with immortality which you pursue as if it were your own flesh and blood . . . Do not talk rubbish about all your previous work being of no consequence, and that only now etc . . . You are one and undivided; and it contains your entire life's journey like a painting with a road shown in perspective, all of which you can see stretching out into the far distance . . .

The affinity of her understanding and her interpretation, her explicit disinterest in the formal trivia of genre and language and her ability to discern "life – in the widest and highest meaning of the word" in his book gave Pasternak very great pleasure.

"My Dearest Olyushka! What a striking letter you wrote," he replied on 30 November 1949:

> Your letter is a thousand times better and more substantial than my manuscript. So it did make an impression on you?! It is not the fear of death but the awareness of the futility of one's best intentions and attainments and of the best available guarantees; and the consequent effort to avoid naïveté and find the right path, so that if something has to fail it should fail free of error and not from any fault of one's own.

Ariadna Efron, then in exile in Ryazan, also read the typescript of the novel. In an extensive letter of analysis, she noted "the fearful jumble" of "personal destinies, epochs, cities, years, events and passions" packed into 150 pages of typescript. She advised offsetting the "lack of room and space" by "filling in the entractes between episodes, providing a rationale for the deeds and cryptic accounts of the characters' actions – thus 'Lara went for a bathe, had a swim, went out in a boat, took part in nighttime picnics by the riverside, let off fireworks in company and danced.'" Ariadna Efron failed to appreciate that Pasternak's deliberately foreshortened approach to the development of the action, and the portrayal of the events of external life by means of pictorial, highly-coloured effects, had also been the device of the Impressionist school of painting. The depth of the inner life of the main characters, the spiritual content of their feelings and thoughts, is treated on a different plane. It is not conveyed by visual effect; and their appearances and personalities are similarly devoid of personalized detail. The contrast discovered by Zhenya Luvers when still a little girl between the picturesqueness of the soldiers' tents and the human spirituality of the men living in them is conveyed in the novel with the utmost sense of acquired mastery. The critics often noted this peculiarity and expressed amazement at the florid portrayals of the secondary characters, their appearances, their ways of speech and behaviour; and at the contrast with the main characters. The latter are delineated by a few indistinct strokes of detail, providing no visual image; their manner of speech is not individually differentiated and their dialogues are left basically as monologues.

14

"I formed a deep new attachment," wrote Pasternak on 2 August 1949 to Olga Freidenberg:

> but as my life with Zina is real I had sooner or later to sacrifice the former and, strange to say, so long as it was all full of torment, ambivalence, and the pangs and even nightmares of a tortured conscience, I bore it without difficulty, and even took pleasure in it. Now my conscience places me inescapably back among my own, I find all that a source of inconsolable gloom: my solitude and my walking on a razor's edge in literature; the ultimate uselessness of my literary efforts as a writer; the strange duality of my fate "here" and "there" etc., etc. At that time I was writing the first chapter of the novel and translating *Faust*, dogged by difficulties and hindrances, with my head elsewhere, with a constant alternation between tragedy and the most carefree exul-

tation and I did not care a rap and it seemed to me that everything was coming out right for me.

What Pasternak had in mind here is the break in his relations with Ivinskaya which came about in spring 1949 when they had reached a painful dead end.

The compassion and concern expressed in the above letter were soon replaced by real alarm on her behalf. The judicial organs started taking an interest in her and after a number of summonses and questionings she was arrested on 9 October 1949. Pasternak absolutely refused to believe that the reason for Ivinskaya's arrest was her involvement in the case against the deputy chief editor of *Ogonek*, Osipov, who had been accused of forging banker's orders. He considered that their relationship was the cause and wished to hear nothing different. His certainty was bolstered by his having been summoned to the MGB* to take possession of his books and manuscripts confiscated during the search made at Ivinskaya's flat. He refused to take them and demanded that they be returned to the person from whom they had been seized.

At this time he was correcting the proofs of *Faust* and tormented by the thought that his Gretchen had got into such a situation, "Life has repeated the last scene in *Faust* down to the very last letter," he wrote on 15 October to Nina Tabidze.

Man's sure rivalry with man has never in my life seemed to me so threatening and dangerous as to provoke jealousy in its most acute and insidious form. But I often in my youth was jealous of a woman's past or her illness or her life being in danger or the threat of her departure, of remote and insurmountable forces. So now I am jealous of her being in the power of coercion and uncertainty, which have replaced the touch of my hand or my voice. But suffering will only lend further depth to my work, will only impart still sharper focus to my being and my consciousness.

The November–December 1949 seven-poem cycle contains indications of his anguish and dread.

> Let the dry leaves let themselves go
> even more gloriously and recklessly.

---

* Ministry of State Security up to March 1953. It re-emerged as the Committee for State Security (i.e. KGB) in March 1954.

Let them add today's galls
to yesterday's brimming, bitter cup. [. . .]

You: the best to emerge from the worst,
when life is the worst kind of illness,
and beauty is founded on courage:
this is what draws us together.

His recollections of their meetings are coloured by the imminent
tragedy.

Snow will fill in the roads
and the roofs will pile high.
I'll stand to stretch my legs:
you'll be standing in the door. [. . .]

The snow blessed on your lashes.
Sadness standing in your eyes.
You are yourself:
nothing to add, or take away.

Like a metal plate
treated with resin,
my heart has been etched
with your presence. [. . .]

When only rumours remain
of all of our years
and we are no longer here,
then who were we? from where?

Four of the poems written at that time develop traditional themes
based on events in the Gospel. They deal with the transcendental
essence of what was then taking place and distil the essential truth
and meaning from the bare facts without any attempt at stylization.

In the last week,
he entered Jerusalem, to be met
by a storm of hosannahs.
Folk ran with branches behind him. [. . .]

But the days grow sterner,
and more menacing: hearts harden,
foreheads frown, the conclusion is come,
and the end is here.

In *Safe Conduct* Pasternak recalls his admiration for Italian art and particularly notes the "feeling of the tangible unity of our culture." "Italy," he wrote, "has for me crystallized what we unconsciously take in in our cradle." Elements of Italian painting and its associative "conscious anachronism" are, of course, present in Pasternak's treatment of New Testament subjects.

Rilke's example of using literary settings of Gospel subjects was the one that most appealed to Pasternak. The former's *New Poems* (1907) provided several examples of this, which he developed further in his *Life of Mary* (1908).

Comparison of Rilke's and Pasternak's treatment of "Mary Magdalene" or "The Garden of Gethsemane" brings out the depth and lucidity of the poems of Yury Zhivago. Pasternak's "Mary Magdalene" follows the traditional form of invoking Christ. In addition, the poem has none of the eroticism customary in dealing with this theme, which also figured in Tsvetayeva's poetic cycle, of which Pasternak already knew in 1928. The darkness and gloom of being abandoned by God in Rilke's "The Garden of Olives" is illuminated in Pasternak's case by faith in "the fearful majesty" of the march of history's centuries as another name for "The Kingdom of God".

> He gave up miracles
> and put off power, easily,
> as if they were loans,
> and was mortal like us.
>
> Now that the long dark night
> stretched like scorched earth,
> empty as all desert places,
> the garden gave life its only hope.
>
> And looking into the void,
> without onset or end, he begged
> his father to let the cup pass,
> his sweat a trickle of blood. [. . .]
>
> But the book of life
> was come to the page more precious
> than all sacred things. What was written
> must come about soon. So be it. Amen.

In his letter to Shalamov of 7 March 1953 Pasternak gave an explanation of the reasons for his conscious rejection of the forces that had shaped his literary career at that far-off time when he had trusted them unequivocally:

> with no fear of anything untoward, without entertaining any suspicion or evil thought of whatever came to him from the world outside, however short-lived and fortuitous it might prove. Since then everything has changed. Even the language people then used is no more. So what is there surprising – after my rejection of so many things, of risk-taking and going to extremes and of the peculiar features of the art of that day – in my trying to set down in present-day language, in a modern, more familiar, more ordinary and calmer projection just some part of that world, maybe even the most precious part of it (though do not think that it is the Gospel theme which makes up that part – that would be a mistake, no, it is not that but the responsive, chromatic, organic perception of life picked up from afar from across the centuries in that theme).

15

"You have probably already seen Akhmatova's poems in *Ogonek* or heard of their being printed," wrote Pasternak to Nina Tabidze on 6 April 1950.

> Remember I showed you part of them, not the best ones at that, a while ago. Those I did not know and which she has used to supplement the ones I did know are the best. I am terribly pleased, as is everyone, at this literary sensation and at this event in her life, and the only thing I find displeasing is that, by analogy, everyone has started to look round expectantly in my direction. But I already said all that she has now said twenty years ago, and was one of the first to say it when such voices were more rarely heard and more to be counted in single numbers. Such things are not for continuous reiteration: either they mean something or they mean nothing, and in the latter event no reiteration can put things right.

The reference was to the cycle of poems printed in three issues of the journal *Ogonek* (Nos. 14, 36, 42, 1950), which were later grouped together under the title *Hail to Peace*. The panegyrics were linked to Akhmatova's intercession on behalf of her son, Lev Gumilev, who had been re-arrested in 1949. Remembering his own civic poems in *Second Birth*, the poem "Not yesterday, but more than a century ago" addressed largely to Stalin, and others from his cycle "The Artist", Pasternak could discern Akhmatova's innate music and the insistent intonation of her voice amid the unfamiliar themes. He hoped that the appearance of these poems in print meant the end of the ban, that the presence of her name in *Ogonek* would remove the black stigma of the critical epithets under which she had always figured for the last five years.

In June Pasternak translated *Macbeth*, the seventh in his cycle of Shakespeare translations. He was later to write that in doing it he could not avoid drawing parallels with Dostoyevsky's *Crime and Punishment*. The "handling of crime by a novelist" was something which had excited Pasternak as a young man, and back in 1913 he had written to Konstantin Loks about it. He now found in Shakespeare a "double dose of the heightened realism of a detective novel", and close attention to detail.

In contrasting the mechanics of Shakespeare's dialogues and those of Goethe, also recently translated by him, Pasternak noted "the degrees of intelligibility demanded from a lyrical-subjective work and a production for the stage."

> When I read something subjective in a lyrical-monological form or listen to its delivery from the stage, the important thing is that I understand it: the text is addressed to me. But when I watch a Shakespeare play, written as a portrayal of life, on the stage, it is not enough that I understand it. The dramatis personae are addressing one another, not me. The dialogue has to be such, not only that I understand it but that I, peeping in and eavesdropping on someone else's conversation as I am, be convinced that those taking part in the conversation understand each other instantly, in mid-sentence, as in life. Scenic dialogue must possess an immediacy and intelligibility over and above the basic intelligibility required of a book, which the spectator observes with his own eyes and is prepared to confirm as an eyewitness.

The contract for the second part of *Faust* was signed in April 1950, but the appearance in *Novy Mir* (No.8, 1950) of an article by T. Motyleva, maintaining that the new translation gave a false impression of the original and took liberties with Goethe's literary-aesthetic views, cast doubt on any further work on *Faust*.

"There was alarm," wrote Pasternak on 21 September to Ariadna Efron:

> when *Novy Mir* scolded my *Faust* on the grounds that the gods, the angels, the witches, the spirits, the madness of the poor girl Gretchen, and all the "irrational elements" had been rendered too well, while Goethe's progressive ideas (which ones?) have been left neglected in the shade.

Even so the contract was not torn up and in the autumn Pasternak started on the second part, which had at first seemed to him "an unmanageably cumbrous mixture of embryonic, barely discernible genius with emergent and triumphant slapstick."

16

Pasternak broke away from his translation work and continued with the novel, so minimizing his exposure to the stifling atmosphere of literary life.

"Of late everything around me has seemed desperately petty," he wrote to Nina Tabidze on 5 December 1950:

> The very least thing might change my life – were that required by someone – and affect it more drastically than does the magnanimity now exhibited towards it, but that is a matter for my unknown benefactor. I for my part cannot conduct myself otherwise and this ineluctability fills my cup full of happiness.

He finished the chapters dealing with the 1917 revolution – "Farewell to the Past" and "Moscow Bivouac". The first reflected Pasternak's impressions of his two journeys in the summer of 1917 to Romanovka and Balashov and established a link between the image of the heroine of *My Sister, Life* and Antipov's sister, who also had taken part in the installation of municipal councils* in country districts.

In a letter of April 1948 to M. P. Gromov, Pasternak defined the character of his hero as "somewhere midway" between himself,

---

* Elective organs of local administration (Zemstvo) introduced under the reforms of 1864. By 1914 they covered over half of the provinces of Tsarist Russia, but were abolished in 1918.

Blok, Esenin and Mayakovsky. This list of poets' names itself explains his new free approach to poetry writing, devoid of his once customary metaphorical impressionism, itself a feature of the "disintegration of form" period which had started with Blok.

As distinct from the above-listed professional poets, the novel's hero is an amateur poet, someone that is, as Tolstoy said of his eldest brother, Nikolay, innocent of the defects which make a person a writer. Pasternak released his hero from the burden of poetic biography, and fashioned him into a composite image of the generation to which he himself belonged, a generation, as he wrote in *Safe Conduct* – "apolitical" in its first statements "about its own science, its philosophy and its art."

Pasternak gave a reading of these two chapters to the family circle which on this occasion included his neighbours, Fedin and Vsevolod Ivanov.

Echoes of this family discussion are apparent in Pasternak's letter of 18 October 1950 to a Georgian acquaintance, Raisa Mikadze:

One hears ever more frequently from one's own kith and kin and one's closest friends that they see my recent interests and my present simplicity, which has cost me so much effort to attain, as meaning that I have lost my way and am resorting to the cult of the banal. Well, even this is no matter for grief. If there is to be suffering somewhere why should my art not suffer and I with it? Maybe my friends are right and maybe they are not. Maybe – and it may very well be so – I have travelled along the same path their fates took them, but a little further, towards respecting human suffering and a readiness to share it.

The writing of the chapter "The Journey" was completed during the spring of 1952 and Pasternak arranged to give a reading of it on 2 June. The Zhuravlevs, Akhmatova and Elena Scriabina, the composer's daughter, were invited. "The majority of those who read the novel," Pasternak wrote to Simon Chikovani on 14 June 1952:

are nevertheless unhappy with it, call it a failure, say that they expected more from me, that it is pallid, that it is beneath me, but I, on learning all of this, give them a broad smile as if this abuse and censure were an encomium.

It was arranged for the reading to take place in Lenya's large room on the upper floor of the flat in Lavrushinsky Lane. Pasternak derived pleasure and comfort from the reaction of his 14-year-old son:

> It was Lenya's first time among my listeners, his first time to be given an idea of what it is I am doing, what I write and what I live for, not because he was then too small and has now grown up but because, as always, the more I love someone the more I have sought to be a source of freedom for that person, and in my house no one should ever have to think the same thoughts as I do or pay me acknowledgement. In addition, I have never considered myself such a stupendous classic* or authority as to impose myself on the children or recommend myself to them. So it was not a matter of indifference to me how today's Pioneer and tomorrow's Komsomol member brought up as he is to a different understanding of certain chronological seams and to a different manner of describing nature, reality and everything on earth, related to how I convey all of this. He had no knowledge of the preceding parts of the novel, and the usual, jealously critical attitude of teenagers to members of the family in the presence of strangers, in company, was a still greater obstacle to intuitive perception on his part . . .
>
> It was a great joy to me when, in answer to my question as to whether he liked it, he said, overcoming his habitual shyness and blushing scarlet: "Very, very much!" And then I heard him, at the other end of the table, already challenging Zina's judgement that this part was not as succinct as its predecessors.

Pasternak's impressions of this reading and of the stereotyped objections which kept cropping up in various quarters come through in his note to Kaverin, with which he enclosed the first four chapters of his novel. Already aware that Kaverin would reiterate the opinion prevailing in literary circles, he jotted down in his note the main points of the novel. In the journal *Oktyabr* (No.9, 1984) Kaverin published this note in a shortened form as Pasternak's own opinion of his book and representing his conscious awareness of its shortcomings:

---

* Ivinskaya in her memoirs, records that her own daughter's affectionate nickname for Boris Leonidovich was "Klassoosha" – an affectionate diminutive of "classic". See *A Captive of Time*, Collins Harvill, London, 1978, p. 24.

2 August 1952

If, after my talk with you and Zhuravlev, I were to consign my promise to oblivion, this would seem remiss to you and be bound to cause you offence. On the other hand, the last thing I should want is for you to fritter away your time as a writer, as a master of the pen, on the work of a person who himself reads nothing, is interested in nothing, and who from spiritual and intellectual sloth idles his days away in the kitchen garden and refuses to give up his vegetal egoism . . . The majority of my friends do not like the work. Some because it is not new and not original to the extent they, in their overestimation of my powers, would like to see. Others because, in declining to tackle the main tasks which are now mandatory, I am evading the main difficulty which all shoulder, and in so doing I render valueless in advance whatever I may succeed in doing. You too, if you are to be sincere with yourself, will be disappointed. Perhaps it is really best to put off the reading until such time as I finish the novel.

That winter, after reading Aseyev's poem "Gogol" and a rabble-rousing attack in an article in *Ogonek*, Pasternak wrote to Aseyev giving his explanation for the sort of approach to the problems of literature which characterized the official attitude to such things as Aseyev's poem and Pasternak's novel:

The distinction between contemporary Soviet literature and all that preceeded it seems to me to be above all that it is bedded down on rock-solid foundations irrespective of whether it is read or not read. It is a proud, self-confiding and self-sufficing phenomenon, sharing with other pillars of State their immutability and infallibility. But genuine art, to my understanding, is far from having such pretensions. How can it set out to give orders or issue instructions when it has more weaknesses and transgressions to its credit than virtues? It nurtures a modest desire to be the reader's dream, the object of his longings, and is in need of his responsive imagination, not in the form of amicable condescension but as an integral element on which the artist is dependent for his formation, just as a ray of light is dependent on a reflecting surface or a refracting medium to enable it to play and sparkle.

These words reveal Pasternak's longing for an unprejudiced reaction from the mass reader without whom, in Pasternak's judgement, there could be no great literature. Pasternak circulated his manuscript widely for reading. He sent it to Kaysyn Kuliev and E. D. Orlovskaya in Frunze, to V. A. Avdeyev in Chistopol, and to B. V. Gubarev in Panyutino in the Donetsk region, and to others in Georgia.

At times he started to have doubts of the correctness of the path he had chosen and in his letters and conversations there are notes of the tragedy of his solitude, of the isolation and ambivalence of his position in literature. Such a mood is reflected in his conversation on 4 May 1952 with Tanya Zhirmunskaya. At the request of her elder, eighteen-year-old sister and her companions, she had borrowed the typescript of the novel from Pasternak. In reply to her thanks and expression of praise, Pasternak wrote sadly that he felt himself "out of tune and at odds with life". Tanya, in her record of their conversation, noted what Pasternak said to her:

Understand me correctly, nothing that is genuine can carry on in this way, at cross-purposes with life. Maybe all of them are poor writers and that is all there is to it, but then it's better to err all together than to err alone. I am now left entirely on my own; that is how things have turned out, and I feel that you understand me. I am somehow completely to one side, completely at variance with life.

Yes, yes, yes . . . I do not feel myself in the wrong and I do not know when it happened. At first we were always together, and I felt nothing of that sort – I, Mayakovsky . . . Mayakovsky and I: and I did not even feel this way during the war. Perhaps after these decrees on Akhmatova and Zoshchenko, I don't know, all of a sudden I was completely alone. That is how it turned out and it's bad.

The first day Andrey Voznesensky got to know Pasternak, he received the typescript of the novel and with it a notebook full of poems.

"Why did he volunteer this to me?" Voznesensky now asks, recalling his visit. "During those years he was lonely, worn out by misfortune, he wanted to find sincerity, candour, to break out of the circle."

This was the time when Pasternak felt most acutely his sense of isolation from the reader and the incipient loss of those friends who readily accepted the de-emphasis on spiritual values of that time and followed in its wake.

But such depressing thoughts left him whenever he plunged back into his work, which never failed to bring him a feeling of joy and happiness.

17

Autumn 1952 arrived. Pasternak was spending a lot more time working in the garden, digging up and gathering in a generous potato crop. He and his family moved back to Moscow. On 20 October, he was taken off to the Botkin Hospital with a generalized coronary thrombosis. He stayed there until 6 January 1953. For the first week he was in a general ward. The head of the ward, Professor Votchal, was seriously afraid for his life.

When the danger had passed, Pasternak was transferred, at Zinaida Nikolayevna's insistence, to the better conditions of the hospital's No. 8 Block,* under the charge of Professor Vovsi. At the end of December he was visited by Anna Akhmatova.

On finally returning home, he wrote on 17 January 1953:

Ninochka! I have remained alive and I am home. Ah, what a lot I have to say to you!

When it happened and I was taken away and lay for five hours during the evening – in outpatients' first and then, at night time, in the corridor of an ordinary, vast, overcrowded city hospital – I was overcome, between losing consciousness and attacks of nausea and vomiting, by such feelings of tranquillity and bliss! I had the thought that in the event of my death nothing untoward or irremediable would occur. Zina and Lenechka had enough to manage on for six months or a year and after that they would look around and do something. They would have friends and would come to no harm. And the end would not catch me out in the throes of work, in the course of getting something finished. The little that could be done amid the obstacles which time had put in the way, had been done (the translations of Shakespeare, Faust and Baratashvili).

Yet alongside me things pursued their familiar course, align-

* Part of the network of special clinics and hospitals for privileged patients run by the Fourth Department (due to be abolished) of the Ministry of Health for the USSR.

ments became more pronounced, and shadings grew sharper! The mile-long corridor with its sleeping bodies, immersed in dark silence, ended in a window giving on to the garden bathed in the inky turbulence of a rain-spattered night and the reflected glow of the night lights of Moscow peeping out above the treetops. And this corridor and the green globe of the lampshade on the night-sister's desk by the window, and the stillness, and the shadows of the nurses and the presence of death beyond the window and behind one's shoulder – it all formed in its concentrated essence such a fathomless, such a superhuman poem. At a moment which seemed the last in one's life, one wanted, as never before, to speak with God, to hail his presence made visible, to catch and capture him. "O Lord," I whispered, "I thank thee for thy language, its majesty and its music, that thou hast made me an artist, that creation is thy schooling, and that my life long thou hast prepared me for this night." And I exulted and wept for joy.

Four years later he gave expression to these feelings in his poem "In the Hospital":

> From the way the nurse was shaking
> her head and the questions she asked,
> he suddenly understood
> he might not get through this alive.
>
> Then he looked at the window,
> grateful for a patch of wall,
> lit by lights from the town,
> which throbbed like a spark. [. . .]
>
> O God, how perfect everything is,
> the patient was thinking,
> the beds, the walls, the death
> at night, the night in town. [. . .]
>
> In the iron light
> failing round my bed,
> the sweet knowledge that I
> and my life are your priceless gift.

On 4 February 1953 Pasternak went into the sanatorium in Bolshevo to recuperate. There he again started to work and his letters from Bolshevo are full of health and happiness.

In a letter of 3 March to Valentin Asmus, Pasternak compared his stay in Bolshevo in August 1935 with his present one. In 1935 he was agonizing over his prose writing, it was making him ill and blocking his every way out. "But now," he wrote:

I have heart trouble, which is not thought simulated, I am in the shadows and not in the limelight; all the attributes have been turned around, and all the pluses have become minuses, but I am happy and free, in good health, gay and cheerful and I am sitting down completely relaxed to work at my Zhivago, which no one needs and which is inseparable from me, at the same window which eighteen years ago was my dead end and at which I was then not able to do a thing nor did I know what I was supposed to be doing.

Pasternak wrote to Varlam Shalamov on 7 March 1953 to draw a parallel between the February Revolution and the silence into which the news of Stalin's death had plunged him.

The February Revolution found me in the depths of the Vyatka province on the Kama River, at a factory. In order to get back to Moscow, I travelled the 160-odd miles to Kazan by covered sledge, part of the journey at night along a narrow forest track with the three horses harnessed to the sledge in single file ahead, just as in *The Captain's Daughter*.* This present tragic event has also found me outside Moscow, in the woods in winter and my state of health will not allow me to travel into town during the leave-takings. Yesterday morning there were folded banners with a black border being carried past in the distance on the far side of the trees and I realized what had happened. It is quiet around here. Every word has become filled up to the brim with meaning and truthfulness. And it is quiet in the woods.

18

When Pasternak was discharged from the Bolshevo sanatorium, he was advised to take care, to live the whole year round outside the city, and, so far as possible, avoid conferences and business meetings. He took up work all the more ardently.

* By Pushkin.

To judge from his letters, he had already put in some concentrated work on the novel in Bolshevo. When he arrived home, *Faust* was awaiting him. It had been listed in Goslitizdat's plan for 1953 and the editor had a lot of comments. As always, Pasternak started revising the manuscript as a whole. He sought not to deal with the specific comments, the arbitrary and haphazard nature of which were apparent to him, but to eliminate the reason for their having occurred – in other words, to put the translation beyond criticism and render it fundamentally congenial to Goethe's intentions. The work was not confined to revision of the manuscript:

"Amendment of both parts of *Faust* is under way," he wrote to Olga Freidenberg on 12 July:

and I have recast no less than a tenth of this 600-page long lyrical torrent on completely different lines. It was a matter of curiosity to see whether I might permit myself the luxury and impudence of wishing to procreate – without any reckoning of hours of day or night – a Faust who would be intelligible and perceptible, who would occupy his rightful physical place in time and space – and not as a mere aspiration, a Faust in accordance with my own present judgement and conception of him.

That summer eleven of the poems in Yury Zhivago's exercise book were written. Two of them – "Insomnia" and "Under an Open Sky" were not included in the text of the book and remained in manuscript form.

The poem "August" reverted to his recent experience of narrowly surviving death. In it the celebration of the major festival of the Transfiguration in Peredelkino church – of which there was a view from the windows of Pasternak's cottage – indissolubly links his miraculous escape as a child, when he had fallen from his horse and remained alive, with the feeling of the inevitable end he experienced in hospital in October 1953.

> Goodbye, Feast of the Transfiguration,
> your azure and the other Saviour shining.
> Sweeten the bitterness of death
> with the brush of a woman's lips.
>
> Harried era, goodbye, and you,
> the one who threw down her challenge
> to endless humiliation. Goodbye.
> I am the field you fought over.

Goodbye to the beat of widespread wings
and the miles of unwavering flight,
to the world in the word,
to creation and creation's miracles.

"Suddenly after the hospital, the sanatorium and the restrictions," he wrote to Olga Freidenberg:

things happened which were not provided for in the regime prescribed me – a wave of happiness, at having my hearing restored to me and my eyes reopened for me, whereupon I ran through *Faust* anew before its final editing and wrote these things and a few more too.

He read his new poems to Fedin and Livanov who came to see him at that time. They cried, as his letter of 18 September to Nina Tabidze indicates:

Nina, what have I done to deserve this ecstasy, this joy that comes to me from my work. At times I feel just as if I were not my own master but being moulded by the hands of the Lord which are making me into something of which I know not, and I am fearful, as you are. No, that's not so – unfearful.

Work on the prose part of the novel was approaching completion: "The main bit is already written in rough form," Pasternak wrote to Nina Tabidze on 16 November:

The hero has already parted from the main heroine and will see her no more. It remained for me (from the first draft version) to describe the doctor's stay in Moscow, from 1922 to 1929, how he sank down in the world and let everything go and, then, how he died, and after that to write an epilogue relating to the end of the Patriotic War. The one and only time in life I wrote like this, at a single go, without pausing to fill in the detail but leaving it till the overall polishing, was *The Childhood of Luvers*, but the same conditions of freedom, spontaneity and gladness did not recur later.

19

Stalin's death induced hopes of the rapid return of people who had been arrested. In those cases where there had been no news for many years and any certainty that the person in question was alive had tended to vanish, the waiting became almost unbearable.

"My dear, dear, dear friend!" wrote Pasternak to Nina Tabidze on 7 August 1953:

> You know I have long ceased to believe in the possibility of Titsian being alive. He was too great, too special a person, spreading brightness wherever he went, for him to be kept hidden without the signs of his presence making themselves felt whatever the bars and bolts. Your reborn faith that maybe we shall see him momentarily infected me. If he is alive, he will without fail return into my life and into yours. It would be an unthinkable joy: such a thing – this one thing and nothing else – would completely turn my life upside down for me. It would be precisely the reward, the compensation from fate which I shall never, never obtain; when, after enormous investment of soul and nerve on a Faust or Shakespeare or the novel, I desperately want something equivalent in return and no money or pleasure or recognition or anything in the world can compensate me for the effort expended.

In October 1953 Olga Ivinskaya returned, under the amnesty. Pasternak wrote that "mere acquaintances have started to talk more animatedly and make more sense, and it has become more interesting to go out visiting and meet other people." His rhyming inscription to P.I. Chagin on a copy of Faust, which had come out in the New Year, combined the basic events of the time into one extended play on words:

> What a lot of years were lost
> while we waited for this Faust.
> Yet the little book got born
> as all on earth must get a turn.
>
> Change had happened in the queue:
> sometimes by this haphazard route
> a book can find its own way out,
> and now and then a person, too.

"For me, in fact, nothing has essentially changed," Pasternak wrote on 30 December 1953 to Olga Freidenberg:

> except one thing – the most important thing in the lives of all of us. The daily, indiscriminate disappearance of names and

personages has stopped, the fate of the survivors has become easier, and some are returning.

Pasternak expanded on the same thought in his next letter:

Even earlier when things were at their most fearful, I had asserted my right to a sort of independence, for which I might at any moment have had to pay a terrible price. Now I can exercise it with much less risk . . . But outwardly nothing has changed. My time has not yet come. I shall not write stupid things for the sake of getting them published. And what I am writing, which gets closer and closer to what I think and feel, is not yet fit for publication . . . In order for it all to exist, to have meaning, to be set in motion (Faust, I myself, work and joys) air is needed. It is unthinkable in an airless expanse. And there is still no air. But I am happy even without air. Do please try and understand that . . .

Pasternak's translation of *Faust* is considered his highest achievement in that field. It has evoked many reactions and much analysis in our country and abroad, principally in Germany.

In his work Pasternak succeeded in conveying the "highest degree of courage – the courage of invention, and creation where a vast plan is encompassed by creative thought," as Pushkin wrote of *Faust*. Previous translations had not transmitted the effective strength of the tragedy, the energy imparted to it by the element of lyrical poetry which illuminates "the remote and inaccessible recesses of our existence in ways not at the disposal of philosophy".

In the "perfection of superform" of *Faust* Pasternak saw:

an attempt to create new elemental matter, an alchemy of lyric poetry, never satisfying – that is, appeasing – the thirst of its creators but accompanying the very highest strivings of artistic feeling, as with Michelangelo, Beethoven and Gogol.

In his letters of this time Pasternak often voiced regret that he was not given a possibility of "retelling the contents in a lively and accessible form, in fluent, concise prose" and uncovering an explanation for "the genuinely bizarre features of the original" in an "honest, committed way".

"I might, for example," he wrote to E. D. Orlovskaya and Kaisyn Kuliev:

have tried to do so in a foreword or a commentary, had I been allowed to write them (and how often did I ask to be allowed to write them, but was it conceivable that I a private citizen without official status or any police rank should be allowed to tackle tasks with so high an ideological content!) – I might have tried, I repeat, to investigate for myself a little more deeply and freely what I had started to investigate in my translation and thus taken – together with other people, with the readers – a few steps towards throwing greater light on a dark and difficult work and on its rationale. But how can one expect any such thing from the present ungifted authors of commentaries and forewords who so readily and enthusiastically accept the licensed mediocrity favoured by those who commission prefaces and those who follow in their wake.

The foreword and footnotes to *Faust* were written by Nikolay Vilyam-Vilmont, whose youthful zest and radiant creative gifts had enthused Pasternak early in the Twenties and inspired hopes of a brilliant future. His article on *Faust* was put together in an oppressive era of total ossification of form and suffocation of thought. He later told us how, out of fear of a profound and free interpretation of Goethe he had compelled Pasternak to go to undue lengths to make his translation conform to the original, so consciously sacrificing the beauty and clarity of understanding attained in the translation. He was also distressed at the revised version of "The Spinning Wheel Song", amended at his insistence, which, in its first version, had rendered the high lyrical quality of burgeoning emotion:

> Only trouble. No peace
> and no sign of strength:
> things I can't retrieve
> or return to ever again.

Pasternak later recalled how Nikolay Vilmont and the editors had protested against Faust's use of the words "filthy tricks" to describe Mephistopheles' retorts. In support of his subconscious feeling about the rightness of these words, Pasternak had somehow discovered its having been used in *The Brothers Karamazov* to define the offers made by the Devil in his conversation with Ivan.

Pasternak wrote to Maria Yudina on 18 January 1954 to say how difficult it was to convey the eloquence of Mephistopheles, which constituted the "stylistic ballast" of the tragedy:

> His oratory is avowedly limited, consciously inferior and yet so sweeping and so brilliantly argued; and these are its ambivalent

and internally contradictory attributes which completely thwarted my best efforts in relation to the text and poisoned my joy in my work.

The significance of the final scene, where the Mother of God appears as the protector of the fallen, is that it brings together the central propositions of the philosophy of Pasternak and Goethe.

The formula "All that is transient is but a symbol", which played so large a part in Symbolism's philosophical constructions, acquired in Pasternak's case the sense of the transition of the finite into the eternal, of the dissolution of "the mortality of an individual element in the immortality of its general meaning". He rejects the word "symbol", involving a long history of various philosophical in-terpretations, and substitutes the concept of "simile".

> Symbol, simile:
> all things in spate.

(Originally it read: "All things in spate are only a simile".)

> The endless goal
> is here: accomplished.
> Is here: undeniable
> in the greater truth.
> The eternal feminine
> urges us on.

The thought concerning the uplifting and spiritualizing quantity of womanly love in the striving after the eternal mysteries of existence originally came out more distinctly:

> The divine nature of the mystery
> is right before our eyes.
> The eternal feminine
> urges us upward.

"I know that there is a lot that is good in the translation," Pasternak wrote on 7 January 1954 to Olga Freidenberg:

> but how can I put it: this Faust was all a part of my life, he has been translated with my heart's blood; that I was conscious that the image of the prison and the rest of it and all these horrors and guilt and fidelity figured both in my work and along-side it.

20

In the spring of 1954 the April issue of *Znamya* carried ten poems from *Doctor Zhivago*. This publication was accompanied by an announcement signed by the author:

> It is anticipated that the novel will be completed by the summer. It covers the period from 1903 to 1929, with an epilogue relating to the Great Patriotic War. Its hero, Yury Andreyevich Zhivago, a doctor, a thinker, a seeker after truth with a creative and artistic cast of mind, dies in 1929. After his death there remain his notebooks and, among his other papers written in his youth, poems in finished form, part of which are presented here and which, taken all together, form the last, concluding chapter of the novel.

This publication meant a great deal to Pasternak not only because "the words 'Doctor Zhivago' have been imprinted on a contemporary page," as he put it, but also because people started talking about the completion of the novel.

Konstantin Simonov commented in his article, "Man in Poetry", on the great formal simplicity and accessibility of the new poems. However, he wrote, Pasternak had not progressed in his understanding of people and the epoch. If his previous poems allowed an over-all glimpse of "What millennium is it out there, my friends", his latest ones disclosed no sign of it. The deduction was that, previously, Pasternak "had shown himself to be a man of broader views than in his poems published in 1954."

Pasternak spent the spring and summer finishing off the first pencilled editing of the last chapter and the epilogue.

In Leningrad Kozintsev was putting on *Hamlet* in Pasternak's translation and sent him an invitation to the premiere. "I shall not go," wrote Pasternak on 20 March 1954 to Olga Freidenberg:

> I need and want to finish the novel and until it is finished I am a fantastically, maniacally unfree person . . . It is much easier to write them [poems] than it is to write prose, but only prose brings me closer to the idea of the absolute which sustains me and governs my life and my norms of conduct and so on and so

on; and creates that inner, spiritual edifice, one of whose tiers may provide a lodgement for what, without this refuge, is the pointless and ignoble art of versification.

In August he enthusiastically set to writing out a fair copy of the section about the partisan unit. The chapters devoted to partisan warfare in the Urals had been put together from original material. He had borrowed books of popular reminiscence and historical studies from libraries and his friends. There still remained leaflets of the time carrying messages of various kinds.

The scene of Larisa Fedorovna's parting from Komarovsky took on special depth. The original drafts retain rough outlines of Yury's monologues expressing the agonized torment of jealousy. Larisa's act of betrayal has been highlighted and deepened by reference to the symbolism of the eternal theme of Eve's fall from grace. The impression of the last twelve months comes out on the pages of the "Lament for Lara". Pasternak was, as previously, continuing to support Olga Ivinskaya's family financially. At his request A. P. Ryabinina gave her a certificate, which she needed to obtain a Moscow residence registration, attesting that she was under contract to Goslit to do translation work on the literature of the national minorities; but their relationship did not resume. Pasternak did not want to return to their old relationship, which he had painfully broken off at the time. He did not want them to see one another and repeat past experience. After Ivinskaya's stay in camp, Pasternak felt he owed her an unpaid debt of conscience and this put him in a position where he was unable to refuse her anything. In the summer of 1954, at her insistence, it started up all over again: their meetings (at first infrequent), Zinaida Nikolayevna's tears, Pasternak's pangs of conscience and his feeling of guilt towards his son.

In 1983 material relating to the joint translation work of Pasternak and Ivinskaya was handed over to the Museum of the Friendship of the People in Tiflis. Of special interest are the interlinear versions on which outline translations have been jotted down in Pasternak's handwriting – versions subsequently issued in Ivinskaya's name. In some cases a start has been made on the translation of a poem together with the words "Carry on in the same way." Some of these jottings have fallen into the hands of collectors in the guise of unknown poems by Pasternak. The works bear the signs of inaccuracy and haste and these translations cannot be reattributed, for they are consciously designed to suit another's aptitudes.

Ivinskaya gradually took over Pasternak's commitments on the publishing side, negotiation with editors and control over payments, which freed him from the necessity of going up to town.

21

"This last winter we had the repairs done to the fabric of the dacha which we rent from Litfond," wrote Pasternak to Olga Freidenberg on 12 July 1954;

> it has been refurbished and turned into a palace. Running water, a bath, gas and three new rooms. I feel uncomfortable in these surroundings; it is above my station. I am ashamed at the walls of my enormous study with its parquet floor and central heating.

That winter, spent in Peredelkino without a break, was devoted to rewriting the final chapters of the novel, much of which was shortened or redone as new. He was in a hurry to finish the work. It had grown in scope and he was afraid of overloading it with detail. On 2 April 1955 when sending the manuscript of the completed chapters to N. P. Smirnov, whom he had known from *Novy Mir* since the Twenties, Pasternak anticipated possible criticism of the novel:

> I have lost my artistic coherence and let myself inwardly sag, like a bowstring or violin string that has gone slack – I have written this novel in an unprofessional way, without a consciously sustained creative aim in my sights; in a homespun way – in the bad sense. with a dullness and a naïveté for which I gave myself both permission and indulgence . . . But I could not do otherwise. It would have been even worse had I, in circumstances of a natural renunciation of literature, without any prospects of ever returning to it, and while solely engaged on translation work, continued as before to "serve the muses", write for the purpose of getting into print and so forth, faithful to my calling and inspired by my mastery of it.
>
> . . . In the public plane this solitude is a fact of destiny and immutable, it is prejudicial and lamentable. But inwardly, I have nothing for me to complain of. In terms of fullness and clarity of

life and preoccupation with the work I love, my life these last years has been one long spiritual holiday for me. I am more than content with it. I derive joy from it and the novel is the outcome and expression of my joy.

The hastiness and cursoriness in the narrative already noted by Ariadna Efron in 1948, grew much more marked in the final chapters. This feature exasperated Akhmatova, who was pleased only with certain of its "descriptions of nature" and called the novel as a whole a failure. She was not alone in her opinion.

The relationship between the narrative and the lyrical elements in prose was a lifelong preoccupation for Pasternak. He had complained to Bobrov back in 1916 that the "utter technicality of his 'The Mark of Apelles' excludes the possibility of a surge in the narration by diverting overmuch effort towards vertical satiety so leaving nothing for horizontal impetus."

His knowledge of musical composition prompted this comparison with the laws of symphonic music governing the relationship between the canto fermo of the melodic line and the continuum of the vertical harmony.

In *High Malady* he had been learning how to manipulate his lyrical material "from a distance" and had complained of his difficulty, as a lyric poet, with the epic narration in *Lieutenant Schmidt*, of how in his "pursuit of the elusive spirit" of his hero, he had been caught up in the lyrical details of his emotional stirrings. Now, in *Doctor Zhivago*, declining the bright colours appropriate to a time of peace, he was using a frugal graphic palette to sketch the years and fates "caught up in the frame of the revolution", the world "of a new restraint, a new severity and new ordeals". When interrupting *An Essay in Autobiography* at that point, Pasternak candidly admitted that he was not in a position to write about it in the vivid, arresting way used in the "portrayals of Petersburg by Gogol and Dostoyevsky".

His attempts to "write as if writing a letter – not in the modernistic way" had dogged him ever since his first 1918 novel about Luvers, and now he was not dismayed by the failure of "people in present-day arts" to understand his growing indifference to "the question of form in my work which is becoming more and more grounded in content alone, personal and eternal content, content not yet fully fermented, still new . . . still unassimilated."

"My whole life," he wrote in 1958 to the well-known musicologist, Petr Suvchinsky:

went on what is called modernism, on fragmentism, on responding to forms – political, aesthetic, universalist forms, and to
trends – left-wing or right-wing, or to disputes between trends.

In the meantime, life (meaning wars, the ascendancy of hare-
brained theories, the hecatombs of human lives, the advent of
new generations) – life pursued its own course, accumulated five
decades of evidence, mountains of new, undesignated material,
not all of which could be grouped under the old classification
(political, aesthetic, left-wing, right-wing and so on and so forth)
and a part of which – the most vital part – still defies classification,
as does a child's awareness. One has to pity those who cling to
their fidelity towards the useless deviousness of the old received
principles, to ideological competition and the behests of what
used to be regarded as novelty but has since been expended on
useless diversions, and fail to do homage to the simplicity and
infantile artlessness of the new, the newly-conceived message
of eternity. One needed to stop paying attention to routine,
established themes – themes of totally spurious significance; one
needed to give one's inner soul – with its conscience, its passion,
its loves and its hates – the right to make a long overdue about-
turn which would release it from its awkward, cramped confinement and give it space in which to breathe freely.

That, in effect, is the whole essence and meaning of *Doctor
Zhivago*.

22

At the height of his work on rewriting the last chapters of the novel
came news from Leningrad that Olga Freidenberg had fallen ill.
The contracts signed in July 1955 with the Maly Theatre for *Henry
IV Part I* and with the Arts Theatre for a translation of *Maria Stuart*
required immediate compliance. Pasternak rejected the idea of going
to Leningrad and on 7 July wrote to his cousin, M. A. Markova,
who was looking after the sick woman:

You must be astounded at my letters. It must seem that I am
without any feeling for Olga and her fate and that I am calmly
burying her while she is still alive. O, how mistaken you are!
But I have been giving such a lot of thought to my own end and

the end of all I love, and I have so long since been prepared for it all – what can we do about it? The only thing that we can do, taking everything into consideration in relation to the events that are dear to us and in response to this costly, foredoomed loss of life, is to pour out all our love into the creation and development of the living, into useful labour, into creative work.

The following day a telegram arrived with the news of Olga Freidenberg's death.

The pages of the epilogue written during those days are tinged with the bitterness of this loss and faith in the creative immortality of the spirit.

It has already happened several times in history. The idealistic, lofty conception has turned into a crude, materialistic reality. In this way Greece became Rome, Christianity the Vatican and Russian enlightenment Russian revolution. Take Blok's "We, the children of Russia's terrible years", and you immediately spot the difference in epoch. When Blok said it, it needed to be understood as a manner of speaking, figuratively. And the children were not children but sons, offspring, intelligentsia, and the terrors were not terrible but anticipatory, apocalyptic, and these are different things. But now the figurative has become the literal and the children are children and the terrors are terrible – that is where the difference lies.

These words convey his recollection of the generation of "boys and girls" of the 1910s who had grown up on Blok's works and to whom Pasternak dedicated his novel:

Those who heard my previous songs
will not hear the next.
The close circle has drifted apart.
That first approval has faded.
The voice of the outsider
carries no weight. Such praise
is frightening, while the old connoisseurs
are strewn right across the back of beyond.

Pasternak wrote:

Although the enlightenment and liberation which people had expected after the war had not materialized together with victory, as they had thought, all the same the tidings of freedom were in the air throughout those post-war years, constituting their sole historic content.

It had seemed to friends at the window, now grown old, that this freedom of the soul had come about; that that very evening the future had displayed itself in tangible form down below in the streets and that they themselves had entered into this future and were henceforth part of it.*

For want of time to check the manuscript as a whole, Pasternak handed it over for typing in mid-July and warned that it was not yet in its final form. Final corrections to the text were made at the end of 1955, immediately before the manuscript was handed over to *Novy Mir* and *Znamya*.

---

* *Doctor Zhivago*, "Epilogue", pp. 462–30.

IV

WHEN THE WEATHER CLEARS

(1956–60)

I

In the summer of 1955 Goslitizdat proposed to Pasternak to publish a small collection of his poems. Pasternak, who was busy on the novel, sought to put off the "realization of this proposal", as he wrote on 14 July 1955 to V. B. Sosinsky, "owing to a lack of time (and a paucity of desire)." Immersed in the "magic art" of prose writing, he tended to express himself at that time particularly sharply and pointedly on the subject of his "distaste for verse" both his own and others'.

"I do not care for 'verse in general' and I know nothing about what is usually called poetry," he wrote to M. G. Vainstein on 5 December 1955. "The world in which people love, appreciate, understand, relish and discuss poems, write the and read them" was diametrically opposed and remote from him:

"I am in sympathy with the Platonic concept of art," Pasternak wrote to Vyacheslav Vsevolodovich Ivanov on 1 July 1958:

(and the exclusion of artists from the ideal society and the notion that the majority should not trespass across the threshhold of poetry), with Tolstoyan intolerance of art and even, as a form of venting their vehemence, with the iconoclastic, barbaric ways of Pisarev* and his followers . . . Art is not prowess but shame and sin, almost forgivable in its perfect innocence, and it can be restored to its proper dignity only by the immensity of what is at times purchased by this shame. One must not think that art is

---

* Dmitry Ivanovich Pisarev (1840–68), a philosopher and revolutionary democrat who preached socialism through industrialization, was imprisoned for revolutionary propaganda.

in itself the source of that which is great. In itself it is an aspiration justifiable only in relation to the future.

Preparation of the book of selected poems began with the winter of 1956. The young Goslitizdat editor, Nikolay Bannikov, was appointed its compiler and Olga Ivinskaya took an active part in the work. Following Pasternak's directions, they located poems by him in old periodicals which had not been reissued in later collected editions. By way of introduction a piece which subsequently received the title *An Essay in Autobiography** was written for the book. On 4 August Pasternak informed M. K. Baranovich:

> This winter, after putting the final touches to the novel, my involvement in a book of selected poems and its preparation became my next concern. The emergence of an introductory essay is due to Bannikov, the compiler, who asked me for an article. In addition to that, he needed new poems for the last additional section of the book; they had to be written, and I had to turn my hand to them almost before I had finished the article. I am writing them without going into them too deeply, without straining over them as was the case long ago, before the revolution. I am totally without appreciation or feeling for their quality and I have already got quite a lot of them down on paper. A number of them will, I am promised, appear in the September issue of *Novy Mir* and of *Znamya*.

The introductory essay contained an expression of gratitude to Bannikov and ended with words which characterize the attitude of the author to the book:

> . . . quite recently I have completed my main and most important work, the only one of which I am not ashamed and for which I answer without a qualm – a novel in prose with additions in verse, *Doctor Zhivago*. The poems assembled in this book, which are scattered across all the years of my life, constitute preparatory stages to the novel. Indeed, I view their republication as a preparation for the novel.†

In May 1956 a broadcast in Italian was put out by Moscow Radio about the forthcoming publication of a novel by Pasternak, *Doctor*

---

* An earlier title was "People and Circumstances" (Lyudi i Polozheniya).
† *An Essay in Autobiography*, pp. 61–2.

Zhivago. Shortly afterwards a representative* of the Foreign Commission of the Union of Writers brought S. d'Angelo, a member of the Italian Communist Party and employee of Radio Italia based in Moscow, to visit Pasternak at the latter's dacha in Peredelkino. Pasternak was working on the vegetable plot, and they went to sit in the garden and had a talk.

The manuscript of the novel was handed over to d'Angelo in the atmosphere of an official visit, for him to study.

What had seemed unimaginable only a year before, now, after the Twentieth Congress which had lightened the stifling atmosphere with an injection of fresh air, became a reality. The resuscitation of publishing activity was marked by new initiatives. A writers' "cooperative" volume entitled *Literary Moscow* was compiled, the editors of which wanted to show new Soviet literature to the best advantage. Pasternak offered them "Comments on Translations from Shakespeare".

Later on, when the 1956 poems had been written, the question came up for discussion of where to publish them – in *Znamya*, the *Literary Moscow* volume, or *Novy Mir*. In deciding between *Literary Moscow* and *Novy Mir*, Pasternak gave his preference to the latter – the position of the "new", "independent" authors' publication seemed to him false and in no way distinct from the old "official" publications. His autobiographical essay, written as a preface to the Goslitizdat collection, was also switched, at the author's wish, from *Literary Moscow* to *Novy Mir*. Vsevolod Ivanov sought an agreement with Pasternak for the publication of the novel to be assigned to the projected writers' publishing house. He undertook to edit the text himself.

2

Twenty-one poems were written by the end of 1956. The original version of "It's vulgar to be famous" is dated 5 May. The poem represented the author's credo, and a handwritten entry by him in the book was headed "I believe". The intention set out here – "to

* It has not yet been possible to identify from other sources the name of the man from the Union of Soviet Writers (though it is doubtless available in the Union's files to which access is virtually impossible). The account in Ivinskaya's memoir is inaccurate on this point.

look ahead and rely for one's intake on what life itself provides" was based on the Gospel precept: "except a corn of wheat fall into the ground and die it abideth alone: but if it die it bringeth forth much fruit."*

The triumphant notes of a man who has fulfilled his mission are audible in the poem. Pasternak was renouncing his past in favour of the future.

> It's vulgar to be famous.
> That isn't what makes you great.
> No need to establish an archive
> or get in a flap over manuscript drafts. [. . .]
>
> You must work at your work,
> not dream of your destiny,
> which should be full of blanks,
> of chapters unachieved, places crossed out.

In his 1956 poems Pasternak again returned to the basic themes of his creative work: faithfulness to life as the highest principle; the artist's calling; nature quickened into vigour by man's fruitful activity. There were special genetic links tying these themes in with the "Peredelkino" cycle of 1941. The discovery made by Pasternak at that time of the special effectiveness "in poetry of direct, transparent speech unloaded with metaphor" has been put to successful and widespread use in the description of the much-loved and ever new pictures of life in the country on the outskirts of Moscow. Pasternak's landscape scenes of Peredelkino have become the leading figure in a book of poetry, a book which succeeds in communicating nature with the fidelity of detail of a portrait. In his last poems the Samarin pond, the meadow in front of the house, the village the other side of the stream, the gullies and the roads – all compete with the real thing in authenticity.

The partially surviving drafts of these poems show that they went through several stages of intensive working. The severity of selection is evident from the fact that interesting images and lines and entire rough versions were frequently left unused and ended up in the wastepaper basket. This primarily concerned Pasternak's poems written in direct reaction to public events which he always discarded as being casual verse, insufficiently profound and too lightweight, not qualifying as lyric poetry but as widely popular "stimulants". In this way his

* John XII. 14.

immediate response to Khrushchev's speech at the Twentieth Congress and to Fadeyev's suicide shortly afterwards ended up in the wastepaper basket. The poem has not survived in manuscript form. Olga Ivinskaya published it from memory. We came across a somewhat differently worded version of it:

> The cult of personality
> is clogged with dirt, forty years on,
> but the feral cult of conformity
> is still in demand.
>
> Even *Pravda* is unbearable:
> truth a group photograph
> of piggy faces. Every day.
> Still in demand, the cult
>
> of denunciation by philistines,
> so people shoot themselves
> because they're drunk,
> drunk because they cannot bear it.

It was during those months that Pasternak had the idea of writing a poem "to commemorate the dead and the murdered on the lines of a litany such as that used in the burial service". This idea was incorporated in his poem "The Soul":

> My sorrowful soul,
> mourning all my dear ones.
> You are the communal grave
> of all those life wore out.

Casting back in his mind to those democratic moral principles which governed the spiritual searches of a generation, Pasternak sharply condemned, in himself above all, the betrayal of the humanist ideals of youth. This was the theme of the poem "Change":

> Once I courted the poor,
> not for highfalutin principles,
> but because their lives
> were free from pomp and circumstance. [. . .]
>
> And I have been impoverished
> since corruption ate into the age
> and petit-bourgeois optimists were rooted out
> and grief became a badge of shame.

3

The manuscript copies of the novel sent to the monthly journals lay about there as so much dead weight. There was no reply either from *Znamya* or from *Novy Mir*.

The copy handed to d'Angelo had not been returned. He had immediately sent it on to the Milan Communist editor, Giacomo Feltrinelli, who shortly afterwards informed Pasternak that he wanted to publish the novel and was looking for a translator. After consulting his sons,* Pasternak replied to him on 30 June 1956 that he was glad that the novel would appear and be read and warned him:

> If its publication here, which has been promised by many of our journals, is held up and you pre-empt that event, the situation will be tragically difficult for me.

But, he added,

> thoughts come into being not for them to be hidden away and suppressed but for them to be voiced.

Through the Foreign Commission of the Union of Writers Pasternak offered *Doctor Zhivago* to a Czech publisher who had expressed a desire to print it. In response to a request from Emmanuil Kazakevich and Veniamin Kaverin, he had handed over the text of the novel for the second volume of the collection *Literary Moscow*. Anticipating the editorial board's objections, he wrote to Konstantin Paustovsky on 12 July 1956:

> You will all be deterred by the unacceptability of the novel, I think. Yet it is in fact only the unacceptable that needs printing. All that is acceptable has long since been written and published.

Pasternak understood what a large role literature was due to play in the spiritual development of society by its portrayal of a variety of characters and situations; by the conflicting points of view it offered; by the way it taught people to see and think. The debate over Vladimir Dudintsev's novel *Not By Bread Alone*, the attempts

---

* i.e. Evgeny and Aleksandr.

to raise the subjects of "lack of conflict", "the lacquering of reality", and the need for sincerity in Soviet literature were the first signs of an awakening of Soviet public thinking, to be abruptly cut short in the autumn of 1956.

In mid-September 1956 *Novy Mir* refused to publish the novel, backing up its verdict with a collective letter signed by five members of the journal's editorial board – Boris Agapov, Boris Lavrenev, Konstantin Fedin, Konstantin Simonov, and Aleksandr Krivitsky. Their critique noted the distortion in the novel of the role of the October Revolution and of that part of the Russian intelligentsia which had supported it. Tendentiously selected quotations were adduced to support this incorrect and superficial assertion.

The patent tendentiousness of the literary criteria of the 1940s and 1950s demanded from the author a clearly defined ideological position and a discriminatory didacticism, both of which were completely absent from Pasternak's novel. The artistic depth of its communication of reality and the portrayal direct from nature by an eyewitness and participant in the events under review combined to create a realistic picture of the misfortunes borne by the country during the First World War and the Civil War. Tolstoyan non-acceptance of violence and cruelty, which permeated his short story "Aerial Ways" and the poem *Lieutenant Schmidt*, found comprehensive embodiment in *Doctor Zhivago*.

According to Simonov's memoirs, it was he who wrote the basic text of the critique and his co-authors then made corrections and proposed addenda of their own. The draft contributed by Fedin made accusations against *Doctor Zhivago* of hypertrophic individualism and of "self-glorification of his own psychic persona". Fedin found backing for this proposition in Zhivago's remark concerning his friends:

> Dear friends, O how hopelessly commonplace you are and the circle you represent and the lustre and art of the names and authorities you admire. The only thing about you that is alive and burning bright is that you lived at the same time as I and knew me.

This part of the novel had evidently scandalized Fedin when he read it the first time, for the rebukes on the score of egotism and absence of concern for mankind had been voiced by him earlier on in spring 1956 at the Easter celebrations in Peredelkino. Irakly Andronnikov, who was among the guests in Pasternak's house, had proposed a toast in honour of the new leadership, hinting at Fedin's recent appointment as First Secretary of the Moscow Writers' organization. Stung by this formula, Fedin, in his reply, contrasted the writers who sacrifice their talents for the good of others with those who choose to cultivate them egotistically, shunning society and its needs and transferring the burden to the shoulders of others. The insinuation was too obvious and I got to my feet wanting to disabuse Fedin and ask what a writer's talent was for and what was expected of him, but my father broke in on my observations with a pre-emptory gesture and changed the subject of the conversation.

Novy Mir's in-house editorial critique, written from the position of the received truths of the 1940s in support of Dudorov and Gordon* who idealized, to use Pasternak's words, "their own captivity", determined the fate of *Doctor Zhivago* for thirty years to come. But at that time, in the autumn of 1956, Pasternak, after learning what it said, tried as soon as possible to forget it and told no one of it. Rumours circulated among writers about the critique and so alarmed Anna Akhmatova that on 15 September she tele-phoned Pasternak to come and see her; and he confirmed it all. Fedin was bidden to Sunday lunch on 23 February as if there were nothing up, but the message from Pasternak contained a request not to speak in the house about the editorial board's missive.

4

Work on the collection of poems was going ahead at full steam. The 1936 cycle "From My Summer Notebooks", which had come out in a shortened form in 1943, now included poems dedicated to Paolo Yashvili and Titsian Tabidze. It also contained "In Memory of Marina Tsvetayeva", all of the wartime poems, and some of those from the novel. Eighteen of the poems composed in 1956 rounded it off, by way of "protecting one's rear", as Pasternak put it to Simon Chikovani.

The poems selected from his earlier books were the descriptive, pictorial ones, those more readily intelligible to the changed reader of the 1950s, grown unaccustomed to poetic language. The weeding out was very strict: long poems were shortened, difficult images and metaphors eliminated and individual stanzas completely rewrit-

---

* Characters in *Doctor Zhivago*.

ten. The easy-going attitude towards biographical detail and lacunae and to the deletion of entire chapters of one's life formulated in the poem "It's vulgar to be famous" was reflected in the work done on this collection.

In the summer Pasternak received a letter from an Italian Slavist in Rome, A. M. Rippelino, who was preparing a collected edition of his poems in translation. Pasternak explained the unintelligible phrases and images of his earlier poems and at the same time made appropriate alterations to the text. The manuscript had already been sent off to the printers and some of the new versions were simply dictated over the telephone and left to the discretion and abilities of the compiler. One must give Bannikov, who had opposed changes to things which had long become classics, his due. Many of the versions rejected by him remained only in manuscript and were not included in the final text.

The September issue of *Znamya* contained a selection of eight poems from the new cycle. *Den Poezii** published "Dawn" and "A Winter's Night". The poem "Bread" appeared in *Novy Mir* (No. 10, 1956). It was proposed to print *An Essay in Autobiography* and four fragments about Blok in issue No. 12, but at the last minute the material was removed from the issue.

Autumn 1956 was marked for Pasternak by excursions into the realm of the theatre. Ruben Simonov put on *Romeo and Juliet* at the Vakhtangov Theatre. Andrey Voznesensky recalls Pasternak inviting him to the premiere. Yury Lyubimov played Romeo and Tselikovskaya Juliet.

The Arts Theatre started rehearsals of the play he had translated a year previously, Schiller's *Maria Stuart*. Pasternak wrote to Nina Tabidze how moved he became at "the sight of the evening city" when arriving to attend rehearsals from the snowbound fields of Peredelkino. He called his first draft of a new poem: "On God and the City".

> We know God only in translation
> from originals restricted to the few.
> And yet we know Him face to face
> in city streets these winter months.

* *Poetry Day* – a yearly collection of Soviet poetry, published by Sovetsky Pisatel Publishing House, starting in 1956, on the initiative of Vladimir Lugovskoy.

November numbs us. Birdless skies
filled with factory smoke. Winter comes
with the Presentation of the Blessed Virgin,
comes and leaves the roofs immaculate. [. . .]

Like the entrance to the tomb, the city
ceases. To the throng in a sidestreet,
God attends. The season of theatre starts
with the storm's controversial premiere.

From surviving jottings and manuscript drafts one can see how
Pasternak's design for a "winter poem" in which he, as always,
wanted to combine all his impressions from these journeys, fell
apart into separate aspects of the theme and re-emerged as different
subjects. The prolonged period of gestation of this design is
ironically brought out in his poem "After the Interval", dated 17
February 1957:

Three months ago,
when the first blizzards flocked
and fell in a frenzy
on our unguarded garden,

I could already sense
in the thick flying snow
a poem about winter tingle
and melt at the back of my brain.

Four days later, on 21 February, the poem "It is snowing" was
written. It represents the endeavour to convey the never-ending
movement of falling snow.

The design behind the "Poem about Winter" acquired a new,
additional thrust from certain events at the end of February.

The Arts Theatre was organizing a formal celebration of Anas-
tasya Zuyeva's sixtieth birthday. To mark the occasion of his getting
to know her, Pasternak composed an impromptu rhyme and wrote
it at her request in her scrap book which was in the form of a
telephone book:

To an actress of great repute,
a respectful, sincere salute,
in this book that remembers
friends' telephone numbers.
Our dacha's leafy drive is dense

223

but, as Mount Athos monks
live celibate in silence,
we've renounced locals and trunks.
Our telephone stays in Moscow
where our faces seldom show.
But just in case – it's V
One Seven Seven Five Three.

Below the rhyme is an entry:

> But this is all nonsense. But how your artiste's sacred fire,
> your Divine spark mingles with the lights of the street, the
> street lamps, the footlights in the theatre and the evening
> glow into one twinkling chiaroscuro of the city at night, of
> warmth and light, artistic tension and mystery! That is what
> happiness is about and no other is needed. Yours, B.P.

Pasternak was invited to attend the evening's ceremonies in the
Arts Theatre. He did not turn up but sent a poem dated 22 February:

I'm sorry that I can't be there myself,
but in my thoughts I'll be
a spirit at your jubilee,
the presence in Row H seat 12.

Two days later came the birthday celebrations of Vsevolod Ivanov
and Konstantin Fedin which were traditionally arranged jointly.
Tamara Ivanova has described the evening of 24 February 1957 in
her book *My Contemporaries As I Have Known Them*. Pasternak pronounced rhyming toasts in honour of those around the table, addressing himself in impromptu verse to each one in turn. Tamara Ivanova
wrote them down at the time and has reproduced them in her book.
Pasternak's direct impression of the evening was captured in the
following verses:

Chains on the chandelier glister,
the table is crowded with wine.
Uncles, brothers, nieces, sisters,
proclaim a name day, drink and dine.

Baskets of flowers: counterclaims
of cyclamen and lilac.
Pictures leaning from their frames.

In this way the design for "Poem About Winter" acquired a new motif which was given the title of "Bacchanalia".

While participating in the general merriment on an equal footing with all, Pasternak noted with his artist's eye the features connecting this celebration in his mind with the ancient pagan rites in honour of Dionysus "the god of winter fertility", as Pasternak called him in his student exercise books. At one time he had been deeply interested in the Dionysiac cult; the sensuality of the orgies of the cult "spills over into culture", into tragedy and becomes part of immortality.

His sideways glance at his merry-making friends was inspired by the emotional estrangement which he had been unable to conquer since the *Novy Mir* critique. Although Pasternak was at pains to conceal how hurt he had been, Fedin, as before, came visiting and they saw in the New Year together; the bitterness at the loss of a close friend of many years' standing against one's wishes broke through in Pasternak's half-worked jottings:

> Friends, intimates, dear dross,
> you've acquired the taste of the day,
> a gain that will count as a loss
> when I've said what I have to say.
>
> Perhaps it is God's will
> and the reward for all your sins,
> this task of eating swill
> from government garbage bins?

5

A contract for the publication of *Doctor Zhivago* was signed with Goslitizdat on 7 January 1957. A. V. Starostin was appointed its editor and he together with the chief editor of the publishing house, A. I. Puzikov, made the journey to Peredelkino to settle the dates and agree on the text. Pasternak gave his agreement to certain cuts. In February 1957 the publishing house approached Feltrinelli with the request that he put off publication of the novel until September when the book would come out in Moscow.

At the Moscow Arts Theatre rehearsals were going on for *Maria Stuart*.

"On 12 March", Pasternak wrote to Alla Tarasova:

> I was setting out from the dacha to go into town for one of the last preparatory rehearsals before the general rehearsal. I had already seen you in a number of extracts and I had a fairly good idea of what a total revelation your Stuart would be . . . And, suddenly, having taken one step down from the cottage porch, I yelled out in unbearable pain from the very knee which I had expected to bow before you in the near future; and the next step I was no longer in a position to take.

His sudden handicap, hospitalization and then a stay in the sanatorium, interrupted work on the book of poems. The last poem before his setback, "After The Blizzard", was written on 7 March and it was not until 5 August that Pasternak sent Tarasova the finally polished version of "Bacchanalia". A letter accompanied the poem:

> Although I have lately been feeling better and have a lot of time at my disposal in the sanatorium, I have done nothing in the course of those four months as I do not believe in there being any substance or authority in what an invalid or anyone considered an invalid may write, and I have not permitted myself to write. But now I want to resume my interrupted activity and I shall not be able to progress a single step until I have done duty to my latest impressions received on the borderline between health and sickness. My intervening impressions on that particular dividing line were the preparation of *Maria Stuart* in the theatre and two wintertime evening family celebrations in town (both winter and summer I live in our country dacha) at the end of February. I had the urge to pull together these variegated and highly diversified elements into one whole and to write about it there and then in a single composition covering the entire theme. I visualized it as coming under the rubric of bacchanalia in the antique sense, in other words in the form of licence and revelry of the sort that may be considered sacred and which formed the basis for Greek tragedy and lyric poetry, and the best part as well as a major – and the best – element in Greek culture in general.
>
> I am sending you my "Bacchanalia" for, as you will yourself see, one part of it is indirectly connected with you. But, please, do not apply any measure of exactitude either to the portrayal of the artiste or to the understanding of the image of Maria Stuart herself. There are no statements about individuals nor any resemblance to anyone

in this poem, although the artiste in the poem is, of course, you –
but in a free treatment of the sort which I would never allow myself
in speaking to you or in talking of you. If the thing as a whole
displeases you or you find it improper, do not be angry with me
and forgive me for having placed you in such a context.

When my father gave us his manuscript notebook to read he
explained that in "Bacchanalia" he had set himself the task of
conveying differing sources of light emerging from below: the faces
of the faithful illuminated by candles, the face of the actress in the
light of the footlights and the face which glows red with shame.

The lighting effects of the city at night time and of the lit
up theatre were already set out in Pasternak's entry in Zuyeva's
scrapbook. It gives an early indication of the contents of the future
"Bacchanalia".

The rays of light, lights, lamps and headlights blaze out from the
drafts of the poems:

> From under the arch of the gateway,
> a sudden sheaf of headlights. [. . .]

> The fan of headlights
> from various makes of car.
> Arches absent, roofs invisible,
> but pavements palpable with light.

The appearance of this "wintertime poem in summertime", as
Pasternak described it in a letter to Nina Tabidze on 21 August
1957, was preceded by verses devoted to his recent stay in the
Uzkoye sanatorium. Up to the revolution, it had been the property
of the Trubetskoy brothers, well-known professors of philosophy
and law. Pasternak had known from his highschool and university
days the philosopher's son, Nikolay Trubetskoy, who later became
a famous philologist. On a walk through the park Pasternak showed
us the windows of the room where Vladimir Solovyev had died.
His jottings on this period that still survive include:

> Even before the rise in the road,
> the park fence and the manor
> where the rest home is housed
> rise into sight.

> Such spacious grounds.
> You won't find anything like them.

The old sanatorium is spread
across the old Trubetskoy estate.

6

The collection *Poems, Lyric and Narrative* was due to come out in
the spring of 1957. But it was at that time that Anatoly Kotov, the
director of Goslitizdat, died while in Leningrad on business. In June
it became known that the collection was not going to be printed.
The printers kept the type intact for several years afterwards.
Publication of the novel was also halted. In answer to Goslitizdat's
enquiry, Feltrinelli confirmed in his letter of 10 June 1957 his
intention not to issue the novel until its appearance in Moscow in
September. He wrote of the splendid qualities of the novel as a
work of art not only from a publishing but also from a political
point of view and that for him, a Communist, the two were
inseparable. He wanted to settle the matter with the Soviet authorities without causing major trouble and assured Goslitizdat that he
had not the least intention of making an international scandal out
of this publication.

These assurances reassured no one.

"Here we had several very frightening days," Pasternak wrote
to Nina Tabidze on 21 August 1957:

Something had happened concerning me in spheres to which I
had no access . . .

Togliatti suggested that Feltrinelli return the manuscript and
renounce publication of the novel. The latter replied that he
would sooner leave the Party than break with me and in fact did
just that. There were several other complications unknown to
me which added to the commotion.

As always, O.V.* took the first blows. She was summoned to
the CC† and then to see Surkov. Then they laid on a secret
expanded session of the secretariat of the presidium of the USW‡
to deal with my affair, which I was due to attend but did not turn
up to; a "'37" type of meeting, with infuriated yelling about this

* Ivinskaya.
† CC = Central Committee.
‡ USW = Union of Soviet Writers.

228

being an unprecedented occurrence, and demands for retribution, also attended by O.V. and An.Vas. Starostin (who were not allowed to speak) who were appalled by the speeches and atmosphere, and at which Surkov read out aloud (with feeling and very well) entire chapters from the novel. The following day O.V. arranged for me to have a talk with Polikarpov in the C.C.. This is the letter I sent him via her still earlier on, that morning:

"People who are morally scrupulous are never happy with themselves; there are a lot of things they regret, a lot of things of which they repent. The only thing in my life for which I have no cause for repentance is the novel. I wrote what I think and to this day my thoughts remain the same. It may be a mistake not to have concealed it from others. I assure you I would have hidden it away had it been feebly written. But it proved to have more strength to it than I had dreamed possible – strength comes from on high, and thus its further fate was out of my hands. I shall not interfere in it. If the truth which is known to me has to be atoned for by suffering, that is nothing new and I am ready to accept any suffering."

P.* said that he regretted reading such a letter, and asked O.V. to tear it up in front of his eyes. Later on I spoke to P. and yesterday, the day after my speaking to him, I had a conversation with Surkov. There was no difficulty about talking to them. They spoke to me very seriously and sternly but politely and with great respect, completely ignoring the crux of the matter – my right to see and think as I deem fit; they did not challenge me on anything, but only asked that I help avert publication of the novel, i.e. hand over to Goslitizdat the negotiations with Feltrinelli and send off a request for the manuscript to be returned for further work to be done to it. I will do so, but in the first place they exaggerate the harmful potential of the novel's appearance in Europe. On the contrary, our friends there think that the printing of the first non-tendentious Russian patriotic work by an author living over here would contribute to a greater drawing together and would deepen mutual understanding . . . In the second place these sudden requests from me will exert not a pacifying influence but the opposite – suspicion of my acting under duress etc . . . Finally, in the third place, no requests or

* Polikarpov.

demands in the legal form which people here are now devising for them have any effect or legal force nor will they achieve anything . . . Over these last few days – as has happened before in such cases – I felt a happy, uplifting sense of inner peace and inner rectitude . . .*

It was indeed the case that Feltrinelli failed to react to Pasternak's telegram containing the request to return the manuscript and stop publication. The Italian translation had been completed. Before starting printing Feltrinelli had re-equipped the printing works with new machinery and he was not prepared to make concessions of any kind. As subsequent events were to show, he was a man of decisive action and an adventurous disposition. When he left the Communist Party, he proceeded to print Mao Tse Tung's *Selected Quotations*, went off to Bolivia to rescue Debray and Che Guevara, was found guilty of organizing the blowing-up of a cinema, went into hiding, subsidized terrorism, and was killed in mysterious circumstances.

In October 1957 Surkov travelled to Italy to try to prevail on the inflexible publisher to renounce publication. But it had no effect. On 15 November 1957, *Doctor Zhivago* came out in Italian.

A month later, on 16 December, Pasternak wrote to Elena Blaginina:

They say the novel has come out in Italian, and will soon come out in English, and then in Swedish, Norwegian, French and German, all within the space of a year. I do not know whether you know that about a year ago Goslitizdat signed a contract with me for the publication of the book; and had it in fact issued it in a shortened and censored form, half the inconvenience and embarrassment would not have occurred. But even now, when, by exaggerating the significance of the awkwardness that has occurred, people thereby contribute to the commotion being stirred up over this affair in various parts of the world – even now the issuing of the novel in an openly censored form would have a calming and soothing effect on the whole business. In the same way Tolstoy's *Resurrection* and many other of our books published here and abroad before the Revolution came out in two sharply different forms; and no one saw anything to be ashamed

* From the private papers of Lydia Chukovskaya, published in *Novoye Vremya*, No. 29, p. 29, 1987.

of and everyone slept peacefully in their beds, and the floor did
not give way under them.

7

As the process of putting the final touches to the poems progressed,
they were written out into a specially-bound album which was given
the name of *When the Weather Clears*. The cover bore an epigraph from
Marcel Proust's last prose work, *Time Regained*. Pasternak had read a
number of books in the Proust series in the 1920s. A copy of the 1925
edition of the first volume *Swann's Way*, with an extract from a letter
from Rilke about Proust's death inscribed on the flyleaf in Pasternak's
writing, has survived from that time. He recalled later having been
unable to read *Remembrance of Times Past* without setting it aside as it
was "too close" to him. Only after finishing his work on *Doctor
Zhivago* was he able to permit himself to read Proust with due attention, with the aim of understanding what "time past" and "time
regained" meant to him. He would say to us that for Proust the past
is always part of the present and exists within it, in the images and
thoughts of people now living – as their memories.

The same attitude to the past constitutes the essence and meaning
of the book *When the Weather Clears*.

The epigraph from Proust refers to the book as an old graveyard
with half-erased inscriptions of forgotten names, so relating it to a
life "apparently meagre in content but significant in terms of losses
endured". In this context the image of "my soul the burial vault"
acquires special significance.

The scenes and themes of the book are irradiated by the light and
experience of the past, by the feeling of the nearness of the end, of
duty accomplished, and of dignified awareness of being master of
one's fate. Pasternak wanted to identify and single out from within
the present life-giving moments of the immediate future in so far as,
in his opinion, the present correctly understood is itself the future.

After recuperating from a recurrence of his ill health, Pasternak
wrote to M. K. Baranovich on 3 May 1958:

> Dear Marina Kazimirovna, I am so at fault! But do not be offended
> with me. I have only just started getting back on to my feet.
> There is no point in wasting words on ill health but you can

measure the appalling havoc caused by these illnesses, hospitals, and months torn out of one's life, each time they recur anew, without hope that this will sometime have a happy outcome.

I now want and need to get a lot done. Everything is now conducing towards it and making it incumbent on me! . . . I must gather strength for a great new prose work; in addition, I must make an early opportunity to write something like an article on the place of art in eternity's design for living, maybe in French for the French edition, in the form of a preface. But instead my burgeoning thoughts start off, as always, with poems. They too need to be written along profound, important thematic lines. Yet all around is mud, spring, empty woods, birds twittering away without response, and it is this that gets into your mind, putting off more valid intentions, taking up space to no good purpose and wasting your time. And I have nothing to send you other than the two I enclose and you will again be right, as always, in not liking them on sight, since these "birdies" are unforgivably banal and feeble. I send a kiss.

Yours, B.P.

The letter was accompanied by two poems of March 1958, "Beyond the Turning" and "Fulfilment", in which the life-affirming theme of a realistically tangible, regained future rings out distinctly. Many first drafts, and pages of workings, initially remote indeed in spirit from the final versions, have survived. They are infused with the anxiety aroused by the tragic ambivalence of his position: on the one hand, the publication of the novel abroad and the growing interest in it in the world as a whole, and on the other, the destruction of the type for printing his collection of poetry and the refusal to publish the novel with Goslitizdat. In the partly finished verses of his poems Pasternak gradually moves from emotional invective to total refusal to judge anyone whatsoever, to the theme of the future and belief in it.

These verses invest the book's title – *When the Weather Clears* – with significance: the thoughts of death being nigh are not at variance with the orientation towards the future, they evoke the feeling of joyful intimacy with eternity.

> And I won't stand there
> and be insulted. However lame,
> I'll take to the road,
> taking the future like a torch. [. . .]
> When I have carried
> unhappiness with honour,

a different time will shine
like a light in the forest.

I'll remember how, long ago,
a way was started here
towards that goal where,
distantly, a torch now alters shape.

I'll know my own house
by a series of signs:
upstairs, second from the end,
my study door.

Here's the way down, the treads,
and the way up, the banisters,
where I hid so many thoughts
all through that pedestrian time.

Gradually the early versions came to revolve around the image of
the little bird guarding "the gates of the forest" with its song. The
danger which lies in wait for it from all quarters links it to that other
bird which Pasternak had unintentionally winged in the Urals in
1916. In his article "Some Propositions" he had presented the image
of "the capercailzie engrossed in its mating call, deaf and oblivious to
all around it" as the symbol of the defencelessness of literature. He
would tell us how hunters used to kill these birds, who saw nothing
and heard nothing in their state of ecstasy, pointblank at a distance of
two paces. "Powerful hunter, accurate shot" was seen by Pasternak
in 1928 as a poetic analogy for violent death.

Let me escape a commonplace death.
Let darkness adorn me in willow and ice.
Let morning flush me out of the reeds.
Take aim. It's all over. Fire as I fly.

His desire to keep things inviolable, "to refrain from distorting life's
voice, resonant within us" found reflection in many early drafts of
his poems of spring 1958 which were later given the titles "High
Audibility", "Readiness", "The Future", "Beyond the Turning"
and "Fulfilment":

The rules of any epoch
can be disobeyed.
Life and all its mysteries
are like this breath . . .

In order to breathe,
to be rid of this weight,
I won't break a single rule
but every rule there is.

Of the numerous sketches, outlining the depth and seriousness of the theme, two poems which were included in the book and dated March 1958 gradually came to stand out.

On 11 June 1958 Pasternak wrote to Nina Tabidze:

I feel fine, my leg is giving me much less pain but still aches whenever I start sitting down . . . But my general state of health is very good and this is no time to be idling; one must profit from one's health and freedom and get something done . . . O.V., Bannikov and many others think I should now write poems in my former style, that from before my illness took over. I have done some writing but I am not only unsure that their judgement is right but convinced of the reverse. I think that despite the familiarity of everything that continues to confront us and of which we continue to hear and read, it has all ceased to be, it has passed by and has had its day; a vast period which cost unprecedented effort has come to an end and is now behind us. Space has now been made to admit what is new, what has not happened before – an immeasurably large, as yet unoccupied space, making room for the divination of the independent, fresh workings of genius, for the intervention in and contribution to our life of new quantities and new days . . . This difficulty exists for me too. *Zhivago* is a very important step, is a great joy and good fortune, of the like of which I had not dreamed. But it is accomplished and this book, together with the period of which it is the expression more than anything written by others – this book and its author are receding into the past. In front of me – whilst I am still alive – a space is becoming vacant, the non-utilization and virginity of which has first to be made to yield up its meaning and then be reinfused with this meaning. And whence am I to derive the strength for this? To substitute old trivia for this, the one essential thing, would be shortsighted and purposeless. Thus my re-emergent poetry writing does not please me, and all that I am sending you is pretty feeble. In all probability, if it came to that, what is now needed is a more sharply differentiated, new mode of poetry characterized by a single, markedly distinct and new criterion.

The thoughts expressed in this letter were reflected in the poem "After the Thunder", dated July 1958:

> Imperceptibly, without a struggle,
> leaving the foundations intact,
> a site has been cleared in the century
> for fresh feelings, subjects, words.

It was at this time that Pasternak felt a strong urge to do new major work. He again experienced the wish to try his hand at drama, to write a play.

8

Lars Gillensten, the Nobel Committee secretary, maintains that Pasternak was put forward for the Nobel Prize each year from 1946 to 1950, in 1953 and in 1957. The 1957 Nobel Prize laureate, Albert Camus, devoted a great deal of attention to Pasternak in his award speech and again nominated him for the prize the following year, the eighth time in all. The prize was awarded on 23 October 1958 with the citation: "For outstanding achievements in contemporary lyric poetry and in the traditional field of great, Russian prose."

On receiving notification, Pasternak thanked the Nobel Committee, in the supposition that the award to a Soviet writer would be a source of pride for his native country and its literature. His numerous previous nominations were a basis for considering that the prize was not connected with the publication of the novel. However the USA Secretary of State, John Foster Dulles, stated in a speech made shortly afterwards that the Nobel Prize had been awarded to the Soviet citizen Boris Pasternak for the novel *Doctor Zhivago*, condemned and not printed in the Soviet Union. This was reported in those very same terms to Nikita Khrushchev.

Zinaida Nikolayevna was busy with preparations to receive guests when Fedin arrived and walked through into Pasternak's study. After Fedin's departure she rushed upstairs and found her husband had fainted away on the settee. Fedin had come to try and persuade him to renounce the prize, failing which a public campaign against him would start the following day. Korney Chukovsky and his granddaughter later came to offer congratulations. The Ivanovs had called the previous evening.

On 25 October, *Literaturnaya Gazeta* reproduced *Novy Mir*'s critique which had served as the journal's reason for refusing to publish the novel in the Soviet Union at the appropriate time. An expanded meeting of the Secretariat of the Union of Soviet Writers expelled Pasternak from membership on 27 October. Pasternak did not read the newspapers: they were full of invective and crude misquotations. The signatories openly acknowledged their ignorance of the novel but confidently abused the book and its author. Much alarmed, we went to see him. He was in good spirits, master of himself, joking, and one sensed an inner uplifting of spirit. Just before this he had started to translate a play by Juliusz Slowacki – the third "Mary Stuart" in his life.* Goslitizdat had been forbidden to sign any new contracts with him or reissue anything at all from his old works. But the Poles had managed to obtain the possibility of giving Pasternak this translation on the basis of refusing to have anyone else do it. In those fearful days at the end of October he did not allow himself to give up work.

He did not go to Moscow till the fifth day, 27 October. He sensed that he would be unable to stand up to the inquisition in store for him, and gave up the idea of attending the meeting of the Secretariat, to which he had been summoned, and sent a letter instead. It contained twenty-two points in which he briefly set out his attitude to the misunderstanding that had taken place, explained the reasons for his actions, and signified his acceptance of the censored edition and of the criticism. He considered the award of the Nobel Prize a high honour for himself and for Russian literature and was ready to donate the money to the Peace Fund. At the end of the letter he added that he did not expect justice and was prepared to be destroyed or exiled but asked them not to be in a hurry over it and to remember that later they would have to rehabilitate him. The letter ended with the words: "I forgive you in advance."

Before returning to Peredelkino, Pasternak looked in on us to tell us what had happened. We were then living near the Kiev Station.

The next day but one Academician Leontovich asked me to go with him to Peredelkino. That same day, 29 October, an article appeared in *Pravda* about the outstanding discoveries made by the Soviet physicists I. M. Frank, P. A. Cherenkov and I. E. Tamm, who had been given the Nobel Prize for Physics. The article, signed by six Academicians, contained a diffuse passage to the effect that

---

* The first *Mary Stuart* was a translation of Swinburne's *Chastelard*, done in the winter of 1916–17.

the award of the Nobel Prize for Physics was objectively grounded but that for Literature was based on political considerations. Leontovich considered it his duty to assure Pasternak that such was not the physicists' opinion and that the tendentious phrases had been inserted into the text against their will.

We met Pasternak in the street. My father was unrecognizable. Grey and dishevelled, he said that all this was now of no importance because he had that morning sent off a telegram to Sweden declining the prize.

In view of the meaning which the award made to me has acquired in the society to which I belong, I am obliged to decline it. Do not take my voluntary renunciation amiss.

On the way back I wanted to explain to Leontovich that my father's depression and confusion were completely unexpected to me, but he interrupted me to say how he admired his exalted spirit and the nobility of his actions.

The same day the Litfond polyclinic sent round a doctor with a pharmaceutical kit for rendering first aid. He was accommodated in the drawing room for a few days. Pasternak was having pain in his left arm, shoulder and shoulder blade. The doctor attributed this to over-exhaustion and asked him temporarily to stop working.

Three days later the General Meeting of Moscow Writers unanimously approved the decision of the Secretariat to expel Pasternak from membership of the Union of Writers and addressed a request to the Presidium of the Supreme Soviet for him to be deprived of citizenship and exiled abroad.

According to Ehrenburg, who had just returned from Sweden where, in an atmosphere of international uproar, he had handed over the Lenin Peace Prize to the Swedish writer, Lundkvist, a sudden, drastic change in the course of events came about when Nehru, who had agreed to head a public committee in defence of Pasternak, telephoned Khrushchev and stated his point of view. Tass guaranteed the inviolability of Pasternak's person and possessions and his unhindered right of passage to Sweden.

On the initiative of the Head of the Central Committee's Cultural Department, Dmitry Polikarpov, Pasternak signed agreed texts of messages to Khrushchev and *Pravda*.

"It is a very painful time for me," he wrote on 11 November 1958 to his cousin, M.A. Markova. "The best thing now would be for me to die, but I shall probably not lay hands on myself."

9

The ensuing dead silence and alarming uncertainty were even harder to bear. The completed translation of Slowacki's *Mary Stuart* was lying around idle in Goslitizdat. No money was being paid for it. Pasternak's translations were immediately excised from Shakespeare's Collected Works, contracts with him were torn up and theatrical performances cancelled. The only source of comfort was his mail which had grown sharply over the past year. Each day brought 20–50 letters. Unknown correspondents wrote to him exhorting him to keep up his spirits, to retain his health, magnanimity, purity of heart and clear conscience as an artist. Those who had managed to read the novel, handwritten and photo-copies of which were going the rounds, expressed their gratitude to him for its truthfulness and courage and their admiration of his bold struggle in support of the writer's right to express his opinion. During the ignoble campaign against him, they congratulated Pasternak on the award of the Nobel Prize and thanked him for remaining in his native country.

"The storms and anathema of local origin are nothing in comparison with the sympathy and support I receive from the world as a whole," he wrote on 12 December 1958 to L. A. Voskresenskaya.

Words of support, expressions of love and pride, alternated in other letters with requests for material help. The lies in the newspapers about the millions he had received drove the poor and needy to apply to him. But he now had nothing with which to help them, driven as he himself was to seek means of support for those close to him and to borrow money from his friends.

"Have I really done insufficient in this life not to have at seventy the possibility of feeding my family?" he asked.

The greater part of the correspondence was made up of letters from abroad. There were more frequent letters addressed to his sisters. Pasternak's previous pupil, Walter Phillip, wrote to him. He kept in touch with B. K. Zaitsev, F. A. Stepun, and P. P. Suvchinsky. Albert Camus became, as he wrote to Suvchinsky, a "cordial acquisition". He had direct and indirect tokens of the interest of Hemingway, Eliot, Steinbeck, René Char, Spender, Nehru, Thomas Merton and Aldous Huxley. He struck up new cordial friendships.

The four concluding poems for the book *When the Weather Clears* were completed in the last days of January 1959. Two of them are shot through with a profound bitterness, alien to Pasternak:

> There's a shortage of life,
> of what has been, of what will be.
> It should fill the room forever,
> an everlasting Christmas tree.

"Winter Holidays" – a favourite theme in Pasternak's poetry, but instead of customary joy and uplift of the spirit, it now bears a distinct imprint of dissatisfaction and exasperation. If in 1941 the Christmas tree was an excited actress to whom the author was addressing a declaration of love, now, in 1959:

> Its top like a chimney brush
> in a dirty ball, the fir tree
> flares out like a woman
> twirling layers of skirts.

"The house like a leaky hovel" shudders from the snores; dusk succeeds dusk, and the sun is a cripple and drunkard "with a fuzzy mug".

The poem "The Nobel Prize" reflected the fearful days of mid-January and his lonely winter walks. In one of his letters of that time he wrote that he felt as if he were living on the moon or in a fourth dimension. There were the conflicting elements of his universal fame and, at the same time, the odious notoriety of his name in his own country, his pennilessness and uncertainty in the future and the hundreds of incoming letters begging for financial help from those funds to which he could have no access. To all this was added Ivinskaya's insistence on the legalization of their relationship, while he was unable and unwilling to make any changes in things as they stood:

> Which way? I'm like an animal trapped.
> Somewhere: people, freedom, light.
> Behind me, the howls of the hunt,
> but the exit eludes me.
>
> What am I supposed to have done?
> Am I a murderer? A criminal?
> The whole world wept
> over my beautiful world.

Even so close to death,
I still believe that kinder times
will come and overcome
the angry power of spite.

Pasternak suffered constant pain and anguish at the pressure he had undergone and the concessions he had made: his renunciation of the Prize and his public statements. As he knew beforehand, it turned out to be a pointless sacrifice.

After the publication on 11 February 1959 in the *New Statesman* of his poem "The Nobel Prize" in an English translation, Pasternak was summoned to the Prosecutor General, R. A. Rudenko. He was charged, under Article 64, with treason to the Fatherland and threatened with arrest if he should meet foreigners. In view of the scheduled visit to Moscow of the British Prime Minister, Macmillan, Pasternak had to undertake to be absent from Peredelkino for the period of the British Prime Minister's stay.

On 20 February Pasternak and Zinaida Nikolayevna arrived in Tiflis by air. He found it difficult to depart from the routine he had set himself, from his correspondence, which demanded a lot of his time and from which he derived moral support. Nina Tabidze, with whom they stayed, did her best to create a familiar atmosphere of work and quiet in the house. He had brought Proust and Faulkner with him. He did a lot of walking round the town. Nina Tabidze's daughter, Nita, accompanied him. In the evening her young friends would visit them.

Pasternak found interest in Mtskheta and the role of that town in the history of the coming of Christianity to Georgia. He was told of the recent excavations and of the finding of the tomb of Serafita, a young girl whose remains had, by a miracle, retained a live impression of her beauty right up to the present day. Simon Chikovani dedicated a cycle of poems to her.

His acquaintanceship with the family of the artist, Lado Gudiashvili, continued and grew closer. Lado arranged a candle-lit evening in the museum-like surroundings of his house in Pasternak's honour. Pasternak inscribed his poem "After the Storm" into his host's scrapbook:

The artist's hand is more powerful still.
It washes all the dust and dirt away
so life, reality, the simple truth
come freshly coloured from his dye works.

A tender friendship grew up between Pasternak and the artist's pretty young daughter, Chukurtma. He tried to dispel her strange ways and sadness by talking to her and, after his departure, by sending her letters. ". . . If by the time I die," he wrote to her on 8 March 1959, "you have not forgotten me, and you still need me for something, remember that I have placed you in the front row of my best friends and given you the right to mourn me and think of me as someone very close to you." His getting to know her gave Pasternak the idea of writing a work devoted to archaeological excavations and to new life reviving after an intervening span of a thousand years.

They returned home on 6 March. Soon afterwards Pasternak wrote to Georgia asking more than once to be sent books on the period of the apostleship of Saint Nina and her disciple Sidoniya.

Pasternak was giving increasingly serious attention to the idea of a play, *The Blind Beauty*, about a serf actor, whose fate recalled that of Shchepkin or Mochalov.* The action was to cover three periods. A prologue related to that of harsh serfdom of Nicholas I, of Saltychikha†-type landowners, of Arakcheyev‡ and his despotic regime, of brigandage and peasant uprisings. The central part dealt with the preparations for the 1861 reforms, the clash of opinion and the tragically wrong solution of the question, and the liberation of the peasants. A third part was due to take place at the end of the century. The hero of the play, the talented actor, Petr Agafonov, becomes head of a famous theatre. He succeeds in finding a doctor to perform an operation on his mother, blind as the result of a tragic accident, and so gives her back her sight.

Work on the play assumed a regular character in the summer of 1959. The title came from a Symbolist reading of Gogol's *The Terrible Vengeance* and an interpretation by Andrey Bely, of "the image of the sleeping Katerina, whose soul had been stolen by a horrible sorcerer." "In the tremendous images of Katerina and the old sorcerer," wrote Bely, "Gogol gave immortal expression to the languish of the homeland – the Sleeping Beauty."

* Shchepkin, Mikhail Semenovich (1788–1863): Actor and major dramatic figure in early history of Russian theatre, who was, himself, a serf up to 1822. A forerunner of Nemirovich Danchenko. Mochalov, Pavel Stepanovich (1800–48): leading Moscow actor, specialized in tragic roles, who was also originally a serf. A member of the Maly theatre at the same time as Shchepkin.

† Saltykova, Darya (1730–1801): Landowner in the area south of Moscow, notorious for brutality to her serfs. Ended up in a monastery prison.

‡ Arakcheyev (1769–1834), General, Minister of War under Alexander the First, and from 1815–25 virtual ruler of Russia. Disciplinarian.

Blok, in the second chapter of his poem *Retribution*, depicts Russia as the Sleeping Beauty, bewitched by Pobedonostsev:*

> Holding her look with the unblinking look
> of a wizard, he made a magic circle
> round about Russia. It isn't that hard
> to get a pretty girl to drop off to sleep
> with clever talk of a fairy tale,
> so she began to get a little bit drowsy
> and lay on her hopes, her ideas, her passions.

On 17 October 1959 Pasternak wrote to Nina Tabidze:

> I have managed to get to love my work on the play and to believe in it. If I stay alive and there is no unforeseen interruption, it will be something no worse and no slighter than the novel . . .
>
> The play is a living future and, together with everything that branches out from it and is connected with it, is my sole passion and concern. The rest is of no interest at all to me, as if it were something that happened two hundred and fifty years ago.

Nikolay Lyubimov helped Pasternak to get translation work. The Iskusstvo Publishing House signed a contract for him to do Calderon's mystery play *The Constant Prince*. At first Calderon disappointed Pasternak and seemed colourless by comparison with Shakespeare, whose profundity and richness he accepted as a habitual norm. The first drafts were written in the summer. But as he gradually familiarized himself with the world of early Spanish Catholicism, Pasternak was amazed at the profundity and clarity of form he uncovered.

> I am furiously translating Calderon from morning to night, as I once did *Faust*. After so long a life and getting to know such diverse literatures of different epochs, I have found pleasure in happening upon an entirely unknown phenomenon, unlike any other. It is a world entirely of its own. Very highly elaborated, masterly and profound.

His extensive correspondence took up a great deal of time. He wanted to put into it all that he had left unsaid, that he had turned over in his mind and comprehended. He sent the basic outlines of his

---

* Pobedonostesev (1827–1907), a lawyer and extreme reactionary, who was influential under Aleksandr III.

unwritten article on *Faust* to the Faust Museum in Stuttgart. He wrote about Tagore to the Indian poet, Amia Chakravarti, through whom he conveyed his thanks to Nehru for the latter's crucial part in deciding his future. To France went a letter on the mission of modern poetry.

The English poet, Stephen Spender, published in the journal *Encounter* a number of articles by Edmund Wilson on allegories and symbolism in *Doctor Zhivago*. On learning indirectly that Pasternak was surprised by this interpretation, he asked him to write to the journal giving his views on art. To avoid unpleasantness Pasternak replied to him in a personal letter.

The journal *Magnum* asked him to complete a questionnaire containing the question "What is man?" In doing so, he was called on to formulate his attitude to Nietzsche. Drawing on his memories of his youthful impressions of Nietzsche and filling them out with some more reading, Pasternak "again came up against the old failure of understanding. His rejection of Christianity is itself taken from the New Testament. Only a dilettante, a thoroughgoing dilettante can be so blind! How did poor Søren Kierkegaard, a less well-read and well-educated person, succeed in grasping this?"

Behind the rhetorical props of hymns in praise of man and "the mysticism of superhuman morality", Pasternak discerns the void of spiritual emptiness and inhumanity. For him man is the hero of the performance which is called history or historical existence;

> Man is real and authentic when he is doing something, when he is an artisan, a peasant or a great, unforgettably great artist or scholar, arriving creatively at the truth.
> . . . Each person, each in his own right is unique and unrepeatable. Because the whole world is mirrored in his conscience . . .
> The Greeks knew this and it is recognized in the Old Testament. This is what is signified by the miracle of sacrifice of self, related in the New Testament.

The famous American conductor and composer, Leonard Bernstein, arrived in Moscow on a visit in early autumn. He and his wife made the journey to Peredelkino. Bernstein spoke of his concert the previous evening and of his wrangles with the Minister of Culture.

"How can you live with such Ministers?" he exclaimed.

"What are you saying?" replied Pasternak.

What have Ministers got to do with it? The Artist talks to God and the latter puts on various performances for his benefit so that he should have something to write about. It can be a farce, or, as in your case, a tragedy – which it is, is of secondary importance.

Bernstein was delighted at this way of putting the question.

The Hamburg Dramatic Theatre came to Moscow on tour in December 1959. On 12 December Pasternak was invited to their performance of *Faust* with Gründgens in the role of Mephistopheles. The photographs taken at the time show the meeting of the real biographical incarnations of these two heroes of Goethe's design.

Work on Pasternak's play went ahead with enthusiasm. Many studies on the history of the serf theatre and the reforms of the 1860s were read through and set aside. The principal figures started to come to life, to acquire their own characters. The figure of Prokhor, who had made the transition from serf to merchant and employer, acquired much importance. An interesting portrayal came into being of Sasha Vetkhopeshchernikov, a nihilist and future revolutionary-populist. One scene was based on Alexander Dumas' journey round Russia.

"Everything is well with me in both the visible and invisible parts of my life," wrote Pasternak to Chukurtma Gudiashvili on 15 January 1960.

The elements which comprise it have long since expanded beyond the point where folly, connections, chance, rumours or stupidity could affect or change anything. These factors threaten me no longer. My new work is now at the stage where the artist starts to get to love his new design and it seems to him that the slowly developing work is larger and more important than he, and that if it were a matter of choosing and making sacrifices, rather it should live than he. That was how it was previously, when everything was so clear. And so it is now, with this new work. But how slowly it moves! How far it still is to the finish! It will be a sort of fragment of nineteenth-century Russian history, covering some fifty years, in dramatic form. I am not even bothered about how far it will be scenically suitable or where and when it will be staged. What does now concern and sustain me is the hope that this will be a kind of succinct and concentrated creative certificate of authenticity or inner verisimilitude. I need no more than that.

In the winter he started to have constant back pain. He had to alternate between work and lying down. Pasternak was in a hurry to finish the first act so as to be able to read it to his friends. He cut down significantly on his correspondence: his last letter to Chukurtma Gudiashvili is dated 5 February 1960. It conveys notes of farewell and the understanding of the seriousness of what lies ahead.

> . . . some beneficent force has brought me up face to face with a world where there are no circles, no fidelity to youthful memories, no distaff points of view – a world of tranquil, unprejudged reality; with the world where, finally, you are weighed and tested for the first time, and – as if at the last judgement – appraised and measured and rejected, or retained; with a world for entry into which the artist has been preparing himself his life long, and into which he is born only after death; with the world of the post-mortal existence of the creative energy you expended and the performances you accomplished.

Soon after Easter, in the last week of April, Pasternak took to his bed. At first the doctors talked of rheumatism. He could no longer climb the staircase to his large room on the second floor and a bed was made up for him in the small ground-floor sitting room where the piano had stood.

We visited him on 2 May. He told us about the play which his brother, Aleksandr Leonidovich, had brought down to him from the room above. He had finished writing out the fair draft of the first act, was looking at some part of it and going on further with his drafting. He knew better than the doctors the seriousness of his illness.

The cardiogram showed a heart attack but it was the daily deterioration of his condition that was alarming. An ambulance was sent to take him off to hospital. He refused.

Litfond sent a doctor and a nurse who watched over the sick man. Pasternak bore his sufferings manfully and in full awareness of the end, endeavouring to console his family, the doctors and the nurses who had been looking after him. An x-ray was taken on 26 May and lung cancer diagnosed. The day before his death he complained to us of how worried he was by his knowledge of the insignificance of what he had accomplished and the ambivalence of world recognition, of which the corollary at that time was total anonymity at home and the wrecking of his relations with his friends.

He had defined his life as a one-man struggle against rampant and triumphant vulgarity in favour of man's free and active talent. "My whole life has gone into this," he said sorrowfully in conclusion.

In the closing hours of 30 May 1960 my father died.

Chronology

1890 Boris Leonidovich Pasternak born in Moscow, 10 February (29 January, old style).

1893 Birth of brother, Aleksandr Leonidovich.

1900 Birth of sister, Josephine Leonidovna.

1900 First meeting with Rilke.
First meeting with Tolstoy.

1901 Enters the Fifth Gymnasium in Moscow.

1902 Birth of sister, Lydia Leonidovna.

1903 First meeting with Scriabin.

1905 During 1905 Revolution is among student demonstrators and is whiplashed by a mounted cossack.

1906 Visits Berlin with his family.

1907 Joins the experimental literary and artistic circle, "Serdarda".

1908 Tutors Ida Vysotskaya.
Graduates from Gymnasium with Gold Medal.

1909 Enters Faculty of Law at Moscow University.
Scriabin gives him an audition.
Transfers to philosophy.

1910 Accompanies father to Tolstoy's deathbed.

1911 Participates in the futurist group, "Centrifuge".
Pasternaks move to new accommodation on Volkhonka Street.

1912 Studies philosophy under M. Cohen at Marburg.
Proposes to and is rejected by Ida Vysotskaya.
Visit to Italy.

1913 Graduates from Moscow University.
Takes post as a private tutor in the family of Moritz Philipp, a wealthy German businessman resident in Moscow.

1914 First meeting with Mayakovsky.
Publication of *A Twin in the Clouds*.
During summer, takes post as tutor at the country estate of the poet Baltrushaitis.

1915 Travelling in the Urals.

1916 Briefly takes management post in a chemical factory on the Kama river.

1917 Returns to Moscow.
Publication of *Above the Barriers*.

1918 Works as a foreign press screener in the Soviet Commissariat of Education.

1921 Leonid and Rosa Pasternak emigrate to Germany.

1922 Travels to Berlin and Marburg.
Marries Evgeniya Vladimirovna Lurye.
Publication of *My Sister, Life* and *The Childhood of Luvers*.

1923 Birth of his son, Evgeny Borisovich.
Publication of *Themes and Variations* in Berlin.

1924 Publication of fragments of *The High Malady*.

1925 Publication of *Aerial Ways* ("The Childhood of Luvers", "The Mark of Apelles", "Letters from Tula" and "Aerial Ways").

1926 Publication of long poem, *Lieutenant Schmidt*, in serial form.

1927 Publication of *Nineteen-Five*.

1928 Publication of *The High Malady* in *Novy Mir*.

1930 Pasternaks holiday with Asmuses and Neigauses in Irpen.

1931 First trip to Georgia in company with Zinaida Nikolayevna Neigaus.
Separation from wife (who goes to Germany on health cure).
Publication of novel in verse, *Spektorsky*, and autobiography, *Safe Conduct*.

1932 Publication of *Second Birth*.
Visit to Sverdlovsk region under the auspices of the Union of Soviet Writers.

1933 Second trip to Georgia.

1934 Marries Zinaida Neigaus (in a civil ceremony).
Trip to Georgia.
Publication of *A Tale* (*The Last Summer*) and translation of *The Snake Eater*.
Intervention on behalf of Osip Mandelstam, following latter's arrest, leads to phone call from Stalin.
At first Congress of Soviet Writers Pasternak is singled out for praise by Nikolay Bukharin, and makes a speech.

1935 Begins regular work as a translator with translation of Georgian poetry.
Obliged to attend anti-Fascist Paris Writers Conference;

meets Marina Tsvetayeva while in Paris; visits Anna Akhmatova in Leningrad on return to Russia.
Publication of translation of *Georgian Lyric Poetry*.

1936 Moves initially into Writers' Union apartment block on Lavrushinsky Lane and is also assigned a dacha in the Peredelkino writers' settlement; spends increasingly more time in the latter.
Important speech at Minsk conference of Soviet Writers on need for artistic independence of writers.

1937 Refusal to sign denunciation of Marshal Tukhachevsky.
Learns of Tabidze's arrest and Yashvili's suicide.

1938 Birth of his second son, Leonid Borisovich on night of 31 December/1 January 1938.
Execution of Bukharin, Pasternak's erstwhile champion.

1939 Nazi-Soviet non-aggression pact.
Tsvetayeva returns to the Soviet Union.
Pasternak's mother dies in Streatham Hill, London.

1940 Publication of *Selected Translations* (poetry).

1941 Soviet Union enters Second World War.
Evacuation to Chistopol in Urals in October.
Learns of Tsvetayeva's suicide.
Publication of translation of *Hamlet*.

1942 After return to Moscow rejoins family in Chistopol.

1943 Pasternak resettles in Moscow.
Visit to the Orel front with other writers.
Publication of *On Early Trains*.

1944 Publication of translations of *Romeo and Juliet* and *Antony and Cleopatra*.

1945 Publication of *Earth's Vastness* and translation of *Othello*.

1946 Beginning of Zhdanov era.
Criticized by Fadeyev, Secretary of the Union of Soviet Writers.
First meeting with Olga Ivinskaya in offices of *Novy Mir*.

1948 Publication of translation of *Henry IV*.
Reads seven of the *Doctor Zhivago* poems to actors in a Moscow theatre.
Death of Zhdanov.

1949 Publication of translation of *King Lear*.
Olga Ivinskaya arrested and held for a year in Lyubyanka Prison where she suffers a miscarriage; subsequently sentenced to five years in a Siberian labour camp.

1950 Pasternak suffers two successive heart attacks.

1951 Ivinskaya transferred from Lyubyanka to camp in Potma.

1952 Pasternak suffers from insomnia, and following fourth heart attack is hospitalized.

1953 Suffers further heart attack.
Death of Stalin.
Olga Ivinskaya released under amnesty.
Publication of translation of Goethe's *Faust*.

1954 Ten poems from *Doctor Zhivago* published in *Znamya*.

1955 Manuscript of *Doctor Zhivago* completed.

1956 Khrushchev's secret speech to the XXth Party Congress damning Stalin.
Feltrinelli's representative contacts Pasternak with a view to publication of *Doctor Zhivago* abroad.
Suicide of Fadeyev.
Novy Mir refuses *Doctor Zhivago*.
Pasternak falls ill and is taken to Kremlin clinic.

1957 One volume selected edition of Pasternak's poetry set in type; additional poems commissioned; *An Essay in Autobiography* written as an introduction to the volume.
Doctor Zhivago published in Italy.

1958 Publication of *Doctor Zhivago* in Britain and the USA and in most West European languages.
Awarded the Nobel Prize for Literature, accepts, but almost immediately compelled to renounce the prize.
Expelled from the Union of Soviet Writers and almost from the Soviet Union. Writes a letter to *Pravda* acknowledging his "mistakes".
Publication of translation of Schiller's *Maria Stuart*.

1959 Increasing political pressure. Health declines.
Last visit to Georgia (to keep him away from British Prime Minister, Macmillan).
Begins work on play, *Blind Beauty*.

1960 Following prolonged bout of illness (diagnosed as cancer) and a heart attack, Pasternak dies at Peredelkino, 30 May 1960.

Select Bibliography

POETRY

Fifty Poems, trans. Lydia Pasternak, Unwin Books, London, 1963.
Poems 1955–1959, trans. Michael Harari, Harvill Press, London, 1960, republished in paperback (together with *An Essay in Autobiography*) as *Poems 1955–1959 and An Essay in Autobiography* (introduction by Craig Raine), Collins Harvill, London, 1990.
Pasternak: Selected Poems, trans. Jon Stallworthy and Peter France, with a preface by Evgeny Pasternak, Allen Lane, Harmondsworth, 1983; Penguin, Harmondsworth, 1984.

FICTION

Doctor Zhivago, trans. Max Hayward and Manya Harari, Harvill Press, London, 1958, republished in paperback, Collins Harvill, 1988.
The Last Summer, trans. George Reavey, Peter Owen, London, 1959; revised translation, Penguin, Harmondsworth, 1960.
Zhenia's Childhood (i.e. "The Childhood of Luvers", with "Il Tratto di Apelle", "Letters from Tula" and "Aerial Routes"), trans. Alec Brown, Elek Books, London, 1958; Allison & Busby, London, 1982.
"Aerial Ways", "Letters from Tula" and "The Childhood of Luvers", trans. Robert Payne in *Safe Conduct: an autobiography and other writings*, ed. Robert Payne, New Directions, New York, 1949.
"Xhenia Luvers' Childhood", "Aerial Ways", "The Mark of Apelles", "Letters from Tula", trans. C. J. Barnes in *Boris Pasternak: Voices of Prose*, "Vol. 1. Early Prose and Autobiography", C. J. Barnes, Praeger, New York, 1977, and Polygon, Edinburgh, 1986.

PROSE

An Essay in Autobiography, trans. Manya Harari, Harvill Press, London, 1959; republished in a revised paperback edition with *Poems 1955–1959*, as *Poems 1955–1959 and An Essay in Autobiography* (introduction by Craig Raine), Collins Harvill, London, 1990.
Letters to Georgian Friends, trans. David Magarshack, Secker & Warburg, London, 1968; Penguin, Harmondsworth, 1971.
Safe Conduct: an autobiography and other writings, trans. Beatrice Scott, Robert Payne, C. M. Bowra, ed. Robert Payne, New Directions, New York, 1949.
Boris Pasternak: Voices of Prose, ed. C. J. Barnes, Praeger, New York, 1977, and Polygon, Edinburgh, 1986.

Letters Summer 1926: correspondence between Pasternak, Tsvetayeva, Rilke, trans. Margaret Wettlin and Walter Arndt, ed. Evgeny Pasternak, Elena Pasternak and Konstantin M. Azadovsky, Jonathan Cape, London, 1986, and Oxford University Press paperback, 1988.

DRAMA

The Blind Beauty, trans. Max Hayward and Manya Harari, Harvill Press, London, 1969.

BOOKS ABOUT BORIS PASTERNAK

Pasternak: Modern Judgements, ed. Donald Davie and Angela Livingstone, Macmillan, London, 1969.
Boris Pasternak: his Life and Art, Guy de Mallac, University of Oklahoma Press, 1981.
Boris Pasternak: a critical study, Henry Gifford, Cambridge University Press, 1977; paperback edition 1981.
Meetings with Pasternak, Alexander Gladkov, Collins Harvill, London, 1977, and Harcourt Brace Jovanovich, New York, 1977.
Nightingale Feaver: Russian Poets in Revolution, Ronald Hingley, Oxford University Press, Oxford, 1981.
Pasternak: a biography by Ronald Hingley, Weidenfeld & Nicolson, London, 1983; Unwin Paperbacks, London, 1985.
Pasternak's Correspondence with Olga Freidenberg, trans. Elliott Mossman, Secker & Warburg, London, 1982.
A Captive of Time, Olga Ivinskaya, Collins Harvill, London, 1978.

GENERAL

Conversations with Akhmatova: 1938–41, prose trans. Barry Rubin, poetry trans. Harry Willetts, Collins Harvill, London, 1990.
Hope Against Hope, Nadezhda Mandelstam, trans. Max Hayward, Harvill, London, 1971; republished in paperback, Collins Harvill, London, 1989.
Hope Abandoned, Nadezhda Mandelstam, trans. Max Hayward, Harvill, London, 1974; republished in paperback, Collins Harvill, London, 1989.
A Vanished Present, Aleksandr Pasternak, trans. Ann Pasternak Slater, Oxford University Press, 1984.
Memoirs, Leonid Pasternak, trans. J. Bradshaw, with an introduction by Josephine Pasternak, Quartet Books, London, 1987.

Select Index of Persons Mentioned in the Text

AGAPOV, BORIS NIKOLAYEVICH (1899–   ): poet and author. Twice winner of the Stalin Prize.

AKHMATOVA, ANNA ANDREYEVNA (pen name of ANNA ARKADYEVNA GORENKO) (1889–1966): great Russian poet, associated with Mandelstam, Pasternak and Tsvetayeva. She married Nikolay Gumilev, founder of Acmeism, in 1910 and divorced him in 1918. Her first book *Evening* appeared in 1912, but it was her second, *Rosary* (1914), that established her popularity. Three further collections, *White Flock* (1917), *Plantain* (1921) and *ADMCMXXI* (1923), appeared in the early years of the Revolution. In 1935 her son, Lev Gumilev, and second husband, Nikolay Punin, were arrested and then released almost immediately (see footnote on p. 73), but both were rearrested: Punin died in a camp in 1953; Lev Gumilev, after fighting for his country in the Second World War, was arrested for a third time in 1949, sent to a labour camp and only finally released in 1956. During this period, Akhmatova wrote "patriotic" verse in an effort to protect her son. However, apart from these enforced eulogies, between 1923 and 1940 (when wartime conditions allowed greater leniency towards writers and a severely censored selection, *From Six Books*, appeared), and between 1946 (when she was expelled from the Union of Soviet Writers following Zhdanov's denunciation) and 1965 (when a major new edition of her work, *The Flight of Time,* finally appeared) she was able to publish nothing in the Soviet Union at all. In 1965 she was permitted to travel to Oxford to receive an honorary D. Litt. She died in Leningrad the following year. Her two greatest works (*Requiem* (Munich, 1963) and *Poem without a Hero* (The Hague, 1973)) were published abroad.

ALEKSEYEV, MIKHAIL NIKOLAYEVICH (1918–   ): novelist and critic.

ANDRONIKOV, IRAKLY LUARSABOVICH (1908–   ): literary scholar of Georgian extraction, well known for his studies of Lermontov (and his impersonations of all and sundry).

ARDOV, VICTOR EFIMOVICH (1900–76): writer of humorous stories, film scenarios and satirical sketches for the variety stage.

ASEYEV, NIKOLAY ("KOLYA") NIKOLAYEVICH (1889–1963): poet of the same futurist group (formed in 1913) as Mayakovsky. He wrote an introductory article to Pasternak's first published collection, *A Twin in the Clouds* (1914). He published a collection of verse during the First World War and revolutionary verses during the Civil War. In 1923 he helped found the journal *LEF* and in 1926 published a notable poem on a revolutionary theme, *The Twenty-six* (i.e. the 26 Baku Commissars executed in 1918). Awarded a Stalin Prize for a poem in honour of Mayakovsky (1941), he wrote patriotic verses in 1941–45 and anti-American verses and songs after the war. After Stalin's death he helped some of the younger poets, but was very conformist in his public utterances.

ASMUS, VALENTIN FERDINANDOVICH (1894–1975): philosopher and logician who was a close friend of Pasternak.

AVERBAKH, LEOPOLD LEOPOLDOVICH (1903–39): Literary critic who was a militant proponent of the concept of "proletarian" literature, and one of the leaders of RAPP (see footnote on p. 10). As such, he was virtually dictator of Soviet literary affairs from about 1927 until his downfall in 1932, when Stalin abruptly changed the policy to acceptance of all writers, whatever their background, who were willing to accept the Party line without question. Averbakh disappeared during the purges, accused of being a Trotskyite.

AZARKH, RAISA MOISEYEVNA (1897–): prose-writer.

BAGRITSKY (DZYUBIN), EDUARD GEORGIEVICH (1895–1934): epic and lyric poet, translator of Burns, Rimbaud and others. After serving in the Red Army, he organized the first "proletarian" literary circle in Odessa, but moved to Moscow in 1925. He was a member of RAPP.

BANNIKOV, NIKOLAY VASILYEVICH (1914–): editor at Goslitizdat who encouraged Pasternak to prepare the ill-fated 1956 one volume edition of his poems (for which *An Essay in Autobiography* was commissioned as an introduction and many of the poems in "When the Weather Clears" were especially written). He contributed the afterword to a small volume of Pasternak's poems which appeared in 1966.

BARATASHVILI, NIKOLOZ (1817–45): outstanding Georgian lyrical poet, famous for his poem *My Steed (Merani)*.

BEBUTOV, G.V.: literary scholar and the editor of the last of Pasternak's books to come out while he was still alive, *Verses on Georgia. The Georgian Poets* (1958).

BELY, ANDREY (BORIS NIKOLAYEVICH BUGAYEV) (1880–1934): major Symbolist poet, novelist, and critic, and (after the Revolution) writer of important memoirs on literary and intellectual life in the first years of the century. His novels, notably *The Silver Dove* (1909) and *Petersburg* (1913) were a new departure in Russian prose and their experimental manner was influential in the early Soviet period.

BERIYA, LAVRENTY PAVLOVICH (1899–1953): Head of the Soviet secret police from 1938, in succession to Yezhov, a Mingrelian. Executed after Stalin's death in 1953. Accused of being a British spy.

BERGGOLTS, OLGA FEDOROVNA (1910–75): poet and prose-writer, known for her long poems on the siege of Leningrad.

BESPALOV, IVAN PETROVICH (1915–): Party official; Order of Lenin. Between 1952 and 1961 he was chief engineer of a plant in Kirov, of which region he later became First Party Secretary.

BEZYMENSKY, ALEKSANDR ILYICH (1898–1973): Soviet poet noted for his political conformism. He was a leading member of RAPP.

BLOK, ALEKSANDR ALEKSANDROVICH (1880–1921): leading Symbolist poet. His first volume of verse (1904) celebrated the semi-mystical "Beautiful Lady", partly inspired by Vladimir Solovyev's vision of Holy Sophia. In later verse Blok bitterly mocked his own romantic delusions, but in his great poem about the Revolution, *The Twelve* (1918), he reverted to his visionary manner. He died broken and disillusioned.

BOBROV, SERGEY PAVLOVICH (1889–1971): poet, critic, and translator (of Voltaire, Stendhal, Hugo, Shaw). He was for a time associated with Pasternak in the literary group "Centrifuge". After the Revolution he wrote several futuristic novels. His prose tale, *The Revolt of the Misanthropes* is, like Zamyatin's *We*, a horrifying vision of the collectivist future. He was also the author of popular books on mathematics for children.

BOKOV, VIKTOR FEDOROVICH (1914–): poet; interpreter of the "back to nature tendency" in the post-Second World War period.

BRIK, LILIA ("LILI") YURIEVNA (1892–): wife of Osip Maksimovich Brik (friend and associate of Mayakovsky) and sister of Elsa Triolet (wife of Louis Aragon) who was the inspiration for many of Mayakovsky's love poems.

BRYUSOV, VALERY YAKOVLEVICH (1873–1924): major poet, editor, translator (Poe, Goethe, Virgil, Maeterlinck) and theoretician of the Symbolist movement, who joined the Communist party in 1919 and published some 80 books in his life time. He introduced free verse into Russian poetry and was the first to use peasant dance tune rhythm (*Chastushki*).

BUGAYEVA, KLAVDIYA NIKOLAYEVNA: wife of Andrey Bely.

BUKHARIN, NIKOLAY IVANOVICH (1888–1938): old Bolshevik and member of the Politburo from 1919 to 1929, when he was defeated by Stalin over the issue of collectivization. He was editor of *Izvestia*, 1934–7. After his arrest in 1937 he was tried at the last great Moscow "show trial" in 1938 and sentenced to be shot. Bukharin, more cultivated and moderate than most of the Bolshevik leaders, took a genuine interest in poetry. At the end of the Twenties he helped Osip Mandelstam to get published, and in 1934 exercised his vestigial influence with Stalin to obtain a reprieve for him. At the first Congress of the Union of Soviet Writers he went out of his way to praise Pasternak.

BULGAKOV, MIKHAIL AFANASEVICH (1891–1940): outstanding novelist, short story writer and playwright, whose novel *The Master and Margarita* is one of the landmarks of Soviet prose.

CHAGIN, PETR IVANOVICH (1898–1967): editor and director of several Soviet publishing houses, including Goslitizdat.

CHIKOVANI, SIMON IVANOVICH (1902–66): Georgian poet, some of whose work was translated into Russian by Pasternak. Awarded the Stalin Prize in 1947 for glorifying the benefits of the revolution in Georgia.

CHUKOVSKAYA, LYDIA KORNEYEVNA (1907–): editor at Goslitizdat who worked on *From Six Books* with Anna Akhmatova and who became her friend and confidant. The daughter of Korney Chukovsky, she was also a friend of Pasternak. She is the author of two powerful novels, first published abroad, *Sofia Petrovna* and *Going Under*. Expelled from the Union of Soviet

Writers in 1974, she was prevailed on by them to accept reinstatement in 1989. One of the rare species: a resident indomitable. Her three volume memoir of Akhmatova is now being published in English (see bibliography).

CHUKOVSKY, KORNEY IVANOVICH (1882–1969): critic, popular author of children's books; quietly influential man of Russian letters; awarded a doctorate by Oxford University in 1962.

CHUKOVSKY, NIKOLAY ("KOLYA") KORNEYEVICH (1905–65): son of Korney Chukovsky and a novelist.

DOLMATOVSKY, EVGENY ARONOVICH (1915–): poet whose collection *Far Eastern Poems* (1937) alternates patriotic subjects with love lyrics.

DUDINTSEV, VLADIMIR DMITRYEVICH (1918–): novelist whose *Not by Bread Alone* provoked fierce controversy in 1956 because of its outspoken portrait of a Stalinist bureaucrat. It was passionately defended by Paustovsky at a closed meeting of the Union of Soviet Writers but, after the Hungarian uprising in November 1956, its opponents prevailed; it was, however, never banned, and in later years came to be accepted (by Khrushchev himself among others) as a legitimate critique of bureaucratic high-handedness under Stalin.

DURYLIN, SERGEY NIKOLAYEVICH (1877–1954): a poet and critic, who wrote under the pseudonyms S. Severny and S. Rayevsky. In 1916 he wrote a study on Lermontov from the standpoint of Andrey Bely's theories. His important later books included *Repin and Garshin* (1926), *From Gogol's Family Chronicle* (1928) and *About Tolstoy* (1928).

EFRON, ARIADNA SERGEYEVNA (1912–75): daughter of Marina Tsvetayeva and Sergey Efron. She was arrested in 1939, shortly after her mother's return to the USSR, and spent the next sixteen years in camps or in exile.

EFRON, SERGEY YAKOVLEVICH (1893–1940?): Marina Tsvetayeva's husband, whom she married in 1912. He came from a Jewish family well known for its publication of the Brockhaus-Efron encyclopaedia. He served in the White Army and emigrated to Prague, then to Paris. Forced to flee France in 1937 as a suspected Soviet agent, he was arrested in Moscow in late 1939, and died or was executed in prison.

EHRENBURG, ILYA GRIGORYEVICH (1891–1967): novelist and journalist of prolific output; originally hostile to the Bolshevik regime, he became a fervent propagandist for it in later decades, but after Stalin's death he played an important part in the "liberal" movement, first by his novel *The Thaw* (1954), which involved him in heated polemics with several Soviet writers, especially Konstantin Simonov, and then in his memoirs, *People, Years, Life* (1960–65). Despite censorship cuts, these gave a franker account of the fate of the intelligentsia under Stalin than had ever before appeared in print.

ELSBERG, YAKOV EFIMOVICH (one of pen names of Ya. E. SHAPIRSHTEIN) (1901–76): Soviet literary figure, once secretary to Lev Kamenev, the Old Bolshevik purged by Stalin. He was widely believed to have been a secret police informer who was responsible for the arrest and exile of a number of fellow writers under Stalin (see Nadezhda Mandelstam, *Hope Abandoned*, p. 572).

ESENIN, SERGEY ALEXANDROVICH (1895–1925): popular lyric poet of peasant origin noted for his lyrical descriptions of the Russian countryside. He married Isadora Duncan in 1922 and travelled to Western Europe and to America with her. In the Twenties his popularity was rivalled only by that of Mayakovsky. After his initial acceptance of the October Revolution, he became disillusioned and came under increasing attack for his riotous behaviour. In 1925 he hanged himself in a Leningrad hotel.

EVDOKIMOV, IVAN VASILIYEVICH (1887–1941): a late starter, his first novel *The Bells* (1926) was effectively his last.

FADEYEV (pen name BULYGA), ALEKSANDR ALEKSANDROVICH (1901–56): Soviet novelist whose books included *The Rout* (1927) and *The Young Guard* (1945), both held up in the Stalin years as models of socialist realism – though Stalin made him revise *The Young Guard* (revised ed. 1951). He was Secretary General of the Union of Soviet Writers (1946–53) and an effective, even if two-minded, whipper-in. He committed suicide in 1956.

FEDIN, KONSTANTIN ALEKSANDROVICH (1892–1977): member of the Serapion Brethren, leading Fellow-Traveller and, later, veteran Soviet novelist. In 1959 he succeeded Surkov as Secretary General of the Union of Soviet Writers and held the post until 1971, when he was appointed to the honorific post of President. Pasternak's next-door neighbour in Peredelkino, an erstwhile sympathiser converted into latterday critic. Nicknamed the "Stuffed Eagle".

FELTRINELLI, GIANGIACOMO (1926–72): Italian publisher who first published *Doctor Zhivago* in the West.

FREIDENBERG, OLGA (1890–1955): cousin of Pasternak who knew him well and with whom he corresponded throughout his life (see bibliography).

FRICHE, VLADIMIR (1870–1929): influential Marxist critic who wanted proletarian poetry to be written only by workmen and claimed that socialist and industrialist culture must be thoroughly rationalistic.

GABRICHEVSKY, AKEXSANDR GEORGIEVICH (1891–1968): art historian, specializing in Italian Renaissance architecture. Professor at Moscow University and corresponding member of the Academy of Sciences.

GERSHTEIN, EMMA: literary scholar, acquaintance of the Mandelstams and Anna Akhmatova, the author of *Sudba Lermontova* (*Lermontov's Fate*, Moscow, 1964).

GLADKOV, ALEKSANDR KONSTANTINOVICH (1912–76): playwright who once worked with Meyerhold; his memoir, *Meetings with Pasternak*, throws important light on Pasternak's life and attitudes during and after the Second World War.

GLADKOV, FEDOR (1883–1958): novelist and short story writer influenced by Gorky. He joined the Communist Party in 1920 and in 1925 published his most successful novel, *Cement*. The first truly popular work of Communist literature, it was later revised in line with the requirements of socialist realism.

GORBATOV, ALEKSANDR VASILYEVICH (1891–1973): old Communist and Red Army General whose autobiography, *Years and Wars* (1964–65) told how he was beaten and tortured by the secret police and worked as a convict in Siberian mines.

GORKY, MAKSIM (pen name of ALEKSEY MAKSIMOVICH PESHKOV) (1868–1936): major Russian writer, friend of Lenin (and later Stalin); author of the novel *The Mother* (1906), which is regarded as a pioneering work of socialist realism. Gorky did much to help and give material aid to intellectuals during the Civil War. He emigrated in 1921 to Italy, but returned in 1929 to become the chief exponent of socialist realism. Gorky was acquainted with Pasternak's father, who drew a portrait of him. After his death in 1936 Yagoda and Professor Pletnev were charged by Stalin with his "medical murder".

GRANIN (pen name for GERMAN), DANIIL ALEKSANDROVICH (1919–): Soviet novelist whose works include *The Searchers* (1954), *Attacking the Thunderstorm* (1962), and whose story of the mid-Fifties "Personal Opinion" was one of a number of works of fiction (like Dudintsev's *Not by Bread Alone*) that questioned the short-comings of the Soviet system under Stalin.

GROSSMAN, VASILY SEMENOVICH (1905–64): writer and journalist best known for his great novel, *Life and Fate* (1985), which was smuggled to the west on microfilm after all copies of the manuscript except one had been confiscated by the KGB. His other books are *For a Just Cause*, published in the USSR in 1952 which swung successively in and out of favour, and *Forever Flowing*, first published in English in 1973.

GUDIASHVILI, LADO DAVIDOVICH (1896–): Georgian poet, painter and graphic artist whose published works include *Georgian Folksongs* (1946).

IVANOV, VYACHESLAV IVANOVICH (1866–1949): poet and leading figure of the Symbolist movement. His fifth floor apartment in Petersburg, the Tower, was in the 1910s the most famous literary salon in Russia. Emigrated to Italy in 1924.

IVANOV, VYACHESLAV ("KOMA") VSEVOLODOVICH (1929–): son of Vsevolod Ivanov; a polymath and linguist specializing in semantics. He was appointed deputy editor-in-chief of *Questions in Linguistics* in 1956, but lost the post in 1959 – probably as a result of his association with Pasternak.

IVANOV, VSEVOLOD VYACHESLAVOVICH (1895–1963): Russian novelist, short-story writer and playwright. In the 1920s, he was a member of the Serapion Brethren. His play *The Armoured Train* was produced by Stanislavsky in 1922. His early writings are vivid descriptions of his unusual and often dangerous experiences. Later, he conformed to socialist realism. A close friend and next-door neighbour of Pasternak in Peredelkino.

IVINSKAYA, OLGA VSEVOLODOVNA (1912–): editor and translator. Pasternak met her in the offices of Novy Mir in October 1946. She served to some extent as the prototype of Lara in *Doctor Zhivago*, and a number of the poems in the novel (as well as others in the last cycle, "When the Weather Clears"), are addressed to her. Her association with Pasternak led to her arrest in 1949 and sentence to five years in a hard labour camp. She was released in 1953, a few months after Stalin's death. After Pasternak's death in 1960, Ivinskaya and her daughter were arrested on a trumped-up charge of currency smuggling and sent to forced labour camps. She was released in 1964 well before the expiry of her new, eight year sentence, and still lives in Moscow. Her account of her years with Pasternak is published in English as *A Captive of Time* (see bibliography).

KAMENSKY, VASILY VASILYEVICH (1884–1961): Russian poet, novelist and playwright; a colourful personality who dabbled in painting, was a travelling actor and an aviator. He joined the Futurist movement at its beginnings, experimenting with transrational language neologisms. His novel *Stenka Razin* (1915), combines prose and songs (some of the latter written in an imaginary Persian language). He belonged to the inner circle of LEF, but contributed little to their journal. A close friend of Mayakovsky, he published the memoir *Life with Mayakovsky* in 1940.

KATANYAN, VASILY ABGAROVICH (1902–   ): literary historian who wrote extensively about Mayakovsky.

KAVERIN (pen name of SILBER), VENIAMIN ALEKSANDROVICH (1902–   ): distinguished novelist who in the post-Stalin years played an important part in trying to obtain greater freedom of expression for writers. He was one of the editors of *Literary Moscow* (see Kazakevich) and has written several novels about the persecution of scientists under Stalin.

KAZAKEVICH, EMMANUIL GENRIKHOVICH (1913–62): a novelist who wrote originally in Yiddish, but began to write in Russian after the Second World War, publishing *The Star* in 1947. He was chief editor of the two volumes of the almanac *Literary Moscow*, in one of which he published his own short novel, *The House on the Square*, about the first period of the postwar occupation of Germany.

KERZHENTSEV, PLATON MIKHAILOVICH (1881–1940): journalist and historian, served in commercial posts abroad, and wrote on the history of the revolutionary movement.

KHARDZHIEV, NIKOLAY IVANOVICH (1903–   ): literary scholar and art critic, who edited (with V. Trenin) the first volume of the posthumous edition of Mayakovsky's complete works. A close friend of Akhmatova and Mandelstam.

KHODASEVICH, VLADISLAV FELITSIANOVICH (1886–1939): poet, critic and literary historian, who published his first poems in 1908 but won general recognition only after publication of post-revolutionary books, *The Way of the Grain* (1920) and *The Heavy Lyre* (1923). His poetry expresses the contradiction between the freedom of man's immortal soul and its slavery to matter and necessity. He emigrated in 1922, lived in Paris and became a brilliant literary critic and an expert on Pushkin.

KIROV, SERGEY MAKSIMOVICH (1886–1934): member of the Politburo and Party Chief of Leningrad. His assassination was probably engineered by Stalin, who used it as a pretext for the mass terror that followed (1936–8).

KIRPOTIN, VALERY YAKOVLEVICH (1898–   ): literary scholar and critic.

KLYUEV, NIKOLAY ALEKSANDROVICH (1887–1937): peasant poet who was arrested in the 1930s and died in Siberia.

KLYCHKOV (LESHENKOV), SERGEY ANTONOVICH (1889–1940): peasant poet and novelist arrested in 1937.

KLYUCHEVSKY, VASILY OSIPOVICH (1841–1911): famous historian and professor at Moscow University and at one time Leonid Pasternak's part-time colleague at the School of Painting, Sculpture and Architecture.

KOROVIN, KONSTANTIN ALEKSEYEVICH (1861–1939): landscape painter, but particularly famous as a designer of scenery for theatre and opera, who later became an impressionist. He died in emigration.

KOTOV, ANATOLY KONSTANTINOVICH (1909–56): literary scholar and editor, who was head of Goslitizdat from 1948 until his death. He played a "liberal" role after Stalin's death; one of the editors of *Literary Moscow*.

KRUCHENYKH, ALEKSEY ELISEYEVICH (1886–1968): Futurist poet noted for extreme linguistic experimentation.

KUDASHOVA, MARIYA PAVLOVNA (née MAYA CUVILLIÉS): contributor to a Centrifuge anthology and later married to Romain Rolland.

KULIEV, KAYSYN SHUVAYEVICH (1917–   ): author and poet, whose works include *Greetings, Morning!* (1939) and *My Neighbours* (1957).

KUZMIN, MIKHAIL ALEKSEYEVICH (1875–1936): poet whose work influenced the transition from Symbolism to Acmeism.

LAVRENEV, BORIS ANDREYEVICH (1891–1959): poet, prose-writer and playwright.

LAVUT, PAVEL ILYICH (1893–   ): painter and ex-actor, who arranged Mayakovsky's reading tours from 1926–30 and wrote a memoir about him.

LEBEDEV, VLADIMIR VASILYEVICH (1891–1967): artist and illustrator.

LEONOV, LEONID MAKSIMOVICH (1899–   ): leading novelist and playwright. His play *The Golden Carriage*, written in 1946, appeared only after Stalin's death.

LEVITAN, ISAAK ILYICH (1861–1900): famous Russian landscape painter.

LUGOVSKOY, VLADIMIR ALEKSANDROVICH (1901–57): talented post-revolutionary poet.

MANDELSTAM, NADEZHDA YAKOVLEVNA (1899–1980): wife of the poet Osip Mandelstam. Her memoirs, *Hope Against Hope* and *Hope Abandoned*, give both a portrait of her husband, his inspiration and his work, and an unvarnished account of literary life in the Stalin years (see bibliography).

MANDELSTAM, OSIP EMILYEVICH (1891–1938): great Russian poet, like Akhmatova an Acmeist, whose collections of poetry include *Stone* (1913), *Tristia* (1922) and *Poems 1928*. The Acmeists opposed both the Symbolists and the formal innovations of the Futurists (with whom Pasternak was briefly associated) and were thought to be more conservative, both in poetry and in general outlook. A satirical poem about Stalin led to his exile in Voronezh, where he filled three notebooks in a last creative burst. The story of his life and of the ordeal which ended in his death in a camp near Vladivostok in 1938 has been told by his widow.

MASLENNIKOVA, ZOYA: a sculptress who made a bust of Pasternak in his last years.

MAYAKOVSKY, VLADIMIR VLADIMIROVICH (1893–1930): in many ways the antipode of Pasternak, Mayakovsky combined powerful poetic gifts with a romantic anguish which could find relief only in total service to the Revolution – at the cost of suppressing in himself the urgent personal emotions evident in his pre-revolutionary work (such as *The Cloud in Trousers*, 1913). After the Revolution he wrote many agitprop pieces on topical themes, as well as long epic glorifications of the new order, such as *Mysteria-Bouffe* (1918), *1,500,0000* (1921) and *Vladimir Ilyich Lenin* (1924). His concern at the loss of revolutionary momentum is reflected in two plays, *The Bedbug* and *The Bathhouse*, written not long before his suicide. Before the Revolution he had been one of the leading figures of the Futurist movement, and after the Revolution, from 1922, he headed a group known as LEF ("Left Front of Art"), with which Pasternak was also associated – at least nominally – until 1927, when he broke with it. Mayakovsky was "canonized" in 1936 by Stalin who proclaimed that he "was and remains the best and most talented poet of our Soviet epoch", adding that "indifference to his memory is a crime".

MEDTNER, NIKOLAY KARLOVICH (1879–1951): composer.

MENZEL, ADOLF VON (1815–1905): German realist painter.

MEYERHOLD, VSEVOLOD EMILYEVICH (1874–1940): leading experimental Soviet playwright whose theatre was liquidated by decree in early 1938. Meyerhold defiantly and publicly confronted his persecutors in January 1939. He was arrested the following day; and a week later his wife, the actress Zinaida Raikh, was found dead in their flat from stab wounds, her eyes gouged out.

MINDLIN, EMIL LVOVICH (1900–   ): author of literary memoirs, *Unusual Interlocutors* (1958).

MOCHALOV, PAVEL STEPANOVICH (1800–48): leading Moscow actor, who specialized in tragic roles, and who – like Shchepkin – was also originally a serf. He was a member of the Maly theatre at the same time as Shchepkin.

MOROZOV, MIKHAIL MIKHAILOVICH (1897–1952): Shakespeare scholar.

MOTYLEVA, TAMARA LAZAREVNA (1910–   ): literary critic.

NADIRADZE, KOLAU (1895–   ): Georgian poet, who studied law at Moscow University, and whose first poems appeared in 1916 in the Georgian Symbolist journal, *The Blue Horns*. His early poetry was mystical and nationalistic and at first he was hostile to the Soviet regime, but later wrote on revolutionary themes.

NARBUT, VLADIMIR IVANOVICH (1888–1944): minor Acmeist poet who joined the Bolsheviks but was expelled from the party in 1928. He was editor-in-chief of the State publishing concern Land and Factory (ZIF). He was arrested during the purges, but was posthumously rehabilitated.

NEIGAUS, GENRIKH ("GARRIK") GUSTAVOVICH (1888–1964): eminent pianist and teacher of music. Pasternak first met him at the end of the Twenties when Neigaus was a professor at the Moscow Conservatory.

Pasternak fell in love with Neigaus' wife, Zinaida Nikolayevna, and after his divorce from his first wife, Evgeniya Vladimirovna, he married Zinaida in 1934, but later the two men resumed friendly relations.

NEMIROVICH DANCHENKO, VLADIMIR IVANOVICH (1858–1943): outstanding theatrical director and founder of Moscow Arts Theatre. Introduced to the theatre the works of Chekhov, Gorky, etc.

NEZVAL, VITĚZSLAW (1900–58): Czech poet.

OBRADOVICH, SERGEY ALEKSANDROVICH (1892–1956): proletarian poet.

OSTROVSKY, ALEKSANDR NIKOLAYEVICH (1823–1886): best-known Russian nineteenth century playwright. His heavyweight tragedies explore the seamier sides of everyday Russian life.

PASTERNAK, ALEKSANDR LEONIDOVICH (1893–): younger brother of Boris Pasternak, and author of the memoir *A Vanished Present*.

PASTERNAK, EVGENIYA VLADIMIROVNA (née LURYE) (1899–1965): an artist and Pasternak's first wife.

PASTERNAK, JOSEPHINE LEONIDOVNA (1900–): Pasternak's younger sister.

PASTERNAK, LEONID OSIPOVICH (1862–1945): celebrated painter and illustrator; father of Boris Pasternak. He left Russia in 1921 and, while retaining his Soviet citizenship, lived first in Germany and, from 1938, in England. He died in Oxford in May 1945.

PASTERNAK (NEIGAUS), ZINAIDA NIKOLAYEVNA (1894–1966): Pasternak's second wife.

PASTERNAK SLATER, LYDIA LEONIDOVNA (1902–89): Pasternak's youngest sister who came to England with her parents in 1938 and settled in Oxford.

PAUSTOVSKY, KONSTANTIN GEORGIEVICH (1892–1968): novelist, playwright, memoirist and editor of *Literary Moscow*, who played a prominent part in the liberal movement among writers in the post-Stalin years. He is best known for his autobiography, *The Story of My Life* (1945–63). An influential, goblin-like figure.

PETÖFI, SANDOR (1823–49): national poet of Hungary whose work Pasternak translated in the late 1930s, and eleven of whose lyrics appeared in Pasternak's translation in a collection of Petöfi's work published in Russian in 1949.

PETROVYKH, MARIA SERGEYEVNA (1908–79): poet and translator; at one time a friend of Osip Mandelstam, who dedicated poems to her.

PILNYAK (VOGAU), BORIS ANDREYEVICH (1894–1937): prominent Soviet novelist whose most famous novel, *The Naked Year* (1922), was the first significant literary attempt to write about the Revolution. In *Tale of the Unextinguished Moon* (1927) he hinted that Stalin ("the unbending man of steel") had killed the Red Army commander Frunze by making him undertake an unnecessary medical operation. He was removed from his position as Chairman of the Board of the Union of Soviet Writers following publication of his novel, *Mahogany*, in Berlin. He was arrested in 1937 and is believed to have died that year, probably in a camp.

PLATONOV, ANDREY PLATONOVICH (1891–1951): the son of a railway worker, who lived mainly in Voronezh and later in Moscow. One of the most original writers in the later Stalin years, he was virtually banned, but he has been rehabilitated and his works are now substantially published in the Soviet Union. He enjoys considerable posthumous renown. A linguistic innovator, deliberately mixing neologisms, archaisms and non-standard language. He was a modernist: a pessimistic romantic whose bizarre portrayal of grass roots reality was unrelentingly sceptical and anti-heroic.

POGODIN, NIKOLAY (pen-name of NIKOLAY STUKALOV) (1900–62): journalist who turned his hand to dramas and comedies on the problems of industrialization including: *Tempo* (1929), *The Poem of the Axe* (1930), *My Friend* (1931) and reached the height of his popularity with *The Aristocrats* (1934) a "serious comedy".

POLENOV, VASILY DMITRIEVICH (1844–1927): a painter of country life who was a War artist in the Russo-Turkish war of 1877–78. He was a member for the Society of Travelling Art Exhibitions. He was elected a member of the Academy of Art in 1893, and after the revolution lived in a village now called Polenovo.

POLIKARPOV, DMITRY ALEKSEYEVICH (1904–65): Party official who was appointed head of the Cultural Department of the Central Committee in 1955 and, as such, was responsible for the political supervision of literature.

POLONSKY, VYACHESLAV PAVLOVICH (1886–1932): Russian Marxist literary critic and historian, an editor of *Novy Mir*. He assailed all the Futurists violently, particularly Mayakovsky, for being too obscure.

PUZIKOV, ALEKSANDR IVANOVICH (1911–): literary scholar; authority on French literature; since 1951, senior editor of *Goslitzdat* (State Publishing House for Literature).

POSKREBYSHEV, ALEKSANDR NIKOLAYEVICH (1891–1966): long-standing head of Central Committee's Special Section and Stalin's closest confidant.

RILKE, RAINER MARIA (1875–1926): regarded as the greatest German poet since Goethe. He visited Moscow in 1900 when Pasternak's father painted a portrait of him. (*Safe Conduct* opens with a childhood recollection of him during a train journey to see Tolstoy.) In the few years before Rilke's death, Pasternak corresponded with him through the intermediary of Marina Tsvetayeva (see bibliography).

RIPELLINO, ANGELO MARIA (1923–): Italian writer, translator and critic; professor of Russian at University of Rome.

ROLLAND, ROMAIN (1866–1944): French novelist, poet and biographer, who won the Nobel Prize for Literature in 1915.

RUDENKO, ROMAN ANDREYEVICH (1907–): Prosecutor-General of the USSR (and, hence, its highest "law" officer) since 1953; he represented the USSR at the Nuremberg trial of the Nazi war criminals.

ROZANOV, VASILY VASILEVICH (1856–1919): Russian philosopher, essayist and critic. He had highly original ideas on sex, and mystical religious views, which he presented in an utterly new prose style. He exerted a strong influence on Shklovsky, who wrote a study of Rozanov in 1921.

SCRIABIN, ALEKSANDR NIKOLAYEVICH (1872–1915): composer; as a young man Pasternak was very much under his influence for a time (see *An Essay in Autobiography*).

SELIVANOVSKY, ALEKSEY PAVLOVICH (1900–1938): critic. Leading figure in RAPP. Arrested and evidently executed in the purges.

SELVINSKY, ILYA (1899–1968): earthy and exuberant constructivist poet, fought with the Red Army in the Civil War. His first collection, *Records*, appeared in 1926. For a brief time he was heir apparent to Mayakovsky's place in Soviet poetry – hazy on ideology, strong on descriptive qualities. His novels in verse included *Ulyalayev's Band* (1927) rewritten in 1956 to make Lenin the main figure.

SERAFIMOVICH (POPOV), ALEKSANDR SERAFIMOVICH (1863–1949): veteran Soviet writer of *The Iron Flood*, a famous novel about the Civil War (1924). A one-time associate of Gorky, he was regarded as a "classic" in the Soviet Union.

SEROV, VALENTIN ALEKSANDROVICH (1865–1911): well-known painter; some of his works (e.g. *Europa*) are on classical themes.

SHAGINYAN, MARIETTA SERGEYEVNA (1888–1982): veteran Soviet novelist and (before the Revolution) a minor poet on the fringes of the Symbolist movement. During the 1920s she was known mainly for her attempt to write thrillers and detective fiction in Western style, decried at the time as "Red Pinkertonism".

SHALAMOV, VARLAM TIKHONOVICH (1906–1982): writer who spent, on and off, seventeen years in forced labour camps in Kolyma (starting in 1929) and subsequently wrote of his experiences there.

SHCHERBAKOV, ALEKSANDR SERGEYEVICH (1901–1945): veteran Communist official and associate of Zhdanov. He was appointed secretary of the Union of Soviet Writers in 1934, despite the fact that he had no connection with literature. Later he was in charge of purging provincial Party organizations, and during the war he was a secretary of the Central Committee (and Candidate Member of the Politburo) with special responsibility for political control of the army. His death in 1945 was later attributed to the Jewish doctors arrested on Stalin's orders in 1952.

SHKLOVSKY, VIKTOR BORISOVICH (1893–1984): eminent literary scholar and Formalist critic, a member of LEF. Shklovsky's influence in the 1920s was immense, and he continued to write articles, books, and scenarios throughout the Stalinist era and into the Sixties. He is the author of *Mayakovsky and His Circle*, 1940 (English translation published 1972).

SHOSTAKOVICH, DMITRY DMITRIEVICH (1906–1975): great Soviet composer. In 1934 Stalin walked out of the premiere of his opera *A Lady Macbeth of the Mtsensk District*, which was then attacked in a *Pravda* article entitled "Nonsense Instead of Music". He and other leading composers were again condemned in a Party decree in 1948 for "formalism". Zhdanov is said to have picked out tunes on the piano for them to illustrate the kind of music the Party required them to compose.

SILLOV, VLADIMIR: member of LEF, arrested and executed by firing squad in the 1930s.

SIMONOV, KONSTANTIN MIKHAILOVICH (1915–79): popular Soviet author, best known for his wartime lyrics and novels on the war (such as *Days and Nights*, on the battle of Stalingrad, 1944). After Stalin's death he played a cautiously "liberal" role in Soviet literary affairs. He was editor of *Novy Mir* from 1946 to 1950, and again from 1954 to 1958. The writer Galakhov in Solzhenitsyn's *First Circle* appears to be at least partially based on him.

SIMONOV, RUBEN (1898–1968): theatre director, mainly with Vakhtangov Theatre.

SOLOVYEV, BORIS IVANOVICH (1904–): literary critic and scholar.

SOLOVYEV, VLADIMIR (1853–1900): a religious thinker and poet who was a major influence on Symbolism.

SPASSKY, SERGEY DMITRIEVICH (1898–1956): poet and prose-writer; at one time close to the Futurists. He was arrested in the late Forties – probably in 1949 – and returned from a camp in 1954 (some of Pasternak's letters to him were published in *Questions of Literature*, September 1969, and in the last of them, dated 5 November, 1954, there is a reference to his "return"). In her memoirs, Nadezhda Mandelstam implies that Spassky was also arrested in the prewar terror, but he was certainly at liberty again by 1939.

STAVSKY, VLADIMIR PETROVICH (1900–43): prose-writer and journalist; appointed Secretary General of the Union of Writers after Gorky's death in 1936 and, as such, was active in the purges of writers in the late Thirties. He was killed at the front as a war correspondent.

STEPANOV, NIKOLAY STEPANOVICH (1902–72): literary scholar primarily concerned with Khlebnikov and Mayakovsky.

STEPUN, FEDOR AVGUSTOVICH (1884–1965): stage producer, writer and scholar. Author of several novels and of an autobiography which gives an excellent picture of the artistic and literary atmosphere in pre-Revolutionary Moscow. Emigrated, lived in Germany.

STETSKY, ALEKSEY STEPANOVICH (1896–1938): Party functionary. He was head of the Central Committee's department of Agitation and Propaganda (*Agitprop*), 1930–8.

SURKOV, ALEKSEY ALEKSANDROVICH (1899–1983): poet; editor of *Literaturnaya Gazeta*, 1944–46; Secretary General of the Union of Soviet Writers, 1954–59. A promising poet who became a literary manipulator.

TABIDZE, NINA ALEKSANDROVNA: widow of Titsian Tabidze, who was a staunch friend of Pasternak until his death.

TABIDZE, TITSIAN YUSTINOVICH (1898–1937): Georgian poet, and friend of Pasternak who translated his poetry into Russian. He was one of the founders of the "Blue Horns" group of Georgian Symbolist poets (1915). He rallied to Soviet Regime after 1921 and helped to found Union of Georgian Writers. At the Congress of Soviet writers in 1934 the Blue Horns group was criticised by the chairman of the Union of Georgian writers as still being only Fellow-Travellers. Arrested during the Great Terror, he was tortured and executed in prison. Part of his correspondence with Pasternak has been published in *Letters to Georgian Friends* (see bibliography).

TAIROV, ALEKSANDR YAKOVLEVICH (1885–1950): actor and, later, director of the Kamerny Theatre in Moscow. He was dismissed in 1939.

TAMM, IGOR EVGENYEVICH (1895–1971): Academician, Soviet physicist and Nobel Prize winner.

TARASENKOV, ANATOLY KUZMICH (1909–56): literary scholar and critic, author of the article on Mandelstam in the Soviet Literary Encyclopedia (1932). (For a comment on him as a collector of poetry, see Nadezhda Mandelstam, *Hope Abandoned*, p. 479.)

TESKOVA, ANNA (1872–1954): Czech translator from Russian and friend of Tsvetayeva, who dedicated a cycle of poems to her. Their correspondence was published in Prague in 1969.

TIKHONOV, NIKOLAY SEMENOVICH (1896–1979): Soviet poet, noted for the romantic flavour and themes of his ballads in the Twenties, who was influenced by Gumilev and Khlebnikov, but later adapted to the demands of socialist realism. Like Pasternak a translator of poetry from the Georgian. He was Secretary General of the Union of Soviet Writers, 1944–46, and from 1950 chairman of the Soviet Peace Committee.

TRENEV, KONSTANTIN (1876–1945): dramatist whose best-known play is the "realist" melodrama of the Civil War *Lyubov Yarovaya*.

TRENIN, VLADIMIR VLADIMIROVICH (1904–1941): critic and literary scholar. Collaborated on studies of Mayakovsky with Khardzhiev.

TSVETAYEVA, MARINA IVANOVNA (1892–1941): gifted Russian poet who was a contemporary of Pasternak, Mandelstam and Akhmatova, all of whom dedicated poems to one another. Tsvetayeva's fate was the most tragic of all. Her husband, Sergey Efron, whom she married in 1912, served during the Civil War as an officer in the White Army, but she was stranded in Moscow till 1922. From 1922 till 1925 she lived in Prague, and then in Paris till 1939. As a suspected Soviet secret service agent, Efron was forced to flee France and went back to Moscow. Tsvetayeva followed him there in 1939. Shortly after her return her husband and daughter were arrested. Sergey Efron died or was executed in prison. Ariadna was released in 1955. When war broke out Tsvetayeva was evacuated to the town of Yelabuga on the river Kama, where in August 1941 she hanged herself. In addition to her poetry, she wrote plays and valuable critical essays. A memoir by her on her relations with Mandelstam was published in 1964 in the *Oxford Slavonic Papers*. Her correspondence with Pasternak and Rilke is published as *Letters Summer 1926* (see bibliography).

TUKHACHEVSKY, MIKHAIL NIKOLAYEVICH (1893–1937): Commander-in-chief of the Red Army, who was executed – along with many other military leaders, including Soviet Army Commander Iona Yakir – on trumped-up charges in Stalin's 1937 purge of the army.

TVARDOVSKY, ALEKSANDR TRIFONOVICH (1910–71): poet and editor (of *Novy Mir*). His *Vasily Terkin* (1941–45), written in a simple but very expressive style, achieved enormous popularity during the war. (A satirical, anti-Stalinist sequel to it, *Vasily Terkin in the Other World*, was published in 1963 by special dispensation of Khrushchev, who was well-disposed to Tvardovsky personally.)

TYNYANOV, YURY (1896–1943): scholar and university professor, whose collection of essays, *Archaists and Innovators* (1929), which analysed Pushkin and Tyutchev and others (including Lenin) from a purely stylistic standpoint, challenged academic standards and strengthened his already solid reputation amongst formalist critics. He was popular for his craftsmanlike historical novels including *Pushkin* (1936–7).

VILENKIN, VITALY YAKOVLEVICH (1910–): art historian and writer on the theatre; author of books on Nemirovich Danchenko and Modigliani.

VILMONT (VILYAM-VILMONT), NIKOLAY NIKOLAYEVICH (1901–): critic, literary scholar, and translator (mainly of German literature). His sister married Pasternak's brother, Aleksandr Leonidovich.

VORONSKY, ALEKSANDR KONSTANTINOVICH (1884–1943): old Bolshevik who edited the major Soviet literary journal *Krasnaya Nov* (*Red Virgin Soil*), which in the 1920s was the main outlet for the Fellow-Travellers and Proletarians. Voronsky came under heavy fire from Averbakh's RAPP, and in 1927 he was expelled from the Party. Voronsky finally disappeared during the purges in 1937 and probably died in a labour camp in 1943.

VOZNESENSKY, ANDREY ANDREYEVICH (1933–): lyric poet who attracted considerable attention by his originality and freshness of form, when he first began to publish in 1958. Together with Yevtushenko he played a major part in the revival of poetry in the years following Stalin's death. A selection of his work has been translated into English as, *Anti-worlds* (trans. Max Hayward with W. H. Auden and others, 1964).

VRUBEL, MIKHAIL ALEKSANDROVICH (1856–1910): an outstanding imaginative painter who was also well known as a book illustrator and theatrical designer. He was a member of the Academy from 1905.

VYSOTSKAYA, IDA DAVIDOVNA: Pasternak's childhood love, to whom he proposed in Marburg in 1912 and by whom he was refused. He dedicated several early poems to her including his famous lyric "Marburg" which he rewrote many times. She married a Kiev banker and went to live in Berlin where she was visited by Pasternak in 1923. Pasternak saw her for the last time in Paris during his obligatory attendance at the 1935 Writers Conference.

YAKIR, IONA (1896–1937): Soviet Army Commander, in charge of Kiev Military District, who was executed – along with many other military leaders including Marshal Tukhachevsky – on trumped-up charges in Stalin's 1937 purge of the army.

YASHVILI, PAOLO DZHIBRAELOVICH (1895–1937): Georgian poet who was one of the initiators of the "Blue Horns" group of Symbolist poets. He welcomed the establishment of Soviet power and wrote poems celebrating it, including a poem on the death of Lenin. In the 1930s he wrote poems about the triumphs of socialist construction in Georgia and translated Pushkin, Lermontov and Mayakovsky in Georgian. Horrified at the news of Tabidze's arrest and execution, and fearing a similar fate, he went to the headquarters of the Union of Georgian Writers, whose secretary he was, and blew out his brains with his own double-barrelled gun.

YUDINA, MARIA VENYAMINOVNA (1899–1970): eminent Soviet pianist and professor at the Moscow Conservatory.

ZAITSEV, BORIS KONSTANTINOVICH (1881–1974): writer who emigrated in 1922 and lived in Paris from 1924.

ZALKA, MATÉ (1896–1937): a Hungarian who fought on the side of the Bolsheviks during the Civil War. In the Twenties and Thirties he published short stories and a novel. During the Spanish Civil War he commanded the 12th International Brigade under the name of "General Lukacz", and was killed in action.

ZASLAVSKY, DAVID IOSIFOVICH (1880–1965): journalist noted for his vituperative *feuilletons*, generally published in *Pravda*. He was originally a Menshevik and was violently attacked by Lenin in 1917 for his articles in the Menshevik press. In 1919 he "recanted" and declared his allegiance to the Bolsheviks. In 1929 he wrote a scurrilous attack on Osip Mandelstam, provoking a strong reply by a group of leading writers, including Pasternak. His poisoned pen was much in demand even after Stalin's death.

ZELINSKY, KORNELY LYUTSANOVICH (1896–1970): literary historian.

ZHDANOV, ANDREY (1896–1948): a close associate of Stalin and a member of the Politburo from 1939. He implemented the tough ideological line of the postwar years, both in promoting Communist militancy abroad (the founding of the Cominform, 1947) and in a savage campaign intended to terrorize the intelligentsia at home – this found expression in the series of Party decrees (the "Zhdanov decrees") condemning alleged deviations in literature, the cinema, philosophy, and music. In each case scapegoats were chosen and made examples of (Akhmatova and Zoshchenko in literature, Eisenstein in cinema, Shostakovich in music, etc.). This period 1944–48 is known as the Zhdanov era.

ZHDANOV, NIKOLAY GAVRILOVICH (1909–): writer of Dudintsev's generation whose story "The Journey Home", like Dudintsev's *Not by Bread Alone*, was an example of the thaw in literature in the early years after Stalin's death. His other books included *Sea Salt* (1947), *A New Sea* (1954), *Petrograd Story* (1960) and *The Wind of the Century* (1963).

ZHURAVLYOV, DMITRY NIKOLAYEVICH (1900–): actor (and variety artiste) in the Vakhtangov Theatre, who gave public "recitations" in the Thirties of a wide range of Russian and Western European poetry and prose including: Pushkin, Gogol, Blok, Akhmatova, Mérimée and Maupassant. His memoir of Akhmatova is included in *Life, Art, Meetings*, Moscow, 1985.

ZOSHCHENKO, MIKHAIL MIKHAILOVICH (1895–1958): a popular satirical writer and member of the Serapion Brethren. He was attacked in 1946 by Zhdanov for his "vulgar parody" of Soviet life and, together with Akhmatova, expelled from the Union of Soviet Writers.

INDEX

Abastumani, 49
Abramtsevo, 78
Agapov, Boris Nikolayevich, 220
Akhmatova, Anna Andreyevna (Anna
   Andreyevna Gorenko), 73, 82, 117, 120,
   124, 135, 144, 154, 163, 180, 184, 194,
   198, 210, 221; decree on, 166, 197;
   Litfond grant to, 179; publication of, 191;
   translation work, 179
Alberti, Rafael, 110
Aleksandrinsky Theatre (Leningrad), 114
Alekseyev, Mikhail Nikolayevich, 120
Alexander I, 241n
Alkonost, 169
All-Russia Theatrical Society, 141
All-Union Conference of Poets (1934), 72
All-Union Translators Conference, 64
Altauzen, Dzhek, 102
Andronnikov, Irakly, 220
Angelo, S. d', 216, 219
Anna Karenina (Tolstoy), 144
Apollinaire, Guillaume, 185
Arakcheyev, General, 241
Ardov, Victor Efimovich, 175
Artist, The, 108
Arts Committee, 130, 131, 141
Arts Theatre, *see* Moscow: Arts Theatre
Aseyev, Nikolay ("Kolya") Nikolayevich,
   7, 8, 9, 23, 66, 74, 120, 133; criticism
   of BP, 63, 64, 72; friendship with BP,
   137, 143
Asmus, Irina Sergeyevna, 17, 19, 25, 28,
   37, 42, 166
Asmus, Masha, 18
Asmus, Valentin Ferdinandovich, 17, 25,
   28, 37, 62, 120, 133, 140, 144, 166, 200
Avdeyev, Valery, 137, 146, 197
Averbakh, Leopold Leopoldovich, 10n, 69
Azarkh, Raisa Moiseyevna, 145
Azov, V., 21
Babel, Isaac Emmanuelovich, 5, 81
Bagritsky (Dzyubin), Edvard Georgievich,
   83
Bakuriani, 45, 49
Balashov, 193
Bannikov, Nikolay Vasilyevich, 215, 222,
   234
Baranov, 36
Baranovich, Marina Kazimirovna, 170,
   215, 231–2
Baratynsky, 160
Bebutov, Garegin V., 50, 51, 64
Beethoven, Ludwig van, 204
Bely, Andrey (Boris Nikolayevich
   Bugayev), 42, 79, 174, 178, 241
Bentsionovna, Yulia, 16
Berggolts, Olga Fedorovna, 174, 184

Beriashvili, Elena, 50
Berlin, 9, 21n, 39, 81
Berlin, Isaiah, 161
Bernstein, Leonard, 243
Bersut, 128
Bespalov, Ivan Petrovich, 103
Bezobrazov, General, 15
Bezymensky, Aleksandr Ilyich, 84
Blaginina, Elena, 230
Blake, William, 109
Blok, Aleksandr Aleksandrovich, 94, 119,
   124, 150, 172, 185, 194, 212; influence on
   BP, 152, 162, 168, 182; BP writing on,
   150, 169, 212, 222
"Blue Horns", 46
Blumenfeld, Feliks, 31
Blumenfeld, Natalya Feliksovna, 44
Bobrov, Sergey, 69, 210
Bokov, Viktor Fedorovich, 129
Boldino, 27
Bolshevo, 82, 91, 200, 201
Borisev, B. M., 73, 85n
Borzhomi, 49
Botkin Hospital (Moscow), 198
Bowra, Maurice, 158, 185
Brahms, Johannes, 48
Brik, Lilia ("Lili") Yurievna, 61, 62, 94
British Ally, 160
Brothers (Fedin), 6, 101
Brothers Karamazov (Dostoyevsky), 205
Brügel, Fritz, 93
Bryn, 148
Bryusov, Valery, 63, 182
Bugayeva, Klavdiya Nikolayevna, 170
Bukharin, Nikolay Ivanovich, 73, 74, 85,
   85n, 93
Bukhshtab, B., 70
Bulgakov, Mikhail Afanesevich, 86, 89
Burkov, I. S., 47
Byron, George Gordon Noel, 109; *see also*
   Pasternak, Boris Leonidovich,
   translations
Captain's Daughter, The (Pushkin), 200
Captive of Time, A (Ivinskaya), 171n, 195n
Calderon, Pedro, 242
Camus, Albert, 235, 238
Caucasus, 44, 45, 47, 98
censorship, 3, 67, 92, 93, 99, 131, 152, 153,
   179, 205, 228–30; *see also* Pasternak,
   Boris Leonidovich: criticism, official;
   individual titles and journals
Central Committee, 10n, 76, 180, 228, 229;
   Decree Concerning the Restructuring of
   Literary-Artistic Organizations (1932),
   69
Centrifuge, 27
Chagin, Petr Ivanovich, 117, 137, 138, 203

269

186, 187, 201, 202, 203, 206, 207, 209, 211; death of, 212
Frunze, 197
Gabrichevsky, Aleksandr Georgievich, 120
"Garden of Olives, The" (Rilke), 190
Garkavi, 108
Germany, 47, 55, 96, 204
Georgia, 44–7, 54, 97–9, 197, 240, 241
Georgian Military Highway, 43, 53
Gershtein, Emma, 172–3
Gidash, A., 69, 88
GIKhL, 32, 33, 67
Gillensten, Lars, 235
Girey, Mikhail (Mengli), 15
Gladkov, Aleksandr Konstantinovich, 33, 78, 86, 135, 136, 137, 139, 140, 144
Gladkov, Fedor, 40
Goethe, Johann Wolfgang von, 53, 182, 183, 192, 201, 205, 206, 244
Gogol, Nikolai, 78, 88, 204, 241
"Gogol" (Aseyev), 196
Gluck, Christophe Willibald von, 171
Golitsyno House of Retreat, 120
Golovchenko, 180
Gorbatov, Aleksandr Vasilyevich, 147, 148
Gorbunov, 138
Gorky, Maksim (Aleksey Maksimovich Peshkov), 20–21, 24, 25, 40, 55, 59, 67, 70, 73–4, 75, 82
Gorky Park (Moscow), 76
Goslitizdat publishing house, 109, 117, 119, 137, 153, 201, 214, 216, 225, 228, 229, 230, 232, 236, 238, 268
Gospel, The, 169, 189, 191, 217
Grabar, Igor, 157
Granin, Daniel (Danill Aleksandrovich German), 150
Great Friendship, The (Muradeli), 178
Great Patriotic War (1941–5), *see* Second World War
Great Terror, The (purges, 1936–8), ix, 78, 85, 88, 102, 105–7, 115–17
Greece, 212, 226, 243
Griboedov, 119
Grigoryev, Apollon, 119, 137, 173
Grishina, Anna, 120
Gromov, P. P., 157
Gromov, M. P., 193
Grossman, Vasily Semenovich, 148
Gründgens, 244
Gubarev, B. V., 197
Gudiasvili, Chukurtma, 244, 245
Gudiashvili, Lado Davidovich, 167, 240
Gumilev, Lev, 73n, 192
Gurtyev, General, 148
Hail to Peace (Akhmatova), 191
Hamburg Dramatic Theatre, 244
Heine, Heinrich, 53, 55
Hemingway, Ernest, 238
Highway, The (Tikhonov), 53–4
Histoire de la France (Michelet), 101
Hitler, Adolf, 96
Hoffmann, 138
Hope Abandoned (N. Mandelstam), 172n
Hope Against Hope (N. Mandelstam), 73n

Hora, Josef, translations of BP's poetry, 92–3
Huxley, Aldous, 238
Ibsen, Henrik Johan, 132, 137, 150
Ilovaisky, Serafim, 137
Imperialist War, *see* First World War
Institute of World Literature of USSR Academy of Science (IMLI), 80n
International Writers Congress (1935), 80, 88n
In the Battle for Orel, 145
Invasion (Leonov), 139
Irpen, 25–9, 30
Isaakyan, Avetik, 154
Iskusstvo, 164
Iskusstvo publishing house, 179, 184, 242
Ivanov, Vsevolod Vyacheslavovich, 5, 6, 60, 116, 129, 140, 145, 146, 173, 194, 216, 224
Ivanov, ("Koma") Vyacheslav Vsevolodovich, 7n, 143, 161, 173, 214
Ivanova, Tamara, 7, 173, 224
Ivinskaya, Olga Vsevolodovna, 188, 195n, 228, 229, 234; arrest of, 188; relationship with BP, 171, 176, 178, 208, 239; release, 203; translation work with BP, 209; work on publication of BP's work, 215, 218
Izvestiya, 40, 71, 93, 94, 95
Kalma, A., 66
Kama River, 200
Kamensky, Anatoly, 21
Kannabikh, Professor, 14
Karivelishvili, Shalva, 50
Katanyan, Vasily Abgarovich, 8
Kaverin, Veniamin, 195, 219
Kayden, Eugene, 77
Kazakevich, Emmanuil Genrikhovich, 219
Kazan, 135, 142
Keats, John, 109; *see also* Pasternak, Boris Leonidovich, translations
Kerzhentsev, Platon Mikhailovich, 6
KGB (Committee for State Security), 188n
Khalturin, 129
Khardziev, Nikolay Ivanovich, 70
Khlysty sect, 36n
Khodasevich, Vladislav Felitsianovich, 9
Khrushchev, Nikita, 218, 235, 237
Kierkegaard, Soren, 243
Kiev, 16, 17, 25, 26, 27, 28, 40, 42, 43, 48, 236
Kirov, Sergey Maksimovich, 15, 78
Kirpotin, Valery Yakovlevich, 69, 88
Klychkov (Leshenkov), Sergey Antonovich, 83
Klyuchevsky, Vassily Osipovich, x
Klyuev, Nikolay Aleksandrovich, 83
"Knight Janos, The" (Petofi), 178
Kobulety, 45, 49–50, 51, 53
Kochetkov, A. S., 170
Kodzhory, 45, 48
Koenemann, 18, 19
Koktebel, 120
Kolzhory, 37
Komsomol, 91, 147, 195; Central Committee, 10n

274

207; *Henry IV*, 155, 160, 212; *King Lear*, 151, 178; *Macbeth*, 192; "Music", 110; *Othello*, 151; *Romeo and Juliet*, 127, 131, 136, 141, 222, "Winter", 110

Pasternak, Evgeniya Vladimirovna (née Lurye), (BP's first wife), 13–14, 16, 17, 19, 25, 26, 57, 107, 123, 135, 143, 178; in Berlin, 21, 35, 39; evacuation to Tashkent, 129; and painting, 12, 13, 17, 28; and BP, 19, 29, 30, 31–2, 47, 54, 104
Pasternak, Evgeny Borisovich (BP's son), 73n, 85n, 219, 236, 245; childhood, 13, 14, 15, 21, 26, 54, 104; evacuation to Tashkent, 129; in Berlin, 21; at Military Academy, 136
Pasternak, Fedor (son of A. Pasternak), 19
Pasternak, Irina Nikolayevna (wife of A. Pasternak), 19n, 25, 26
Pasternak, Josephine Leonidovna (BP's sister), 13, 57–8, 81, 161
Pasternak, Leonid Borisovich (BP's son), 109, 121, 128, 129, 135, 138, 142, 153–4, 179, 194–5, 198, 208, 219
Pasternak, Leonid Osipovich (BP's father), xi, 10, 17, 18, 19, 47, 60, 77, 96, 97, 101, 104, 107, 118; death, 157
Pasternak, Lydia Leonidovna (BP's sister), 3, 21, 24, 95, 109, 110, 161
Pasternak, Zinaida Nikolayevna (formerly Neigaus), (BP's second wife), 56, 57, 58, 59, 76, 80, 129, 130, 131, 134, 166, 175, 195, 198, 235, 240; birth of son Leonid, 109; childhood, 58; death of son Adrian, 157; marriage to Genrikh Neigaus, 17, 25, 28–9; in Moscow, 100, 111, 144; and BP 30–31, 35–6, 37, 39, 40, 42–3, 44, 49, 57–9, 82, 91, 108, 178, 187, 208; in Peredelkino, 16, 114, 115, 121, 153–4; war work, 128, 135, 238
Pasternak, Rosa Isidorovna (née Kaufman) (BP's mother), xi, 18, 19, 96, 101, 104, 107, 116, 118
Paustovsky, Konstantin, 219
Pavlenko, Petr, 121
Peace Fund, 236
Peredelkino, 60, 97, 100, 103–4, 107, 111–12, 115, 119, 121–2, 124, 125, 129, 132, 134, 140, 145, 154, 201, 216, 217, 220, 222, 225, 236, 239; BP in (1946–53), 164, 198; BP in (1954), 209
Petersburg, 58, 79, 171, 210
Petrovsky, Dmitry, 102
Petrovykh, Maria Sergeyevna, 170
Phillip, Walter, 238
Pilnyak (Vogau), Boris Andreyevich, 5, 25, 30, 33, 35, 88, 90, 103
Pilnyak, Olga Sergeyevna, 36n
Pioneers, Young, 195
Pisarev, Dmitry, 214
Plato, 214
Platonov, Andrey, 24–5, 140
Ples, 129
Pobedonostsev, 242

Poe, Edgar Allan, 110
Poetry Section, 184
Pogodin, Nikolay (pen name of Nikolay Stukalov), 144
Poland, 99, 236
Polenov, Vasily Dmytryevich, x
Polikarpov, Dmitry Andreyevich, 229, 237
Polonskaya, Veronika, 2, 43
Polonsky, Vyacheslav Pavlovich, 23, 37, 40
Polytechnic Museum, 157, 164
Poputchiki, *see* Fellow-Travellers
Poskrebyshev, 81
Poti, 49
Pozner, 7, 9
Prague, 92
Pravda, 64, 69, 85, 86, 144, 149, 152, 236, 237
Presidium of the Supreme Soviet, 237
Proust, Marcel, 231, 240
"Prowess, Feats and Glory" (Blok), 152
Punin, Nikolai, 73n, 117n
purges (1936–8), *see* Great Terror, The
Pushkin, Aleksandr Sergeyevich, 1, 27, 38, 64, 77, 79, 94, 101, 102, 160, 173, 200n
Puzikov, Aleksandr Ivanovich, 225
Rabelais, François, 138
Rachmaninov, Sergey, x
Radio Italia, 216
Radlova, Anna Dmitrievna, 116
Raikh, Zinaida, 116
RAPP (Russian Association of Proletarian Writers), 10, 33, 69, 70; Second Production Conference (1932), 69
Read, Herbert, 158
realism, 154, 156, 173
Red Army Theatre, 144
reforms (1864), 194n
Rembrandt (Harmenz van Rijn), 112
Remembrance of Times Past (Proust), 231
Renoir, Pierre-Auguste, 167
Requiem (Akhmatova), 117
"Requiem for a Lady Friend" (Rilke), 16
Resurrection (Tolstoy), 230
Retribution (Blok), 242
Reztsov, L., 120
Rilke, Rainer Maria, x, 16, 31, 39, 45, 92, 109, 150, 190, 231
Rippelino, Angelo Maria, 222
Rolland, Romain, 27, 32, 125
Romadin, 13
Romania, 149
Romanovka, 193
Rome, 212, 222
Rovno, 137
RSFSR Union of Writers, 179n
Rudenko, Roman Andreyevich, 240
Rul (The Helm), 21
Ryabinina, Aleksandra P., 117, 120, 208
Ryazan, 186
Rylsky, Maksim, 154
Sachs, Hans, 109; *see also* Pasternak, Boris Leonidovich, translations
"Sacred ties of brotherhood, The" (Chikovani), 46